Archer, Dale.

The ADHD advantage

DATE DUE   AUG 0 1 2015

The ADHD
Advantage

The ADHD Advantage

What You Thought Was a Diagnosis
May Be Your Greatest Strength

Dale Archer, MD

AVERY

An imprint of Penguin Random House LLC
375 Hudson Street
New York, New York 10014
penguin.com

Most Avery books are available at special quantity discounts for bulk purchase for sales
promotions, premiums, fund-raising, and educational needs. Special books or book ex-
cerpts also can be created to fit specific needs. For details, write Special.Markets@penguin
randomhouse.com

ISBN 978-1-59463-351-5

Printed in the United States of America
10 9 8 7 6 5 4 3 2 1

Set in Palatino LT Std Roman

To my father

CONTENTS

Part II. Discovering Your Strengths

Part III. Finding Success

FOREWORD

The time to view Attention Deficit Hyperactivity Disorder through a new lens is long overdue. Dr. Dale Archer's *The ADHD Advantage* redefines all but the most severe cases of ADHD as expectable difference, not medical diagnosis. Hopefully, his work will help reverse the dangerous global trend that seeks to medicalize individual variability and medicate it into oblivion. Dale's view is quite different. Rather than suppressing ADHD symptoms, he finds the adaptive strengths in them that can be leveraged with awareness and the right set of tools. Pills are not always the answer.

As chair of the task force that produced the fourth edition of the *Diagnostic and Statistical Manual*, I have been alarmed by the tripling of ADHD rates in just twenty years. It's not that our kids are getting sicker. Human nature is remarkably constant. Some of the increase may be due to better recognition of real cases, but the evidence is overwhelming that we are in the midst of a fad largely engineered by drug companies' misleading marketing to doctors, stressed parents and overworked teachers, as well as a quick-fix mentality and insurance demands that a diagnosis be made immediately on a first visit.

We are turning our kids into pill poppers. ADHD is now diagnosed in 11 percent of all children ages four through seventeen and is medicated in 6 percent. It is estimated that 15 percent of all children will get the diagnosis before they reach voting age. And the percentages get really crazy for teenage boys—20 percent are diagnosed and 10 percent are medicated. Remarkably, a child's date of birth is the best predictor of whether he gets the label. The youngest kid in the class is almost twice as likely as the oldest to be diagnosed with ADHD. Misplaced diagnostic exuberance has turned age-appropriate immaturity into a psychiatric disease—and treats it with a pill, rather than just letting the kid grow up.

The rates of ADHD jumped because of three events during the late 1990s. First, new and very expensive ADHD drugs came on the market. This provided the means and motive for aggressive marketing. Twenty years ago, sales of ADHD drugs in the United States totaled a modest $40 million; now they have soared to an obscene $9 billion. Most of this money would be better spent to improve schools by reducing class size and adding gym periods so that fidgety kids could blow off steam.

Second, drug companies were allowed for the first time to engage in direct-to-consumer advertising. Ads peddling the ADHD illness to sell the profitable pill soon dominated TV, the Internet and print media. The misleading message was that ADHD is common, underdiagnosed, the cause of all school and behavioral problems, the result of a chemical imbalance and easily treatable with a pill. The marketing was mostly aimed at primary care doctors, who now prescribe the bulk of psychiatric medicines. They usually write quick and unnecessary prescriptions after a very brief visit, being forced into a premature diagnosis in order to get paid. Kids are hard to diagnose and change a lot from visit to visit without intervention—especially since they are often first seen on their worst day. Medication should be a last resort used only for the clearest, most impairing, most pervasive and most persistent disorders. Instead, the medicines are often passed out like candy.

Third, the first report from a multicenter study suggested that medication was superior to psychotherapy in treating ADHD. Subsequent follow-up studies failed to support the long-term effectiveness of medication, but these did not receive very much attention.

It is easy to overdiagnose and overtreat ADHD. It is defined by nonspecific symptoms and behaviors that are widely distributed in the general population: poor concentration, distractibility, impulsivity and hyperactivity. At the poles, the diagnosis is easily made. At one pole, the kid who presents with classic early-onset, severe ADHD is unmistakable. At the other are the kids who clearly do not have ADHD. But in between (at an arbitrary, flexible, fuzzy and heavily populated boundary), it is tough to distinguish clinical ADHD from normal kids who are no more than frisky and difficult to manage. Dale's ADHD continuum describes this in detail—a new way of looking at symptoms that no longer warrants the immediate reflex of a prescription.

Overdiagnosis and loose prescription habits have fostered a thriving secondary market for pills originally intended for ADHD but instead illegally diverted for recreational use and/or performance enhancement. Remarkably, one-third of college students now use stimulants, as do one in ten high school students. Stimulant overdoses have quadrupled in recent years. And more than 10,000 two- and three-year-olds are already on stimulants. Things have gotten so out of hand that two federal agencies are now tussling over control of stimulant distribution: the Drug Enforcement Agency has clamped down on the production of stimulants, causing the Federal Drug Administration to express concern that not enough pills are available for legitimate use.

What started as a childhood epidemic is now also spreading rapidly to adults. ADHD promises to become a very popular diagnosis in this new market because virtually everyone would like to concentrate better and be less distractible. And the differential diagnosis in adults is particularly difficult because nonspecific ADHD-like symptoms accompany virtually every one of the psychiatric disorders. Far too often, ADHD is becoming a common add-on diagnosis—especially used by clinicians prone to prescribing polypharmacy drug cocktails. Adult ADHD should be diagnosed only when symptoms are clear-cut, definitely impairing and had their onset in early childhood. There is no such thing as late-onset ADHD.

So, how can we sort things out? How can we succeed in reducing the overdiagnosis of ADHD without risking underrecognition and undertreatment? This book is a good place to start by recognizing that the ADHD has inherent strengths that, until now, have rarely been discussed. Dale has identified and explored several key advantages, including resilience, an ability to be calm in a crisis, a propensity for multitasking and a penchant for nonlinear thinking. He discusses new research and gives dozens of real-life examples of how these strengths play out in the day-to-day lives of people who have attained a level of personal and professional success in multiple fields, whether they are CEOs, teachers, truck drivers or small-town doctors. In addition, he highlights two fields in which those with ADHD appear to excel: athletics and entrepreneurship.

His takeaway is that by trying to suppress and medicate ADHD out of existence, we risk suppressing the gifts that are part of the package. Dale offers an array of useful and insightful alternatives for leveraging these strengths without the aid of a pill. Overmedicating, he argues, could dim the light that could be the next great business leader, explorer or innovator.

Parents are the first line of protection against the glut of medicating. Increasing physical activity can help fidgety kids. Enroll them in a team sport, swimming, yoga, martial arts, dance or tumbling—anything to let the kid blow off steam and acquire discipline. This book lays out a host of pragmatic options for both children and adults to improve education, career and relationships. Not every difference is a sign of dysfunction. Kids differ in the pace of their development. Immaturity is not a disease. Medications can be helpful, sometimes essential, for clear-cut and severe cases when all else has failed, but only as a last resort, not as a careless panacea.

We don't help our kids by giving them an inaccurate ADHD diagnosis and prescribing unnecessary medication. We help our kids by loving them, accepting them and helping them to find and use their strengths.

—Allen Frances, MD
Chair of the *DSM-IV* Task Force
Author of *Saving Normal*

AUTHOR'S NOTE

To respect the privacy of a few individuals mentioned in this book, names and identifying details have been changed. First and last names are used for those who were willing to be fully identified.

INTRODUCTION

Why ADHD Can Be Your Greatest Strength

Wwhat do David Neeleman, founder of JetBlue; John Chambers, CEO of Cisco; and business mogul Sir Richard Branson have in common? They, along with the singer Pink, Ty Pennington, Adam Levine and countless other high-profile achievers have publicly embraced their diagnosis of ADHD, and for good reason. For many, this trait is a blessing, not a curse.

It's time to dispel the widespread misperception that this is only an affliction in need of a fix. Even its name—Attention Deficit Disorder or Attention Deficit Hyperactivity Disorder—features a double whammy of negative connotations from those two *D*-words, implying that someone who possesses its typical characteristics is both broken and deficient. But this loaded term is a complete misnomer, because ADHD is not a minus. Leveraged and understood, it can be a huge plus! Just consider what David Neeleman has to say about the most overly diagnosed and medicated condition in mental health:

> If someone told me you could be normal or you could continue to have your ADD, I would take ADD. . . . I can distill complicated facts and come up with simple solutions. I can look out on an industry with all kinds of problems and say, "How can I do this better?"

He goes on to state that if there was a pill he could take to make it go away, he'd refuse to take it, and he's absolutely right. Far from being a group of symptoms that need to be medicated and managed, the most common features are, in fact, strengths that some of the world's most accomplished people have leveraged to attain new heights in their chosen fields.

Those with ADHD are life's entrepreneurs, CEOs, leaders, explorers, champion athletes and out-of-the-box thinkers, with extraordinary abilities to work under pressure, rebound from crises, multitask and conceive of ideas outside the restrictions of linear thinking. While people with ADHD can have trouble focusing on any one task, if something piques their interest they can become hyperfocused, able to carry an idea or task through to new heights of achievement. They are also an overwhelmingly positive bunch, possessing an innate resilience, high energy and a sense of humor that allows them to get past the many challenges of day-to-day living, and to keep on trying.

Look closely at many of the world's most cutting-edge CEOs, those who have created new products, transformed their industry landscapes and founded their own businesses from scratch, and chances are you'll find they possess a greater or lesser degree of the ADHD trait. These are the people who push the boundaries of what's possible and refuse to accept the restrictions of the status quo, and that is a good thing.

Simply put, ADHD can be best understood as a brain with a very low boredom threshold. (Yes, this is greatly simplified; I wish it were so easy.) People who have it chafe against the mundane and routine, and yet they excel in chaotic situations. Centuries ago, they would have been the restless ones in the village during times of plenty. But when famine or catastrophe struck, they were the fearless leaders who found new lands or new ways of surviving. A research study found high populations of those with the genetic background for ADHD in far-flung places like Siberia, Tierra del Fuego and Australia, prompting scientists to refer to the dopamine transporter gene associated with ADHD as the "explorer gene," something we'll be *exploring* in more detail in Chapter Four.

Now, I can't say for certain that this set of genes led the dawn of civilization, but there is no question they gave our adaptable and risk-taking ADHD forebears an evolutionary advantage. This genetic trait still exists in our species for a reason. Impulsivity, for example, which gets a bad rap today, could mean the difference between life and death in times of grave danger, when there is no time to waste analyzing a decision. Think about it. Our ADHD forebears were the prehistoric survivors who could calmly make a split-second decision to jump off a cliff to save themselves from a charging saber-toothed tiger. Jumping off a cliff may look crazy. But in fact, this impulsive act, or what some might call a gut instinct, is a split-second calculation based on the odds of survival. After all, a possible broken limb is better than being mauled to death. That quick reaction may be your only real chance of survival.

Today, in these turbulent times of economic, social and technological transition, the ADHD adventurer's moment has come again, and you will meet many who are finding new frontiers as they travel, explore and discover.

These next pages will challenge the standard view that individuals must suppress their adventurous natures and attempt to squeeze into our ever-narrowing definition of what is defined as normal by focusing on the many positives of a condition that, for many, has contributed to the unique position they hold in the world today. We need to recognize, embrace and skillfully use the best of this ADHD trait, not manage or stifle or "normalize" the very qualities that could define our next generation's leaders.

This book explodes the myth that ADHD is a problem that needs to be fixed. Of course, many do struggle with the "symptoms," and need treatment. Yes, there is a flip side to some of these strengths in the absence of self-awareness and the use of certain strategies to overcome the weaknesses. But for too long, educators and mental health experts have been overdiagnosing and overprescribing to the detriment of our nation's children. It's a fact that's only just beginning to get recognition from former proponents of stimulant use among members of the medical community.

In the spring of 2014, Dr. Keith Conners, who was among the first physicians to legitimize ADHD as a diagnosis, called our surging diagnosis and prescription rates "a national disaster of dangerous proportions."

ADHD diagnoses have been climbing exponentially. Statistics vary depending on which study you cite, but in the United States the National Center for Health Statistics reports that 6.4 million American kids (11 percent) ages three through seventeen have been diagnosed. Even more disturbing is the number of children now on medication for ADHD: 3.5 million; up from 600,000 in 1990, according to the Centers for Disease Control and Prevention (CDC).

"The numbers make it look like an epidemic," Dr. Conners told the *New York Times*. "Well, it's not. It's preposterous. This is a concoction to justify the giving out of medications at unprecedented and unjustifiable levels."

"Honor dies where conflict of interest lies," says Dr. Allen Frances, a professor emeritus at Duke University and the former chairman of the *DSM-IV* Task Force (*DSM* referring to *Diagnostic and Statistical Manual of Mental Disorders*, which you will be hearing more about in the coming pages). Dr. Frances, one of the most respected experts in this field, has expressed his outrage at how closely tied the so-called thought leaders in ADHD are to Big Pharma, and has become an outspoken critic of this trend to overdiagnose and medicate even toddlers, which he aptly calls "reckless."

Interestingly, the state-by-state variability ranges from 5.6 percent in Nevada to 15.6 percent in North Carolina. What does that say about the validity of a diagnosis? Why do three times more kids in North Carolina have ADHD than in Nevada? Is it the water, or is the desert a cure? Even more stark is the comparison with the United Kingdom, where the average diagnosis rate is less than 2 percent. Or France, where the percentage of kids diagnosed and medicated for ADHD is less than 0.5 percent!

This profound discrepancy is fueled by Big Pharma, overworked teachers, psychiatrists, stressed-out parents, a pop-a-pill mentality and our microwave culture. In a highly competitive environment where it pays to conform and be "normal," there's an unhealthy tendency for parents, doctors and educators to identify something as a problem in the hopes of finding a cure.

ADHD wasn't even recognized as a condition until 1980, much less treated, but it's since become one of the most searched terms on the Internet, more than *sex* and *death* (but, interestingly, below *Twitter*, *Facebook* and *Google*). When college students are abusing drugs like Ritalin to ace tests and one of the hottest stories in sports involves suspensions of NFL players doping with stimulants, and kids in middle school aren't allowed in class unless they take their medication, something is seriously wrong.

It's time to say the pendulum has swung too far and must head the other way. Look, I'm not suggesting that in severe cases treatment for ADHD is not indicated, but do more than one in ten kids really merit the diagnosis? What's needed is a drastic shift in the way we diagnose, view and handle what is more of a distinctive personality type than a debilitating psychological condition. We need to understand that ADHD isn't just something that flicks on and off like a switch. It exists along a continuum, on a scale from 1 to 10, and only a few with the diagnosis have symptoms that are severe enough to merit the highest ratings of 9, 10 or 10+ and hence require medication, but as a last resort—not first. For most, all it takes is awareness and a few simple adjustments to leverage this trait into your greatest strength.

I am going to give you the tools and information to turn back this tide. As parents, children, teens and adults with ADHD, you deserve a brand-new perspective about this diagnosis, as well as a range of prescriptions (not pills) to help you or your loved one identify the many strengths of this trait. By the end of this book, you will be able to develop a life's path that fits, and enhance the best of ADHD to maximize potential in school, career, relationships and life.

Part I will define ADHD, its history, genetics and pathology, put

it into historical context and speculate on the many extraordinary figures throughout the ages, such as Christopher Columbus, Leonardo
da Vinci, Mozart, Eleanor Roosevelt, Virginia Woolf and Benjamin
Franklin, who probably had this trait in abundance. It will examine
the effect an ADHD diagnosis has on a child, and propose innovative
and practical ways to harness their potential with descriptions of progressive academic programs that could serve as a blueprint for educators and parents.

There will also be a quiz to help you determine where you, or
your child, sit on the ADHD continuum, and data that describes how
ADHD typically manifests according to age group.

This section will also discuss when treatment may be needed and
those last-resort instances when it's appropriate to medicate, with
strong caveats about the potential side effects, the tendency to overmedicate and the abuse of these stimulant drugs. It will also offer
some alternative methods that, instead of suppressing the strengths,
improve the focus and calm necessary to maximize them—including,
but not limited to, mindfulness practice, strategies on how to study,
how to kick into hyperfocus mode and the beneficial effects of exercise. Diet will also be addressed, but not in a way most would expect.
You are not necessarily what you eat!

Part II will focus on the many advantages of ADHD, using success
stories from all walks of life, from real people with everyday jobs all
the way to high-profile celebrities, doctors, lawyers, athletes, CEOs
and entrepreneurs—to highlight these strengths. Conversations with
everyone from small-business owners to business moguls will illumi-
nate how nonlinear thinking can spawn entire industries, and a low
boredom threshold can lead to multiple interconnected businesses
that make up a multibillion-dollar commercial empire.

It's worth noting here that the vast majority of people interviewed
for this book were more than happy to be on the record and share
their stories with the world. This is striking, because for most books
in the mental health field it's almost impossible to reveal identities
due to stigma. The interviewees' eagerness to fully participate shows

that a positive shift in perceptions has begun, helped in part by the high-profile celebrities, athletes and businesspeople who have publicly embraced their diagnoses. The *New York Times* has also done some stellar reporting over the past two years, putting misunderstandings about ADHD and its overmedication in the spotlight. The *Times'* coverage has doubtless helped to raise awareness and change attitudes toward the diagnosis. But make no mistake, the stigma still exists, and can affect perceptions in certain career fields, which is why a small handful of our interview subjects requested anonymity.

Part III will illustrate how these strengths can be leveraged in entrepreneurship, athletics and relationships. It will end with the best advice gleaned from the scores of successful ADHDers on the best way to find your fit. Because, more than most people, those with ADHD must have passion to be truly engaged and stimulated by their life's work.

Because there is no one-size-fits-all tool for a trait that has many individual variables, we have laced this book with dozens of inspirational stories. Men and women of all ages and backgrounds have experiences and insights to share, from Christopher Lauer, the young German politician who stands on the podium and, with little to no preparation, gives some of the most rousing speeches of any Berlin public figure, to fashion designer Kelly Dooley, the consummate multitasker whose brand has become a cult favorite among celebrities. You will meet business moguls and athletes, like NFL quarterback Dave Krieg, one of the most prolific passers in NFL history. And middle school teachers, like Tichelle Harris, who switched from a career in banking to teach and transform the lives of underserved kids, doing all that she can to inspire other young ADHDers like herself, who might not otherwise get the mentoring they need inside the public education system.

Each of these ADHDers has a life and career story as unique as their fingerprints, having carved out jobs and businesses for themselves that are as fascinating as they are unconventional and unexpected. But the one thing they all have in common is a tool kit with specific and practical tips. In their self-awareness, developed through life experience, research or with the support of understanding and educated family members and partners, they have come up with ways that work for them to manage their time, recharge, refocus and follow through. Their particular tools may not work for everyone, but they will inspire you to assemble your own kit to better leverage the strengths of the ADHD trait.

Entrepreneur Shane Jordan, for example, who owns a thriving chain of computer repair shops, talks about how the singular focus of riding his motorbike or landing a plane—his two favorite hobbies—creates a stillness and calm in his mind that's as good as a week's vacation on a beach for someone without ADHD. Trade show and real estate CEO Kenneth "Bucky" Buckman shares how he manages his high energy by listening to his body, which shuts down every six months or so and forces him to rest, so that he can power up again for the next business challenge. Home decorating start-up owner Anita Erickson filters out the distraction of all the thoughts running through her brain by writing them down on lists. The simple act of writing it down helps her to mentally de-clutter, so that she can focus on the main priorities of her day.

Where applicable, we will include these takeaways, to help those with the diagnosis, as well as their family members, spouses, teachers and peers, better leverage their strengths. Specific and practical information will be offered, in quick bullet points, at the end of the relevant chapters, the better to suit fast minds eager to get to the point!

But by far the most important takeaway from the book is that there is a vast world of possibility out there for people with the ADHD trait. The key to a successful life *because of*, not *in spite of*, ADHD is acceptance. Be proud of who you are and recognize that your unique combination of genetics, brain chemistry and personality could land you in the pages of history. No, your brain does not work like a "normal" brain. So what? It's a matter of leveraging its characteristics as strengths, choosing the right career and education path and maintaining an awareness of what works, without struggling to try to fit into a box that teachers, family, peers and the rest of society call "normal." ADHD is not a disorder; it's a difference that, in the right context and with a set of customized tools, can help you or your child become one of life's explorers, leaders, inventors or entrepreneurs. This trait is precisely what can give you the edge. It's your distinct advantage, so go ahead, embrace it!

I should know. I am a psychiatrist with ADHD and, no, I have never taken medication for it. Instead, I've stayed busy, leveraging my restless nature and innate curiosity to establish a thriving practice, develop multiple successful psychiatric programs and launch several successful businesses and author a *New York Times* best seller, *Better Than Normal*.

Interestingly, I did not even realize I was an ADHDer until I wrote the *Better Than Normal* chapter on ADHD. (Physicians aren't always the best at self-diagnosis.) The more I delved into the research, the more I recognized myself, and the many ways I had instinctively leveraged the strengths of this trait over the years. The revelation was transformative, and bringing more consciousness to everything I do has greatly enhanced my life. Sure, I need to work around certain aspects of this trait: I'm easily bored, get distracted and linear thinking does not come naturally. But I've learned alternative ways of achieving my goals that in the end are so much easier for me, and today I consider the ADHD trait my greatest gift.

PART I

Exploding the Myth

CHAPTER ONE

Born This Way

When *Extreme Home Makeover* star Ty Pennington was attending grade school in Atlanta, Georgia, his teachers didn't know what to do with him. It was so bad that, when his mother, who was studying to be a child psychologist, asked the school principal to let her observe the school's ten "most challenging children" in the classroom, he replied, "Mrs. Pennington, I don't think you want to see this."

Within the twenty minutes his mother watched her son from behind the door, Ty tried to climb out the window, swung from the blinds, slapped his classmates on the back of their heads, stripped off most of his clothes and rode his desk around the room as if it were a jeep. It wasn't that he was trying to be a bully. He just needed an outlet for all his pent-up energy, and the extra attention was an added bonus.

"To call me distracting would be an understatement," he shared with me. "I got so bored and far behind what was being taught that I found my entertainment by entertaining the class."

Class Clown

But he suffered for it. Moving from school to school, getting his butt kicked at recess, he gained a reputation for being "a certain type of kid." He became so well known for his boisterous conduct that by the time he hit middle school, his teachers had him permanently sitting in the hallway. It wasn't until his family moved to the suburbs and Ty started at a new school where he wasn't known that his grades started to improve. A new environment and stimuli alleviated his boredom, which in turn helped him focus more. It worked for a while, until the novelty wore off and he began earning the same reputation again.

This was during the seventies, long before ADD or ADHD even existed as a diagnosis, so Ty suffered the pain of not knowing why he was different. He was simply branded a "problem child." Like a multitude of others, his early school experience was tortuous and demoralizing. The *H* in his ADHD—Hyperactivity—was especially pronounced. No one, with the exception of his more enlightened mother, believed he would become a success in life. No one else was interested in making sure he got an education. Instead, they put him on antihistamines to keep him drowsy and under control while they focused on teaching the kids in class they deemed "worthy, with a future."

Ty's self-esteem took a beating. He was the kid who couldn't be trusted not to burn down the house if he was left alone. But as he got older, he saw a glimmer of hope. He took up soccer, which channeled all that extra energy and built up his self-confidence.

"All of a sudden it came together and I could read the field. I went from sitting on the bench to scoring hat tricks repeatedly in a game," he says.

Learning to Learn

After his first year in college, Ty was finally diagnosed with ADHD, and the knowledge that his brain was different from others' helped him to see that he was not necessarily a bad kid, or less capable than his peers. The diagnosis was a shock at first.

"It was not what I wanted to hear at that age," he told me. "I was going through a lot, questioning my parents, authority, the meaning of life. . . . And then to find out I had a mental difference. It was rough."

But his doctor, who also had ADHD, helped Ty to recognize his strengths. This newfound self-awareness was also a relief. He finally understood why he couldn't retain anything he'd read and the words were just a blur. A visual thinker, he'd draw, and those visual cues would remind him of the answers in class. He'd been sketching some macabre scenes of wagons drawn by rats, carrying giant severed fingers—scenes that had him sent to the therapist's office. But his therapist told him he had a gift, which gave Ty the courage to work full-time as a carpenter to put himself through art school, where he excelled.

There were a few years of house painting and modeling to pay the bills before he made it in show business and became a household name. Ty was anything but an overnight success. He modeled for J.Crew and Swatch, and appeared on television spots for Macy's and Levi's. Then he started doing set designs in Hollywood. But when he was eventually approached to be on *Trading Spaces*, Ty knew he'd found his niche.

"They needed someone like me—slightly sarcastic, knows his way around a building site—so I went on an audition and got a job being myself. I was blown away!"

Finding His Fit

Then came *Extreme Home Makeover*, which was originally intended to be no more than a thirteen-part series. When the producers asked him if he could build a house from top to bottom in just seven days, Ty laughed and told them:

"It'd make for a hell of a show, but you'd have to be nuts to try."

Or if not nuts, at least have some of the advantages of ADHD. Rebuilding a home top to bottom, inside and out, in just seven days would leverage every single ADHD strength he had: multitasking, risk-taking, physical and mental energy, calm in the middle of chaos, a desire to move quickly from one thing to the next, as well as the ability to see the whole and all the moving parts of a project, and how they relate to one another. Throughout each project, he could remain hyperfocused because he was passionate about the project and loved the thrill. The pressure of having to do all that work within a tight time frame also stimulated his ADHD brain and left him with no time for boredom.

"It was as if the job created itself for me," he says.

Today, Ty is the perfect poster boy for ADHD. He even wears a T-shirt that reads OMFG ADHD, and named his home décor business Art Design Home Décor (ADHD), ingeniously co-opting the diagnosis as his brand. This is a man whose enthusiasm is infectious, and his high energy and optimism are among the very attributes that can turn ADHD into such a powerful advantage. He not only accepts, he embraces ADHD strengths as a part of who he is and the success he enjoys today. Although it wasn't always apparent to him that it was a blessing to be born this way, he now wears the ADHD label with pride.

Poster Child

Ty took the time to speak with me despite multiple projects on the go, including, incidentally, filming a public service announcement on ADHD awareness immediately after our phone interview. But ADHD advocate is just one of dozens of roles the Emmy-winning television star plays in a career that includes actor, entrepreneur, producer, writer, author, furniture manufacturer, artist and philanthropist. Through his chosen career, or I should say careers, Ty could not have found better outlets for his high energy, intense enthusiasm and curiosity, combined with a restless nature and low boredom threshold.

His is one of many success stories you will read about in these next pages. Instinctively, Ty has figured out how to leverage his traits into a stellar career that is uniquely suited to the way his brain is wired. By going public with ADHD, Ty also sets a great example, proving that you don't have to live inside that box called "normal" in order to make it. In fact, being who he is, allowing his ADHD flag to fly, has enabled him to carve out an extraordinary career path that combines all his passions and strengths and opens him up to a world of possibility.

The lesson here is that the ADHD traits should never be suppressed. ADHD is a natural part of the human condition. Not only is it in the normal range, in many ways it can make us *better* than normal. No, it's not innate to everyone; we don't all jump from idea to idea or embrace spontaneity and risk—that would lead to utter chaos. It takes both so-called normal and ADHD to make the world go 'round. But it's time to recognize that those with the ADHD trait play a tremendously important role in our society as innovators, explorers, leaders and risk-takers. We need them to shake things up a bit and challenge the status quo.

Of course, it's not black-and-white. The world isn't divided up cleanly into those who have it and those who don't, because not all those who have ADHD possess it to the same degree. Like all psychological traits, it exists along a continuum, on a scale of 1 to 10. I am an 8 and I suspect, although I have not formally assessed him, that Ty is closer to a 10.

That means our brains are wired a little differently from those who fall lower on the trait continuum, and at the end of this chapter I will give you the tool—a quiz—to figure out where you or your loved one lie on the spectrum.

It's Not a Disorder, It's a Difference

So what exactly is ADHD? The trait is a combination of brain chemistry and genetics that affect the dopamine transporter gene and its receptors. Simply put, the brain reacts differently to stimulation in someone with an 8 or 9 or 10 on the scale, compared with someone who is calm and well organized or, say, a 1 on the continuum. In effect the risk, the pressure of a deadline, chaos or the possibility that you are about to go off a cliff actually causes a different reaction in those high on the ADHD scale. They actually feel a rush, or euphoria, not the panic, anxiety or dread many would experience who don't have ADHD. These extreme states actually boost a feel-good response in the brain, which is why many with ADHD appear so focused and functional in the middle of a maelstrom.

I'll delve more deeply into the science, diagnostics, demographics and terms in the next chapter, but here is a quick qualifier on the difference between ADHD and ADD:

Simply put, ADHD and ADD are exactly the same thing. ADD stands for Attention Deficit Disorder. In its earlier usage there was a modifier specifying either with or without hyperactivity. In 1987 the official diagnosis was changed to ADHD (Attention Deficit Hyperactivity Disorder). Today the most common usage is ADHD, encompassing all the symptoms of inattention, whether you have hyperactivity or not.

Generally speaking, an ADHD diagnosis means you have some of the following tendencies: difficulty focusing or staying on task; inattention to details; inability to sustain attention; trouble listening; disorganization; avoidance of tasks you don't find interesting; frequently losing things; being easily distracted by external stimuli; and forgetfulness. People with six of these tendencies qualify as having the inattentive part of ADHD, according to the *Diagnostic and Statistical Manual of Mental Disorders* (*DSM-V*).

The Flip Side

But there's another way to look at what most in the mental health field like to regard as symptoms. Flip them around and you have the following: an ability to multitask; a propensity to thrive in situations of chaos; creative, nonlinear thinking; an adventurous spirit; a capacity for hyperfocus on something that fascinates you; resilience; high energy; a willingness to take calculated risks; and calmness under pressure.

Fascinating, the way a different lens can affect the view, isn't it?

Suddenly they become strengths, not debilitating weaknesses or character flaws.

One of the things I have noticed from my conversations with successful patients, interviewees and friends who rank highly on the ADHD continuum is that they have excelled precisely because they embrace their so-called symptoms. Perry Sanders, a highly accomplished entertainment lawyer, television producer and commercial real estate entrepreneur, has a classic case of ADHD, but he doesn't see it as a big deal because this trait has worked so well for him in business that he can't imagine how it could possibly be labeled a "disorder," when it is, in fact, the most powerful tool in his box.

"People may not understand how my brain functions and view it as a problem, but it works well for me," he says.

The same healthy self-regard goes for Ty, who embodies many of the strengths of ADHD and possesses the self-awareness to identify exactly how each aspect of these traits has contributed to his success.

Of course, these are strengths anyone can have. I am not saying that this compendium of characteristics is exclusive to people with ADHD, but in my practice I have seen a striking predominance of these qualities in conjunction with each other. Taken to extremes, or under the wrong circumstances, they can be a problem. Multitasking, for example, might result in an inability to follow one thing through to completion. But they also can be useful, and certainly don't require us to slap on a diagnosis.

Following are a few of the ADHD advantages as embodied by the examples of various success stories, which I will detail further with research and examples in Part II.

Nonlinear Thinking

Professional photographer and soccer dad Freddie, who is at least a 9 on the ADHD continuum, is a classic example of a nonlinear thinker. His brain is on warp speed, zigzagging from one thought bubble to the next, coming up with some incredibly original and creative ideas in the process. It's hard to follow for most people, but makes perfect sense to him, and to everyone else with ADHD.

Freddie's mental agility can also translate into distractibility. He's a late bloomer who ricocheted from job to job on the most unlinear career path you could imagine, from fighting forest fires on the West Coast, to editing a start-up business magazine in Cambodia, to thought leadership consulting and PR for finance companies in Boston. Freddie found elements of each widely differing job description challenging and fun, but focus and follow-through became a problem, particularly in the corporate, nine-to-five roles. It was only when he discovered his talent for photography that it all came together.

Today, he roams to wherever his eyes and imagination take him, leveraging his nonlinear thought processes into profoundly moving visual images that capture moments in a human face, landscape or street scene that others simply wouldn't see.

"It's a way of seeing, using your peripheral vision and being in tune to your environment, and seeing how these seemingly random visual cues come together to tell a story," he explains.

In other words, each photograph offers a glimpse inside his highly creative, nonlinear ADHD brain.

Impulsivity

The tendency to act quickly, sometimes with little thought, on that flash of insight, intuition or gut feeling, which entertainer Howie Mandel possesses in abundance, gets a bad rap. Most people fear this unpredictable quality and anticipate disastrous consequences. But it can reap huge rewards as well.

No one could ever accuse Howie, the hugely successful comedian, actor, producer, *America's Got Talent* judge and game show host, of overthinking. He told me in a recent interview that he never planned on becoming a comedian. In fact, nothing in his life was ever planned.

"Everyone else I knew was charting a path to their future. I wasn't charting, nor did I have a path," he says.

But he had plenty of ambition. Howie wanted to become a millionaire, although he wasn't clear on the specifics. According to the usual standards, he was already doing well before he became a comedian. By the time he was in his early twenties and engaged to be married, his career in carpet and lighting sales was chugging along, albeit with a few bumps, and he was on track to be a business owner with a secure middle- to upper-middle-class lifestyle.

But he was always the jokester. One night, when he and his wife, Terry, were hanging out with friends, one of them suggested he try performing at Yuk Yuk's, a well-known stand-up venue in Toronto, and with no prior experience in performing, Howie signed up to take the stage on the club's next amateur night.

The fact that it was a set date, and he was required to have his five-minute stand-up routine all planned out in advance, filled him with dread. Yet, with little preparation, he stood up on that stage, and had the audience in stitches with some filthy dialogue that just came to him, funny voices, and such a completely winning way of interacting with the crowd that he was invited back as a featured act. At first he genuinely didn't know why they were laughing so hard, and threw his hands up the air, saying, "What, what?" The gesture went down so well it became the signature part of his act, as did his "borderline psychotic" persona, as he puts it. It was the beginning of a passion and obsession that prompted Howie to push further and further beyond the edge.

Within a year, he was on vacation in Los Angeles with Terry and some friends when he decided to go to the famed Comedy Store on amateur night. There he met an acquaintance from the Toronto stand-up circuit, who helped him sign up for a set and introduced him to the executive producer of a comedy game show called *Make Me Laugh*. He did his Yuk Yuk's act, with a few more ad-libs, and impressed the producer so much, he was invited to audition for the show.

Howie attributes his greatest comedic successes to his spontaneity. His unique brand of humor is unexpected and out of the blue. "All those things I've done on impulse that have turned out great were because of ADHD," he told me.

One of his most infamous shticks at that time happened completely on impulse. His "Donny the half man, half chicken" routine included placing a latex glove over his head and using the fingers as a cockscomb. One night, out of the blue, he decided to pull the glove farther down on his face, inflating and deflating it by blowing through his nose. The more the fingers rose up and down on top of his head, the more the audience laughed. His absurd comedic sense is a clear example of impulsivity and nonlinear thinking.

A Willingness to Take Risks

Not to be confused with impulsivity, another key attribute of those with ADHD is risk-taking. It means that some thought goes into certain decisions, although they are decisions most people would not dare to make. Another way of putting it is that they have an adventurous spirit.

In the case of Bradley, a truck driver from Texas, that willingness to put everything on the line and take a flying leap into the unknown gave him a career and a livelihood beyond his wildest expectations. Another late bloomer, Bradley, who is forty-seven, had been struggling to find his fit most of his adult life.

"I had five or six kinda careers, all related to driving and operating trucks and heavy equipment, and it all bored me to death," he says.

He finally fell into long-haul trucking and, while he was good at it and able to hustle the work, the tedium became unbearable. But then he had the chance to drive an oversized load—a specialty kind of transportation that requires escort vehicles, route planning, and a variety of permits depending on the roads and route taken, coupled with the skill to handle a 120,000-pound payload.

Bradley loved the challenge and the fact that you would only have to haul about two loads per month, freeing him to pursue his many other interests. When he looked into it he found there was a need for qualified truckers to haul huge multimillion-dollar electrical control buildings from the factory to locations across the United States, he impulsively decided to go for it. For the first time in his life, Bradley had discovered something that met his need for adventure and that could sustain his interest. So he asked his mother to mortgage her house, and combined his own savings, so that he could buy the specialty tractor-trailer he needed for $250,000.

This was at the start of one of the worst recessions in decades. Other truckers said he was crazy. Without customers, he'd never be able to cover his costs. He saw it differently. Though he barely will admit to having ADHD due to the stigma, he does admit to all the characteristics of the trait. And he saw this as his chance—maybe his only chance—to put those strengths to use. He *had* to go for it. So he put bids on jobs before he even had the truck, and then farmed them out to other truckers until he had his own vehicle. Within a year he was able to pay his mother back, and now makes a comfortable living for his family, bringing in $30,000 to $60,000 per job. Even better, he now has a reputation as one of the top drivers in the field, getting to pick and choose the best and most challenging deliveries.

"It was a big giant gamble," says Bradley, who also happens to be a poker player in his free time. "But I really felt at the time it was my only option to find stability and do something that I loved, that would not bore me to death, and obviously it paid off."

Resilience

Another highly valuable trait that those with ADHD have is resilience. So when they take a risk and, as can often be the case, they fail, they have this uncanny ability to bounce back.

Serial entrepreneur Benjamin Blanchard doesn't mind failing. In fact, he says, "I just don't have the attention span to dwell on setbacks. I get bored so easily." So when a business venture doesn't quite go according to plan, he's not interested in doing a postmortem, because he's already moved on to the next exciting idea. On the one hand, you could argue that he should be more cautious, but not allowing an excess of fear to hold him back is why, at just twenty-seven, he already has three thriving businesses.

This fearlessness and ability to move forward is something that Ben has in common with many of the world's most successful CEOs and entrepreneurs. It's not that they don't learn from their mistakes, it's just that they are not afraid to try virtually anything.

JetBlue founder David Neeleman's first start-up, a tour-operating company out of Salt Lake City that he dropped out of college to run, was a failure, because the airline he'd partnered with went out of business, and all the money he'd paid up front for their services had to be written off. But that just propelled him to the next venture, a partnership with Morris Air, which was eventually sold to Southwest Airlines for $130 million. As the second largest shareholder, that gave him enough capital to start up JetBlue. He also learned valuable lessons from the first failure—the importance of capitalization and never being beholden to an outside entity.

He told me, "It's not what happens to you in life, it's how you react to it, and how you are able to rebound."

Restlessness

Of course, it takes a tremendous amount of energy to bounce from one thing to the next. Most with ADHD have an abundance of physical and mental energy, or restlessness. It's one reason why they often enjoy athletics.

Early on, four-time Super Bowl champion and sportscaster Terry Bradshaw channeled his excess energy into sports. In high school he set the national record for the javelin, and used that powerful throwing arm to win four Super Bowls as the quarterback of the Pittsburgh Steelers.

That restlessness propels Terry into other areas besides sports. In addition to being a two-time Emmy-winning sportscaster, since his retirement from football he has become an author, horse breeder and country singer.

"When you've got something to prove, there's nothing greater than a challenge," Terry has famously said. He has since become an advocate for ADHD and mental health awareness.

The Multitasker

That restlessness translates well into the extraordinary juggling act that describes the careers of many ADHD success stories. A self-described "jack-of-all-trades," Ty Pennington is happiest when he's moving from one project to the next, no matter how exhausting and physically demanding that can be. So I would add this title to his long and varied résumé: master multitasker.

He enjoys it so much that he loses himself in a project or, rather, projects. At the height of *Extreme Makeover*, he spent an average of 240 labor-intensive days a year working nonstop, battling heat stroke, food poisoning and torn muscles because the show must go on, and barely noticing the aches and pains. He was multitasking on steroids!

The work escalated even more after the show's second season, when Ty was doing two homes in one week. He describes tearing down the highway to another location in one state, going back and forth between each family to see the results of the renovations, and loving every moment of it. "Never once was I not being stimulated," he recalls.

For someone like Ty, it's impossible to do just one thing at a time. "I've found the perfect job for someone who doesn't ever want to get bored," Ty told me. "Traveling to a new place, starting a new project, thinking about a new idea, keeps the adrenaline and creative juices flowing. I may be executing plan A, but if I'm not also developing plans B, C and D I fall into a rut and get sloppy."

But just as the ADHD multitasker can buzz from task to task, she also has the ability to hyperfocus when she is truly engaged and passionate about something. Television journalist Lisa Ling, for example, who at forty was diagnosed on her own show *Our America with Lisa Ling*, described it this way when she was speaking with her psychiatrist:

"When I'm immersed in a story, then I feel like I can laser-focus. But if I'm not working, my mind goes in every direction but where it's supposed to go."

Cool Under Pressure

With so much going on in their lives, those with ADHD are remarkably calm in the middle of a maelstrom. It's when they find themselves in their element. There's nothing former college volleyball star and start-up incubator consultant Tatiana finds more engaging than the pressure of many challenges coming at her at once. While traveling around the world for her sport, playing against other Junior Olympic feeder teams, the middle of that volleyball court was her favorite place to be. She relished being under the gun to make the deciding shot, reading the expressions and movements of the other players and processing all that information. It was like being in the still center of the storm.

"My brain is always tuned in to what is going on in the moment," she says. "When things are flashing before my eyes, I feel perfectly in control, because I know how to react faster than anyone else around me."

The twenty-three-year-old Chicago native hopes to translate this strength into her chosen career path as an entrepreneur—although she still enjoys a few games of volleyball on weekends.

That calm amid the chaos can be an asset in a multitude of professions. Chef Alexis Hernandez also thrives under the gun, building his career on ruthless cooking competitions, having faced off with the likes of Bobby Flay, Rachael Ray and Wolfgang Puck and beating out thousands of hopefuls to become a finalist on season six of *The Next Food Network Star*. The New Jersey native reveled in the heat of the kitchen, going against the clock to prepare inventive gourmet meals, never breaking a sweat as the final seconds of each challenge ticked away.

Today, he is executive chef at the Union Hill Kitchen in Atlanta and, when he's not speaking about his ADHD diagnosis to highlight its positive attributes, has appeared on the hit morning show *Café CNN*.

Of course, not everyone with ADHD possesses all of these tendencies, or at least not in equal measure. And many of us share overlapping strengths. We are, after all, individuals. But decades of clinical practice, during which I have treated thousands of patients, has convinced me that the previously mentioned characteristics of ADHD are strikingly common, and recent research in this field bolsters my case. But perhaps the most powerful evidence of ADHD's advantages can be found in the inspiring stories you will read in these next chapters, detailing the real-life successes of those who actually possess the trait and recognize the many ways in which it can be as much a gift as a diagnosis.

Or, as Chef Alexis puts it:

"I have always felt that the way that my brain thinks, there's a beauty in it, and if I'm able to look at the beauty in it, I can live my life the way I want."

THE TOOL KIT: WHERE DO I FIT ON THE CONTINUUM?

If you have not already been diagnosed with it, suspect you may have it, or have been told by friends and loved ones that you do have it, there is an abundance of quizzes that exist online to help you figure out if you have ADHD. Unfortunately, many are sponsored by pharmaceutical companies that sell treatments, and are oversimplified, leading to questionable results. We will talk more about how children are diagnosed in Chapter Three. (Hint: Until now, the standards for a diagnosis have been loose.) But for adults, one of the more comprehensive surveys has been made by the National Resource Center on ADHD, a program of the advocacy group CHADD (Children and Adults with Attention-Deficit/ Hyperactivity Disorder): http://www.help4adhd.org/documents /adultadhdselfreportscale-asrs-v1-1.pdf.

A quiz developed and verified in conjunction with psychologist Dr. Jerry Whiteman in my last book, *Better Than Normal*, can also quickly tell you whether you are a 4, a 9 or a 10+ on the continuum. While none of what follows should be considered official diagnoses, they will give you an awareness and an incentive to look into it further. That self-knowledge can be the first step toward managing the challenges and leveraging the strengths of this trait. So rate yourself on the following scale, and see where your ADHD superpowers lie.

Never   **Sometimes**   **Often**
1   2   3   4   5   6   7   8   9   10

_____ 1. I can't decide what I want to do.

_____ 2. I have a hard time staying focused on a task.

_____ 3. I'm hyperactive.

_____ 4. I'm restless.

_____ 5. I quickly lose interest in many things I usually enjoy.

_____ 6. I'm impulsive.

_____ 7. I try to do many things at once.

_____ 8. I feel like I have 100 things going through my mind.

_____ 9. I get bored easily.

_____10. I don't like waiting.

_____11. Sometimes I act before thinking things through.

_____12. I'm not very organized.

_____**TOTAL:**

Divide your total by 10 to get your ADHD score. That is where you lie on the continuum. If it is over 10 you are a 10+.

CHAPTER TWO

A Diagnosis of Boredom

When Mark Twain's hero Huckleberry Finn was forced to study spelling for an hour every day, he said, "I couldn't stood it much longer . . . it was deadly dull, and I was fidgety." His teacher, Miss Watson, threatened him with eternal damnation if he didn't pay attention. Huck replied that it didn't seem like such a bad alternative. "She got mad then, but I didn't mean no harm. All I wanted was to go somewheres; all I wanted was a change, I warn't particular."

Whether Mark Twain was Huck Finn has been a great literary debate for the ages. But based on all I have read about this author's life, it's my opinion that there are many autobiographical elements to the Huck Finn character, not least of which is his ADHD. So imagine if this literary genius were living out his childhood in today's world. He'd have been diagnosed, put on Adderall, and forced to sit quietly in a classroom, attending each day of school. Because he would be unable to let his childhood imagination roam free, all those early childhood memories of adventures that formed this beloved book might never have happened.

As our perceptions of ADHD are evolving, so is the diagnosis. That's why it's important to understand that the medical community still does not have all the answers. The assumptions parents, teachers and doctors make about the treatment of individuals with these traits are not always appropriate, and can do more harm than good. Too often, even medical professionals are winging it. Criteria for a diagnosis are being interpreted so loosely that almost anyone could qualify, and we're becoming too eager to slap a label on people in order to pull out the prescription pad.

Of course, the awareness that you have ADHD can actually be a good thing. But the problem is that we are calling it a diagnosis, which automatically suggests the need for treatment, which is almost always in the form of meds. A diagnosis also suggests a kind of uniformity to the trait that simply does not exist. We're overlooking too many variables in the range of symptoms and severity. It is *not* one-size-fits-all. While there is no question ADHD is a prevalent trait, it is not black-and-white. There are multiple shades of gray, and yet our culture keeps putting everyone in the same box when the effects of the trait are complex, nuanced and rarely require what has become the standard treatment—a pill.

Evolution of a Label

ADHD did not even exist as a diagnosis until 1980, when the third edition of the American Psychiatric Association's bible, *Diagnostic and Statistical Manual of Mental Disorders*, introduced the term to give kids with hyperactivity, impulsivity, short attention span and easy distractibility a diagnosis, or, if you prefer, a label. Back then it was simply called Attention Deficit Disorder, referring to children under the age of eighteen. The precursor, the 1968 edition of the *DSM*, listed something resembling the disorder which was called the "hyperkinetic reaction of childhood," focusing on hyperactivity, restlessness and a short attention span. It was a way of recognizing that all those restless mischievous kids, like Dennis the Menace, Calvin from *Calvin and Hobbes*, and the boy at the back of the classroom shooting spitballs, were not just being bad. They had a "condition," albeit a poorly understood one.

The *DSM-III* redefined it as a diagnosis that consists primarily of inattention, changing it in later editions to ADD with and without hyperactivity, before eventually settling on ADHD as a catchall in 1994, and listing three subtypes, including:

- ADHD, primarily inattentive.
- ADHD, primarily hyperactive/impulsive.
- ADHD, hyperactive/impulsive and inattentive combined.

In 2000, the revised fourth edition of the *DSM* also added a fourth category, Adult ADHD, which was a great boon to Big Pharma, which we will talk about in the next chapter.

I don't like using the broad term of ADHD in diagnosis, because it is not as clear as ADD with the listed subtypes. However, for the purposes of this book, and to avoid confusion, we will stick with the more widely accepted ADHD label.

If anything, the term has been too widely embraced. Who would have thought that, three decades after its introduction, the National Center for Health Statistics would report that 6.4 million American kids (11 percent) ages three through seventeen, and about 15 percent of school-age boys, would receive this diagnosis, with about half of those on medication? That represents a 53 percent rise in the last decade!

Getting It Wrong

William Evans, a professor of economic statistics at the University of Notre Dame, who published a paper on the subject in the *Journal of Health Economics* in 2010, was among the first to call out the epidemic of ADHD overdiagnosis in the United States. He found that the biggest predictor for the diagnosis of ADHD was the age of the child with respect to their grade. In other words, younger children in a given grade have more ADHD symptoms than older ones. No surprise there—younger kids clearly are more restless and less able to concentrate on a topic, or sit quietly in a classroom all day long. According to his research, "approximately 1.1 million children received an inappropriate diagnosis and over 800,000 received stimulant medication due only to relative maturity."

Let me quickly point out that I'm not opposed to medication to treat those with the most severe symptoms. At the high end of the continuum, some do struggle and need to be on medication, and for this group it may be worth the side effects. But do more than one out of every ten kids really have ADHD?

The Gender Gap

I should also mention that, while ADHD does affect girls, the diagnostic rates are much lower for them, with three boys to every one girl identified as having ADHD. It's possible that just as many girls have the trait as boys, and anecdotally we are seeing that the statistics may be skewed. I was surprised by the number of women who came forward to be interviewed for this book, and it's now becoming clear that girls/women appear to have a different set of "symptoms"—but more on this later.

Many of the ADHD women we've talked with say they did not get diagnosed until later in life, in many cases having been misdiagnosed with conditions like depression first. No research has explained this yet, but the hyperactivity component is less common in women, making it much harder for the nonpsychiatrist to diagnose, and may be confused with the frustration and mild depression often experienced by these women when they lack the awareness to leverage their strengths. Fortunately, most of those I spoke with sought second opinions and did not stay on the prescriptions for the various other disorders for which they were diagnosed.

Although she had some self-esteem issues because she wasn't where she thought she should be in life, Shanna Pearson felt no symptoms of the clinical depression that she was told she had after her first appointment with a mental health professional. Yes, she was feeling a little frustrated, but it was a far cry from that diagnosis. "There was no way I was depressed," says Shanna, who is now a successful Toronto-based ADHD coach and founder of the consultancy One Focus Total Success. Her high energy and zest for life just didn't add up to that cursory diagnosis.

Shanna first looked into whether she had ADHD at thirty-two, after a friend's father, who was in the mental health field, suggested she might have the trait. While she wasn't hyperactive, she was bursting with nervous energy, and mentally she seemed all over the place.

She didn't take his word for it, but she knew he had a point. Shanna, a self-described "scatterbrain," had already lived in eleven cities and four countries in eight years. On her last job, working at a U.S. education center for sixth-graders where about two-thirds had been diagnosed, she'd assumed it was a childhood disorder and didn't make the connection. But hearing the possibility for the first time from someone she trusted prompted Shanna to search further. She always knew she was different. She was always a daydreamer in school, although never disruptive enough to get diagnosed. Shanna was also "allergic to boredom."

As a teen and young adult Shanna couldn't stay in one place for longer than a few months, often purposely "creating drama" in her life and relationships to keep it interesting. "I was on a roller coaster," she says, adding that she found ways to smooth out the ride and work with her strengths without medication as soon as she learned what she had. "Finally it all made perfect sense," says Shanna, who developed ways to work with ADHD that became the basis of her ADHD coaching business, which now has thousands of clientele around the world.

Shanna's diagnostic story is typical among ADHD women. Because the symptoms tend to be less external they can be harder to recognize in girls, who, according to a Harris Interactive poll conducted by the National Center for Gender Issues and ADHD, tend to exhibit different signs and symptoms: poor self-esteem, worrying, perfectionism and nosiness—not necessarily the typical hyperactivity and lack of focus recognized in boys. They are risk-takers too, but in my experience that behavior often tends to manifest differently due to contrasting gender expectations, and perhaps for evolutionary reasons. (Men went out to hunt the woolly mammoth while women stayed behind in the village.) Growing up, women aren't necessarily encouraged to be physical risk-takers, so we may see this play out more in social interactions, such as creating drama. Boredom perhaps drives them to gossip as a type of self-stimulation. But there is much more research needed on ADHD in women, since most studies to date have focused on boys and men.

The same study found that 85 percent of the teachers and more than half the parents and general public believe that girls with ADHD are more likely to go undiagnosed, so now the push is on to increase diagnosis in girls. Yes, it's important to know you have the trait, and where it sits along the continuum, but that shouldn't automatically mean medication. While a diagnosis can bring self-awareness, which is a good thing, pills are *not* the quick-fix answer. In any case, girls are not necessarily underdiagnosed, it's just that health-care professionals and educators have to dig a little deeper to recognize the ADHD, which is what they should be doing with boys and girls alike. It appalls me to think that girls and women could become the new untapped stimulant market for Big Pharma, although I am sad to say it would not surprise me in the least.

In a *Wired* magazine interview in December 2010, Allen Frances (lead editor of the *Diagnostic and Statistical Manual for Mental Disorders-IV*) blamed the *DSM* itself. "We made mistakes that had terrible consequences," he says. One of these consequences has been that diagnoses of ADHD have skyrocketed. Gary Greenberg, psychotherapist and author of the article, writes: "Frances thinks his manual inadvertently facilitated these epidemics—and, in the bargain, fostered an increasing tendency to chalk up life's difficulties to mental illness and then treat them with psychiatric drugs."

The "Normal" Box

It is part of an overall direction in mental health that's troubling: the profession of psychiatry has taken on the role of defining "normal" in our society. Webster's dictionary defines normal as being "free from a mental disorder." As we purposely shrink the box called normal and it gets smaller and smaller, the abnormal universe expands to include almost everyone—hence these ever-loosening guidelines for the diagnosis. It enables us to say, "Don't worry, we can fix that with a pill and make you normal just like everyone else."

As I have said in my last book, *Better Than Normal*, our profession has not only redefined mental health by overdiagnosing and over-medicating an ever-expanding number of diagnoses, we are also taking away the hope of human nature by telling our patients that they are inherently "abnormal" and need to be fixed. The psychiatrist's office has gone from being the place no one would be caught dead visiting . . . to the place where a pill can fix anything. And psychiatry itself has gone from being stigmatized to glamorized.

This trend, which has gained even more momentum since I last visited the subject, ignores the fact that psychiatric conditions do not come with an on/off switch, but rather occur along a continuum, with only those on the highest end of the spectrum requiring treatment and, in some cases, medication. If we tighten up the diagnostic criteria to make them more specific and objective, we are less likely to misdiagnose and overmedicate today's Mark Twain.

ADHD on a Continuum

Let me take this moment to explain the continuum theory in more detail. As I outlined in *Better Than Normal*, there exists a handful of psychological traits that can be part of a normal character but when present in the extreme can be considered abnormal to the point where it can lead to a psychiatric diagnosis. To that end, I developed a scale of 1 (none of the trait) to 10 (superdominant trait) on the continuum—which came from the test you took at the end of the previous chapter. This continuum delineates where so-called normal ends and something diagnosable and treatable begins. For example, in the middle of the bipolar scale, an individual could be considered high energy, but it is by no means a disorder until it becomes a manic episode that interferes with daily function, like nonstop talking, pathologically high energy, no need for sleep, extreme risk-taking behavior and even psychosis.

Likewise, a 5 to 7 on the obsessive-compulsive disorder continuum would simply be a perfectionist, nothing more, but a 9 or 10 might have to open and close a door fifty times before walking into a room. Certainly not everyone who scores a 9 or 10 necessarily faces dysfunction or insurmountable challenges in daily life, particularly when it comes to ADHD. Someone on the high end of the continuum may be extremely energetic, adventurous and different from the norm, yet *still* does not need treatment.

This continuum applies to mental health in general, and ADHD in particular, which has been hit with an avalanche of overdiagnosis and treatment. It forces us to recognize that what we tend to label a disorder or diagnosis is, in most cases, nothing more than a collection of personality traits that exist to a greater or lesser degree and contribute to the uniqueness of an individual. They are the very traits that make us special and define who we are.

False Epidemic

The problem is, we tend to want to treat every aspect of the human condition as a kind of disease. As a recent landmark article in the *New York Times* pointed out, even some of ADHD's leading advocates now say we've been overzealous in trying to treat every ADHD child, and this has led to too many people receiving a diagnosis based on flimsy evidence. According to the *Times* article's analysis of the Centers for Disease Control and Prevention (CDC) data, "This disorder is now the second most frequent long-term diagnosis made in children, narrowly trailing asthma."

Our eagerness to slap a convenient label on kids causes doctors, teachers, even parents, to overlook other potential causes of ADHD-type behavior, including lack of sleep, anxiety or problems at home, resulting in stimulant treatment that makes their problems worse. And yet, not only do school-age children get overdiagnosed, toddlers are now being medicated for ADHD! It seems this has become easier than commonsense parenting skills. Instead of diagnosing and medicating at that age, establish age-appropriate boundaries. You'd be amazed at how much setting rules and sticking to them can improve most behavioral problems among toddlers. Our cultural shift has gone from basic discipline to diagnosis and treatment with a pill.

In a CDC study released in May 2014, the data suggested that more than 10,000 two- to three-year-olds on Medicaid are being medicated for ADHD, and potentially another 4,000 on private insurance. Even more disturbing, according to a report by the watchdog group Citizens Commission on Human Rights that was based on numbers crunched by IMS Health, a health information and analytics company, there are 1,422 zero- to one-year-olds on ADHD medications. Infants! What kind of knee-jerk reaction to a crying baby is that? There aren't even officially accepted guidelines for these infants and toddlers, because being restless, impulsive or hyperactive is developmentally perfectly normal.

The one small consolation is that the *DSM* says medication should only be a last resort for children ages four through five, and the American Academy of Pediatrics recently issued guidelines for diagnosis and prescription that apply to this patient population. They also recommend that parents and teachers must first undergo formal training to improve the child's environment or try other behavioral training—a rule of thumb that should be applied to all potential cases.

Diagnostic Checklist

Until now, there has been no hard science for an ADHD diagnosis, but instead simply a series of questions and assessments that help mental health professionals reach a conclusion. However, this is true for most psychiatric diagnoses. No accepted diagnostic test—that is, blood test or brain scan—exists for the major psychiatric conditions, and ADHD is no different. The *DSM* continues to adjust the standards of assessment with each new edition, but they're still flawed and prone to overinclusion.

Meanwhile, efforts are under way to bring more science to the diagnosis. Researchers at the Medical University of South Carolina have recently discovered that low brain iron *may* be an objective biomarker of ADHD. They used MRIs to measure the brain iron levels in twelve children diagnosed with ADHD who had never taken ADHD medication, and compared them with ten children with ADHD who had taken medication, as well as twenty-seven who did not have the ADHD diagnosis. The scans revealed that the brain iron levels in the children without ADHD was similar to those with the diagnosis who were taking ADHD medication, and that both groups had much higher brain iron levels than the unmedicated ADHD children. The researchers, who also took blood samples, found blood iron levels were comparable between all the study groups, suggesting that iron absorption into the brain may be lower in those with ADHD even when blood iron levels in the body are normal.

It's important to note that there is not yet any evidence that low brain iron is the actual cause of ADHD. But if larger studies confirm these findings, and researchers can replicate the potential of low brain iron as a biomarker, we may be able to use MRIs in clinical diagnoses of ADHD, although we are not there yet, and I am concerned that this is just another way to make it easier to diagnose ADHD and treat with medication. Unless low brain iron is found to be a cause and we can it treat it with iron, I am skeptical about the merits of this study.

Other diagnostic findings are even less significant. A recent study out of Tel Aviv University recently found that adults with ADHD who took a diagnostic computer test were unable to suppress involuntary eye blinks or movements in anticipation of visual stimuli. But on medication those eye movements were suppressed. The researchers argued that this would make for a foolproof diagnostic tool.

But so what if their eye movement is different and then normalizes with meds? That means nothing. And what if the ADHD eye movement is better—a sign that they are more hyperfocused and engaged in the task? Why would you want to suppress that? My point is that association does not prove causality and this study is just another example of how the medical and science community is looking for ways to make it easier to diagnose and then medicate.

Diagnostic Standards

Recent research notwithstanding, currently there is no single or conclusive step in the diagnosis of ADHD in children, and often symptoms can overlap with other issues, like dyslexia, anxiety or depression. Most diagnoses rely on subjective observations by parents, teachers and doctors that tend to emphasize the negative and overlook the strengths. They tend to forget that most of us can thrive with the ADHD traits, given the right environment and support.

Meanwhile, the *DSM-V*—the most recent edition of this manual—has established certain diagnostic standards. Interestingly, the latest edition, May 2013, now says that symptoms may first occur anytime before age twelve, instead of before age six—so there are more kids who can be caught in the diagnostic net. But it also recommends that several symptoms be present in more than one setting, such as school, home, work and among friends. There also needs to be "clear evidence that the symptoms interfere with, or reduce the quality of social, school or work functioning."

And the *DSM* added new descriptions applicable to older age groups that makes it easier to diagnose. Adults and older adolescents need only exhibit five "symptoms" as opposed to the six needed for younger children. Symptoms must also have been present for at least six months, and not confused with behavior that is developmentally appropriate—in other words, while the signs are not necessarily constant, they appear often enough to be noticeable, and to the point where they can interfere with daily function.

Specifically the latest *DSM-V* symptoms list for ADHD, primarily inattentive, are as follows:

- Often fails to give close attention to details or makes careless mistakes in schoolwork, at work or with other activities.
- Often has trouble holding attention on tasks or play activities.
- Often does not seem to listen when spoken to directly.
- Often does not follow through on instructions and fails to finish schoolwork, chores or duties in the workplace (e.g., loses focus, sidetracked).
- Often has trouble organizing tasks and activities.
- Often avoids, dislikes or is reluctant to do tasks that require mental effort over a long period of time (such as schoolwork or homework).
- Often loses things necessary for tasks and activities (e.g., school materials, pencils, books, tools, wallets, keys, paperwork, eyeglasses, mobile telephones).
- Is often easily distracted.
- Is often forgetful in daily activities.

For hyperactivity and impulsivity to the point where they are developmentally inappropriate or disruptive:

- Often fidgets with or taps hands or feet, or squirms in seat.
- Often leaves seat in situations when remaining seated is expected.
- Often runs about or climbs in situations where it is not appropriate (adolescents or adults may be limited to feeling restless).
- Often unable to play or take part in leisure activities quietly.
- Is often "on the go" acting as if "driven by a motor."
- Often talks excessively.
- Often blurts out an answer before a question has been completed.
- Often has trouble waiting his/her turn.

- Often interrupts or intrudes on others (e.g., butts into conversations or games).

But even with the *DSM*'s lists and guidelines, diagnosis in children and adults remains imprecise. And the presentation may change over time. Most children grow out of hyperactivity, for example. It's also an incredibly loose diagnostic criteria when six out of nine symptoms equal a diagnosis, and five out of nine is nothing. Of course it is never that black-and-white! How can it be? Hence a continuum.

A Scarcity of Experts

Ideally, a child psychiatrist who specializes in ADHD should determine whether a child has the trait, but there are not enough of these professionals to go around—just eighty-three hundred in the United States compared with fifty-four thousand family doctors—and often these specialists, who aren't always covered by health insurance, are hard for the average family to afford. Typically, it's the family doctor or pediatrician who makes the call, and most haven't had the kind of formal training necessary to properly question the patient, or family of a patient. In fact, there's been growing concern that doctors in the United States aren't being sufficiently trained to properly diagnose or handle the trait before handing out a pill, with many pediatricians receiving little more than a few hours of instruction on ADHD—usually in the form of a PowerPoint presentation.

"With ADHD that's like showing a slide of how to swim the butterfly and expecting people to go home and swim the butterfly," Dr. Peter Jensen, a leading child psychiatrist, told the *New York Times*. "It takes real, hands-on training."

It takes time to properly diagnose by closely watching the child in different environments—time that most pediatricians don't have. Instead, most draw their conclusions by sifting through different evaluations and reports from teachers and parents, coupled with five minutes of interviewing the child in the office.

In fact, one of the leading predictors of an ADHD diagnosis is the teacher—not the medical professional. Educators in schools and day care tend to be at the front line and the first to suggest a diagnosis, which is not a good thing, as they are far from qualified and may confuse potential ADHD behavior with other factors in a child's life.

And of course they are not the only ones getting it wrong. As it stands now, different medical professionals will often come to completely different diagnoses because so much of the observable criteria are open to subjective interpretation. And once that diagnosis is made, pediatricians and other nonpsychiatric doctors have no other course of treatment—such as therapy—to offer. Just pills. So if you are a hammer, everything you see is a nail—but more on that in the next chapter.

There is some good news. The medical profession is beginning to acknowledge that we have largely failed our patient population when it comes to diagnosing and treating ADHD, and a new movement is afoot to improve training for pediatricians, including seminars by the nonprofit Resource for Advancing Children's Health Institute (REACH)—although much more needs to be done to upgrade doctor training in this field.

The Rare Exceptions

Of course, not all physicians rush to a diagnosis. Dr. Oren Mason, a family physician based in Grand Rapids, Michigan, who in 2001 founded Attention MD, specializing in attention disorders, runs a litany of tests. First, he told me, he does a background history that includes medical history, mental health history, educational history, work history, substance use history and social history. He then asks people for narrative descriptions of ADHD symptoms both recently and—in the case of adolescents and adults—during childhood. For school-age children, he collects reports from teachers as well. For adults, he asks for corroboration from spouse, significant other, boss, parents and even old report cards.

Next, he screens for symptoms of sleep disorders, learning disorders, anxiety, obsessive compulsive disorder (OCD), depression, and other mood disorders. This is followed by several questionnaires specifically detailing ADHD symptoms that have diagnostic-level specificity.

When all of that is collected, he does computerized attention testing. Then he sits down with the patient and family for a ninety-minute visit. The purpose of the visit is to confirm or rule out the diagnosis of ADHD and to begin treatment planning.

In his practice, a typical diagnosis of ADHD involves about two hours of staff time and two hours of Dr. Mason's time, before any treatment is started.

"I wish I could tell you how many people go through this type of rigorous diagnostic process versus the number that are 'diagnosed' within the course of a brief office visit," says Dr. Mason, who is troubled by the number of "uncareful" diagnoses we make in our profession.

Ask Better Questions

Dr. Mason's kind of rigorous questioning and testing should be the standard, but sadly it's all too rare, and improvements in diagnostic training may have to wait until the next generation of medical school graduates. Meanwhile, when making a diagnosis, mental health professionals need to ask themselves some tough questions that take into account the nuances of the traits and the individual strengths and personalities of each patient. We need to consider, on a scale of 1 to 10, what separates an ADHD 7 from an ADHD 10. Who gets medicated . . . and why? How could one person use a set of "symptoms" as a springboard for success while another with very similar symptoms needs meds and therapy?

Indeed, how *are* CEOs like Norm Brodsky, an *Inc.* magazine columnist and founder of CitiStorage; Ingvar Kamprad, founder and CEO of IKEA; and Peter Kight, CEO of CheckFree—public figures whose

ADHD has been widely reported—able to parlay their ADHD into tremendously successful careers, while others are searching for a magic pill and a cure? Innovation is a hallmark of those with ADHD. When children first present with symptoms, why aren't we telling them that they are three times more likely to form their own business, will thrive in disruptive situations, will embrace adventure and are adept at multitasking, as opposed to giving them a diagnosis and a pill?

We must stop thinking about how to give the "patients" what they think they want and start taking a look at what's good about what they have. A diagnosis should not be a stigma. In fact, I wish there was a better word for it than *diagnosis* or *disorder* because, except for the far end of the continuum, this is not an illness that needs to be treated. Again, it's a difference, and something to be embraced as part of people's individuality; their genetic blueprint.

A Family Affair

In fact, there is a high level of inheritability with the trait. Of course, the genetic component of ADHD, which I will detail more in the next chapter, is complex, and still requires further research. One major gene study is currently under way at the National Institutes of Health's National Human Genome Research Institute. Many scientists believe there are at least two genes involved in the trait (I believe there are several), each of which has a myriad of individual variations.

But there is no denying the trait's recurrence in blood relatives. Over the years, I've come across numerous cases of ADHD in children that ultimately led to a discovery of it in one or both of the parents, as well as other siblings, aunts, uncles and cousins . . . I have it, my son, Trey, has it and multiple scientific studies confirm that ADHD is very much a family affair. The research has found that there is a 20 to 25 percent likelihood that if one child in the family has the trait, a sibling will too, and 15 to 40 percent of children will have a parent who shares the diagnosis, according to researchers at the Center for Neurobehavioral Genetics at UCLA. Studies found that identical twins share the condition 70 to 80 percent of the time when either twin is diagnosed, or 30 to 40 percent in the case of fraternal twins.

The Neelemans discovered that ADHD runs in their own family when the youngest child of seven, Mark James Neeleman, was diagnosed at fifteen.

Mark was a troubled teen who was failing out of high school and self-medicating with cannabis. His struggles in school were interfering with his self-esteem, particularly as he was living under the shadow of his incredibly successful older siblings, including Steven, a doctor and CEO of Health Equity who is ten years his senior, and David, the founder of JetBlue and, now, founder and CEO of Azul Airlines in Brazil.

Little was expected of Mark, and one of his four brothers even suggested he become a football coach and sell home security door-to-door, as if that were all he could aspire to.

"People would ask me, 'What happened to you?'" Mark recalls. "I had a chip on my shoulder because of that."

At a parent-teacher conference, one of his high school science teachers told his parents that he might have ADHD, or what was then referred to as ADD.

"My dad went berserk," Mark recalls. Back then the diagnosis was more of a stigma, so his father said, "If he has it, then I have it. Go to hell!"

Soon after, Mark was sent to live with his older sister in California. His rebellious nature had not been going over well in Salt Lake City, where his Mormon family was based. His sister sent him to see a doctor, who diagnosed him. The realization that he had ADHD, along with the new environment and school, where he received extra attention and flexibility in how he learned, helped him graduate from high school and complete a college degree, where he impressed his professor with a paper "suggesting that ADHD and Asperger syndrome are superhuman mutations that exist to push society forward." What an insight! I couldn't agree more.

Soon after Mark's diagnosis, his mother did some research and came across Dr. Edward Hallowell's groundbreaking book *Driven to Distraction*. She gave it to her son David, who after skimming the list of criteria realized in amazement that he had it too. David was thirty-four at the time, and received his "official" diagnosis at forty, when Dr. Hallowell came to visit him at his JetBlue offices. After a two-hour meandering conversation, the doctor got up to leave, and as he was walking through the door it finally occurred to David to ask him, "So, what? Do I have it?"

"Big-time," the doctor replied.

Mark and the rest of the family had long suspected. "We'd be at a family barbecue and David would be grilling meat, then suddenly decide he needed to buy a watch," Mark shares. "We wouldn't see him for the rest of the afternoon!"

Mark's and David's diagnoses gave both of them some peace of mind—an example of how it helps to recognize that you have the trait, as long as it's not being defined as a disorder and immediately medicated.

"I was totally relieved," David recalled. "Although I was running a company, I couldn't spell or write an email and had to have people do all those tasks for me. I thought I was dumb."

Both siblings quickly discovered, and leveraged, the advantages of ADHD. They also shared a desire to inspire and educate others by setting an example and showcasing the strengths of the trait.

"It made me more determined to spread the word and make people realize that, just because scholastically they could not succeed, they could actually be very successful in life. Perhaps even more so than others who can ace all the standardized tests," says David.

"It's amazing to me how many kids need help to channel these powers in their favor," says Mark, who shares his ADHD story with young people all over Brazil, where he now lives, working alongside his brother to help with Azul and running numerous other ventures as well. (More on that later.)

ADHD is a topic that comes up at family gatherings, as the

Neeleman boys have since discovered that their two sisters have it too. It's also apparent that the patriarch of the family, Gary, a former executive at the *Los Angeles Times* who began his career as an award-winning foreign correspondent in Brazil during the revolution, has many of the classic characteristics of the trait. David's daughter may also have it, "but she was too distracted to complete the questionnaire," he says. His son, who just graduated from high school, has already been diagnosed, and David could not be more proud.

"His teacher said he makes comments on a classroom discussion that are so insightful and out of left field, he wonders how he ever came up with that," says David, who has perhaps passed on some of his nonlinear thinking through the ADHD trait.

Mark is equally proud of his brother:

"Now, at thirty-five, and going on twenty years dealing with my ADHD, I have had the perfect example of my brother, who is the grand master of channeling his ADHD," Mark told me. "I am pleased to say I too have embraced and channeled this power."

It's an attitude and approach that has turned this inherited trait into a family treasure.

THE TOOL KIT: UNDERSTANDING ADHD BY AGE

The ADHD brain is the same no matter how old you are. But what makes the difference, and potentially exacerbates the so-called symptoms, is the context. Here's a breakdown of what can happen at different stages of life, and a way to put it into perspective:

Preschoolers (Before Grade One)

When a toddler is running, jumping and climbing over things, fidgeting and being a little chatterbox, it is developmentally normal. This is why it's both difficult and unwise to make a diagnosis at this age. The less structured, free-form context of day care is also a place where these kids do well, so their behavior isn't typically designated a problem. That said, there is a disturbing push toward diagnosing children at this age and even younger—a trend that will be discussed in the next chapter.

WHAT TO DO

If you face pressure from a spouse or day-care administrator to get your child diagnosed, resist! Let your little explorer explore the backyard and expend some of that high energy on the playground. Be glad you have someone adventurous in the family, and encourage that curiosity and free spirit whenever you can. In severe cases before first grade, it's you who would have sought a professional opinion and had your child assessed. But in the majority of cases it's often the school system that will make that call for you. Again, at that point make sure you are seeing a child psychiatrist or child psychologist, preferably one who specializes in ADHD, as there are many treatments out there that don't involve taking a pill, and each child responds differently, so it takes a level of expertise to get it right.

From Grade One Through High School

Not all child ADHDers are necessarily hyperactive, but when present, hyperactivity often increases in the more structured setting of our public education system. By this age, and within the rigid context of the classroom, children are expected to sit still and conform to certain societal norms. Most kids are able to channel energy and control the impulse to fidget, interrupt others or blurt out answers in class, but the ADHDers have more trouble conforming to these expectations. They chafe under authority and struggle with the rules—making them more disruptive, and more of a perceived problem. Grades suffer as they find it difficult to concentrate and forget to do homework and family chores. This is why a diagnosis is more likely to occur in children once they reach elementary school age. But the symptoms manifest more not because of the child but because of the context.

WHAT TO DO

At this age it is even more likely that a teacher will push for a diagnosis. If so, do not go with the school recommendation of a family practitioner, who will almost certainly medicate. Find a child psychiatrist/psychologist with expertise in ADHD and explore every possible alternative—from therapy to behavior modification to classroom structure to how your child does homework. (More on this in Chapter Five.) Do everything possible to avoid medication. If you've already tried the alternatives and they don't work, then yes, consider a stimulant prescription, but only as a last resort, when all other attempts to address the concentration and focus issues have failed.

High School and Beyond

They used to say that we outgrow our ADHD. Not so. As adults we have more self-control, so we often mature out of the hyperactive component of the trait, and self-knowledge helps us learn how to harness the trait. But we are still ADHDers. It is the same brain from birth to death. But often, free from the constraints of middle and high school, and even later in high school when you can take more elective classes and have more free time, ADHD becomes less of an issue. Getting to college can be a huge relief. You can write papers at three a.m. with the television on, taking video game breaks if you feel like it. Interestingly, you are back to the free form of your preschool days. So now you can take the classes you like, study in your own way, discover what really interests you and blossom.

WHAT TO DO

Use this time in your life to explore the things you love. You will succeed when you find subjects that interest you and stimulate your ADHD brain into hyperfocus mode. Foster self-awareness, and figure out which settings and career options work best for you. How? The next chapters will offer you plenty of tools to help you find your fit and leverage your strengths, and there are much better options than taking a pill. Again, remember this mantra: medication is only a last resort.

Medications for ADHD

AMPHETAMINE STIMULANTS

Adderall: Short-acting; 4–6 hours; some loss of appetite, weight loss, sleep problems, irritability, tics. Short-acting medicines require frequent dosing.

Dexedrine: Short-acting; 4–6 hours.

Dextrostat: Short-acting; 4–6 hours.

Dexedrine Spansule: Long-acting; 6–8 hours; some loss of appetite, weight loss, sleep problems, irritability, tics. Long-acting medicines are convenient but may have greater effects on appetite and sleep.

Adderall XR: Long-acting; 8–12 hours.

Vyvanse: Long-acting; 10–12 hours.

METHYLPHENIDATE STIMULANTS

Focalin: Short-acting; 4–6 hours; some loss of appetite, weight loss, sleep problems, irritability, tics. Short-acting medicines require frequent dosing.

Methylin: Short-acting; 3–4 hours.

Ritalin: Short-acting; 3–4 hours.

Metadate ER: Intermediate-acting; 6–8 hours; some loss of appetite, weight loss, sleep problems, irritability, tics. Longer-acting medicines are convenient but may have greater effects on appetite and sleep.

Methylin ER: Intermediate-acting; 6–8 hours.

Ritalin SR: Intermediate-acting; 4–8 hours.

Metadate CD: Intermediate-acting; 8–10 hours.

Ritalin LA: Intermediate-acting; 8–10 hours.

Concerta: Long-acting; 10–12 hours; some loss of appetite, weight loss, sleep problems, irritability, tics. Longer-acting medicines are convenient but may have greater side effects on appetite and sleep.

Quillivant XR: Long-acting; 8–12 hours.

Focalin XR: Long-acting; 6–10 hours.

Daytrana patch: Long-acting; 10–12 hours; skin irritation, some loss of appetite, weight loss, sleep problems, irritability, tics.

Nonstimulants

Strattera: Long-acting (extended release); 24 hours; sleep problems, anxiety, fatigue, upset stomach, dizziness, dry mouth. Rarely, liver damage. There are some concerns about a link between Strattera and suicidal thoughts.

Intuniv: Long-acting (extended release); 24 hours; sleepiness, headache, fatigue, abdominal pain. Rarely, Intuniv can cause low blood pressure and heart rhythm changes.

Antidepressants

Wellbutrin: Short-acting; 4–5 hours; sleep problems, headaches. Although occurrence is rare, Wellbutrin may increase the risk of seizures.

Wellbutrin SR: Sustained release; (long-acting); 12 hours.

Wellbutrin XL: Extended release; (long-acting); 24 hours.

Tofranil: 8–24 hours; sleep problems, anxiety, fatigue, upset stomach, dizziness, dry mouth, elevated heart rate, risk of heart arrhythmias.

Pamelor: 8–24 hours.

Aventyl: 8–24 hours.

Norpramin: 8–24 hours; not recommended for children. Associated with rare cases of fatal heart problems.

BLOOD PRESSURE MEDICINES

Clonidine: 4–6 hours (tablets); fatigue, dizziness, dry mouth, irritability, behavior problems, low blood pressure. Stopping this medicine suddenly can result in high blood pressure.

Catapres: 24 hours (patch).

Kapvay: 24 hours; tablet taken twice a day.

Tenex: 6–8 hours.

CHAPTER THREE

Pop-a-Pill Culture

When he was nine years old, Cameron Alexander's parents noticed their son was unhappy and struggling in school. They'd just divorced, so it wasn't surprising that their child was depressed. Cameron wasn't hyperactive, but he was listless, unfocused, disinterested in most things and socially somewhat isolated. He had trouble accessing his memory and couldn't pay attention when he was supposed to. School bored him because, as he says, "I never felt challenged," and this lack of stimulation caused him to act out and get into trouble. A friend of Cameron's mother was a counselor and suggested that he might have ADHD, and soon enough, he was put on Ritalin.

Cameron hated the stuff. He never quite felt himself on the medication, which caused insomnia, teeth grinding and the sweats. Worst of all was that having to take a pill each morning made him feel like he had an "intangible" handicap.

"Every morning before I used to even get to say hello to my mother, she'd ask me, 'Did you take your medicine?' It used to gall me," he recalls. To him, the implication was that he could not even be addressed without first popping a pill, because, "I had a problem and no one would want to be my friend unless I calmed down and dealt with it." If anything, the medication ritual made him feel more ostracized, introverted and socially inadequate.

"I figured, if I bothered other people so much, then why should I bother with them?"

Sure, taking stimulants helped him with focus, although Cameron was already exceptionally bright and able to complete reading and math assignments well ahead of the rest of his class. With minimal effort, he got B-pluses and A's. Mostly the pills just kept him in line and made him less of an apparent problem to his teachers and family.

"I think that, considering everything else that was going on with me at the time, it was a narrow cure," Cameron says. "Maybe it was somewhat beneficial, but not for the length of time I was on the stuff."

He stayed on the medication through high school as well as his freshman year at Louisiana State University. There was never any discussion about him coming off the meds. He was never informed of any alternatives, like having him channel his energy into things that engaged him, like art, on which he could focus for hours, or animals, "which I loved more than people sometimes." There were small doses of activities, and in retrospect Cameron feels that a more disciplined, sustained routine in which he could have developed his interests would have helped. He's right. A serious exploration of other options would have helped.

"My behavior was never addressed, only suppressed," he says.

At LSU, Cameron started partying, abusing the Ritalin and giving it away to friends—a common story for young people on ADHD meds. He'd received little attention from his peers in high school, and this was his chance to shine socially. "I had something they wanted," he recalls.

Cameron took the pills more and more, because he was developing a tolerance, and excessive amounts made it harder for him to notice the side effects. He was basically numbing himself and, unable to find something he was passionate about, it wasn't long before he dropped out. "I lost my ride there because I was an immature kid unleashed upon the world."

He then moved in with an uncle in Milwaukee, where he took odd jobs for a year in construction and factories. It wasn't for him, so he moved back in with his family in Louisiana, where he partied some more. Realizing that his life lacked direction, and lacking a passion for any particular career, Cameron decided to shake himself out of his apathy and join the military.

A Different Prescription

"I chose it because it was something I had to commit to and couldn't give up on," he says. Enlisting in the military was also an opportunity for him to get off his ADHD medication, since his processing unit had some concerns about his stimulant use. (Generally it's hard for people on ADHD medication to qualify for the military.) No one directly told him to come off the medication, but it was something Cameron had always wanted to do anyway, and he felt he could do it with the right amount of discipline.

Long-term stimulant users can experience withdrawal symptoms, including lower energy, hypersomnia, depression, a loss of concentration and increased appetite. But these effects usually disappear after a few days, and Cameron hardly had time to notice. In fact, the ability to sleep through the night and feel like himself more than compensated for any short-term sluggishness.

In that environment, where there was no option to go home or run off and party, Cameron flourished, as I often see with ADHDers who sign up for the military. Although it seems counterintuitive that they would thrive in such a regimented setting, there is something about those do-or-die, high-pressure situations induced by lots of physical activity, military drills and training that stimulates and engages the ADHD brain—calm under pressure. The physicality and structure gave Cameron a newfound focus. He was forced to adapt and get along with everyone in his unit, and the intense training gave him an outlet for his restless energy and need for stimulation. Because they were all in it together, depending on each other, it improved Cameron's relationships, and he no longer felt isolated. Best of all, he could sleep well for the first time since he was a child.

"I felt like a better, cleaner version of myself, and not someone who had just downed a gallon of coffee," says Cameron.

All he needed was a chance to be physically and mentally challenged in ways that hadn't been happening for him at home or school. The intense exercise, being outdoors and having to deliver and not let down the other men in his unit focused all his restless energy in a healthy way. It made him realize he was perfectly capable of being a valuable team player and accomplish tasks without medication, and that gave him confidence and self-esteem.

Although I have not assessed Cameron directly, I would guess he is about an 8 on the continuum, and probably never needed to be on stimulants in the first place. Regrettably, he had to miss out on the best of his childhood and teen years before he found out how good life could be when he wasn't suppressing his natural strengths with a pill.

Last Resort

That's the case for most ADHDers, and many of the success stories who were interviewed for this book say they have either never taken medication for the trait, or they have tried it, not liked it, and realized over time that there were better alternatives for channeling their superpowers.

JetBlue founder David Neeleman told me that if he could take a pill to make his ADHD go away, he'd refuse; Michael Phelps, who has publicly embraced his ADHD, has launched a fitness program that enables ADHD kids to focus without medication, and sprinter Justin Gatlin, another Olympian ADHDer who has been open about his diagnosis, started winning more races when he gave up his meds.

"Once you learn how to manage it and can control your life through certain mechanisms, you will have a way of looking at the world that others don't have," says Neeleman. "You can see obvious things that aren't obvious to others, and if you can capitalize on this you can be very successful."

Trying those mechanisms and working with your ADHD strengths instead of medicating them out of existence should be the first step for anyone with the diagnosis. Medication should only be a last resort, and even then, treatment should not be full-time or indefinite.

But unfortunately the opposite is usually the case, and these days pills seem to be the answer to every aspect of the human condition. Over the past three decades, we've gone from being reluctant to recognize and treat an ADHD diagnosis in children to a nation addicted to the quick fix, whether there's a real problem or not. Practitioners are handing out Ritalin and Adderall like it's Halloween candy, and perfectly healthy young men and women, be they the college student cramming for a test or the football player looking for an edge on game day, are becoming addicted to stimulants, with tragic consequences. And it's all under the aegis of legitimate medical practice.

Often the patient knows best, even when parents and teachers tell them otherwise. Benjamin Blanchard, whom you met in Chapter One, was told to go on Ritalin in the fourth grade not because his grades were bad but because this bright, inquisitive and energetic boy was constantly interrupting in class. They kept giving him an N for nonsatisfactory conduct, which was the behavioral equivalent of an F, and when Ben went on the meds, that grade went to 0, meaning his conduct was deemed perfect. Teachers praised him for being the most improved student in school.

But Ben didn't feel like himself. This sociable kid, whose people skills are a huge reason why he is such a successful salesman today, turned into a recluse, barely talking to his classmates. He begged his parents to let him come off the drug, and they allowed it when he was in seventh grade—only to put him on another stimulant: Adderall.

"It killed a lot of my best personality traits, so once I got out of high school I was pretty much done with Adderall," he says. "I eventually figured out that I was better off coping and getting stuff done, using my ADD attributes to my advantage, something that I never would have been able to do if I'd stayed on medication."

A Place for Pills

Let me be clear: I am not rejecting the diagnosis and medication of ADHD, although drugs should only be used in the most extreme cases, as a last resort where people are a 9, 10 or 10+ on the continuum and otherwise unable to function.

There are a widely disparate number of drugs for ADHD that are just preparations that work in the exact same way, and the biggest brands are stimulants based on the chemicals amphetamine and methylphenidate. But there are also antidepressants and blood pressure medications that can be effective. (See the list in Breakout I before this chapter.) The fact that dozens of ADHD drugs are out there highlights the importance of having a specialist involved in care, as many general practitioners may know of only one or two big brand names.

The stimulants such as Ritalin, Adderall, and Vyvanse, which are most commonly prescribed to treat ADHD, can be extremely effective. They work by increasing the dopamine and norepinepherine tone in the brain, thus reducing the need to self-stimulate through movement and distractions. This affords children and adults with ADHD the opportunity to sit still and follow directions, and quiets the onslaught of thoughts, acting as a kind of filter for the brain, although I will argue later that there are other nondrug interventions, treatments and exercises that help the distracted to focus. I would also suggest that even for those who arguably do need treatment with stimulants, medication alone isn't an adequate tool.

"Pills without further therapy don't do much at all," says Dr. Oren Mason, whom you met in Chapter Two. "You have to train this newly active part of the brain. You need to start introducing some discipline and structure into your life."

Of course, it's tempting for people using stimulants for the first time to forgo therapy or any other additional "treatment," because this quick fix is often so fast-acting and drastic in its results. Patients liken it to a nearsighted person putting on glasses for the first time. Short-term, this medication can improve performance in everyone from fighter pilots to college test-takers and football players, whether they have ADHD or not. And that's precisely the problem.

A recent Sunday *New York Times* article brought this to the fore with the heartrending story of twenty-four-year-old Richard Fee, a bright, energetic young premed student and class president whose legal prescriptions led to a downward spiral of delusion, anger, depression and suicide.

The article describes how his parents were never convinced he needed Adderall, and pleaded with his doctor to stop prescribing the medication. By then their son was dangerously addicted to prescription medications. Charming, convincing and highly intelligent, he lied to various doctors to keep the prescriptions going, and it was remarkably easy for him to access more pills. Doctors kept upping his dosages even in the face of evidence for his addiction. Even after he'd already spent a week in a psychiatric hospital, he managed to convince his doctor to prescribe three more months of ADHD medication. Two weeks after that prescription ran out, he hanged himself.

As one of his own physicians, Dr. Charles Parker, told the *Times*, this was a classic case of the way the medical system fails young people when it comes to ADHD. "We have a significant travesty being done in this country with how the diagnosis is being made and the meds are being administered," he said.

He is absolutely right. Cases of suicide as a result of stimulant use are rare, but not unheard-of. Increasingly common, however, are accidental deaths caused by poly-drug abuse and alcoholism that can be triggered by the abuse of ADHD medications. In April 2013, about three months after Alan Schwarz's *New York Times* story about Richard Fee ran, there was an op-ed piece written by Ted Gup, a Harvard ethics fellow and father who lost his son through a drug and alcohol overdose.

Like Richard Fee, Ted's son David received the ADHD diagnosis when he was in school. The pressure to put him on medication was unrelenting, and even David's psychiatrist refused to see him until he was on Ritalin. From there, the boy moved to Adderall, and a list of other medications to suppress his irrepressible energy, which his father likens to having a battery that was too big for his small body.

"And so he would leap over the couch, spring to reach the ceiling and show an exuberance for life that came in brilliant microbursts," writes Ted, in what is one of the most eloquent and vivid descriptions I have ever read of what hyperactivity looks like in a child.

Ted writes that his son was known to pass out his Adderall to various classmates in college—again, an all-too-common problem. Ask any high school or college kid if he or she has taken ADHD meds to enhance performance or focus, or knows someone who has, and the answer will likely be yes, followed by a shrug, as if it's no big deal.

David's father also believes that the medical profession's rush to medicate, and the ease with which people can get prescriptions, perpetuates a culture of self-medication that can easily lead to serious drug abuse. So long-term use of a stimulant like Adderall can potentially trigger a spiral and eventually lead to the kind of heroin and alcohol abuse that killed his son—a bright twenty-one-year-old college senior.

Potential for Abuse

David's is not the first, and it won't be the last, of such cases. College students can easily get their hands on all kinds of serious prescription medications these days, trading their prescriptions or what they find in their parents' bathroom cabinets like baseball cards.

A 2009 study by the National Survey on Drug Use and Health found that college students ages eighteen through twenty-two were twice as likely over the previous year to abuse Adderall as their non-full-time counterparts, and that nonmedical users of Adderall were eight times as likely to have used cocaine and/or prescription tranquilizers (without a prescription), and five times more likely to have been users of prescription pain meds. They were also 90 percent more likely to have been binge alcohol drinkers. A 2012 report by the Substance Abuse and Mental Health Services Administration, a federal agency, saw emergency room visits due to nonmedical use of stimulants rise to more than twenty-two thousand in 2010, triple the numbers in 2005.

What appalls me is that the pills that cut short the young lives of Richard and David, and are ruining the futures of so many others, are distributed and sanctioned by the medical community, based on "diagnostic tests" that are so loose they would be laughable if the results weren't so dire.

The culprits are:

- Big Pharma, which has found a new, multibillion-dollar market for stimulants since adult ADHD has been recognized.
- The harried nonpsychiatric practitioners who rely on little more than a questionnaire or a ten-minute interview to make a diagnosis.
- Psychiatrists who today get virtually no psychotherapy training in their residency program. (When I trained it was a fifty-fifty split between psychopharmacology and psychotherapy.)
- Teachers who are doing their best to control a class of thirty-five or more students and need all the help they can get.
- Parents who are both working and stressed out dealing with a rambunctious child.
- And, finally, demand by the consumer for a quick fix.

It's telling that, of the approximately 6.4 million kids who have been diagnosed with ADHD in the United States, about half are on medication. Adults have been another big growth area for stimulant sales. A report by Express Scripts, one of the country's leading prescription drug managers, finds that prescriptions for adults with ADHD rose 53.5 percent between 2008 and 2012, with the greatest increase among women ages twenty-six through thirty-four, up 86 percent.

"The trends here signal a need to look more closely at how and why physicians prescribe these medications for adults and the need for prescribers to fully assess the entire psychosocial landscape of an individual patient prior to reaching for the prescription pad," the report says.

And yet the drug industry continues to find new "patients" to market to, including toddlers, as we mentioned, and people who *think* they might have some new kind of attention disorder. The latest so-called disorder is something researchers are calling "sluggish cognitive tempo," or SCT, according to an April 2014 article in the *New York Times*. This could be a whole new market of people to sell ADHD drugs to. The *Times* article even points out that some of the researchers involved in getting this recognized as a legitimate disorder have helped Eli Lilly show how its drug, Strattera, could treat it. That says a lot about how the drug industry and medical professionals are in cahoots.

Basically, if it's a thing at all, SCT is ADHD without the *H*—or could it simply refer to a child who had a bad night's sleep and struggles to stay awake in class? Not if the drug companies have anything to say about it.

It's staggering. We're turning all kinds of individual traits into medical conditions, and doctors, be they psychiatrists or family health practitioners, only seem to know how to treat them as such. As Ted Gup writes in his *New York Times* article "Diagnosis: Human":

> Ours is an age in which the airwaves and media are one large drug emporium that claims to fix everything from sleep to sex. I fear that being human is itself fast becoming a condition. . . . Challenge and hardship have become pathologized and monetized. Instead of enhancing our coping skills, we undermine them and seek shortcuts where there are none, eroding the resilience upon which each of us, at some point in our lives, must rely.

In effect, we are trying to diagnosis every aspect of the human condition, including and especially the ADHD trait. Putting a label on it invariably means a prescription. A more detailed diagnostic process, along with long-term treatment plans such as behavioral therapy, are methods that just don't pay. Our microwave culture demands the shortcut solution of a pill, despite the fact that research is beginning to show the harmful long-term results of stimulant use in individuals, with or without ADHD.

Layer onto this the tremendous amount of advertising dollars that are being poured into promoting stimulant treatments for adults. Adult ADHD has only recently become a thing, but now it is a cause célèbre, with hugely popular figures like rock star Adam Levine making ADHD public service announcements about "owning it." Mr. Levine says nothing about taking medication, although it's implied. To be sure, there is merit to the fact that he is publicly embracing his ADHD and advocating for accepting and managing the diagnosis. But the fact is that the ad is paid for by Shire, which makes Vyvanse, a prescription treatment for ADHD that Shire is aggressively trying to use to take market share from Ritalin and Adderall.

In the interest of full disclosure, Ty Pennington, whom you met in Chapter One, has also served as a spokesman for Shire, and the posters of a promotional YouTube video in which he appeared in 2008 got slapped with a reprimand by the FDA. When Ty spoke with us, however, he had already stepped back from the role of ADHD medication in his life. After taking stimulants since he was seventeen, he has realized that it's better for him not to be on them full-time.

"You get to a point when you understand what a body needs and what it doesn't," explains Ty. "I wanted to sleep, relax and seem like a normal human rather than that rapid-speaking crazy man for the camera. I was sort of worn out."

The intentions were good. I have no doubt that celebrities like Ty and Adam wanted to put a positive face on a trait that had been stigmatized for so long and let people know that awareness and seeking help can greatly improve quality of life. But one unintended consequence is that it's putting a glamorous face on ADHD treatment with drugs. It's the opposite extreme from where we were a decade ago, with unhealthy consequences.

Big Pharma's Long Shadow

Drug companies have also dangerously oversold the benefits of the pills and turned relatively common behavior, like forgetfulness or impatience, into a disorder. They claim everything from improved academic performance to better-behaved children who take out the garbage. As Alan Schwarz points out in his *New York Times* article "The Selling of Attention Deficit Disorder," the FDA has cited every major producer of ADHD medications for false or misleading advertising, some more than once.

It's not just the television ads and drug-company-sponsored "public service" messages that mislead the public. As Schwarz's *Times* article also points out, doctors are often paid by drug companies to publish pro-medication research, and many undersell the potential risks and side effects of these drugs. Big Pharma even sells directly to children. Shire subsidized fifty thousand comic books with characters that say things like, "Medications may make it easier to pay attention and control your behavior." While there is nothing wrong with raising awareness and demystifying the trait, consider the source and the motive. The result of this aggressive, multifront push for ADHD treatment was more than $10 billion in sales for Big Pharma in 2013, up from $1.7 billion a decade earlier.

This is a trend in Big Pharma overall. For years now, drug makers have been operating on the dark side, financially incentivizing doctors and health-care providers to promote their drugs, and compensating pharmaceutical sales reps based on the number of prescriptions written by the doctors they call on. It's a practice rife with conflict of interest, leading to overprescription of medications that may not even be the most appropriate for patients, and it's been the cornerstone of drug marketing for decades.

The 2000 landmark study on this, titled "Physicians and the Pharmaceutical Industry: Is a Gift Ever Just a Gift?," concluded that simply meeting with pharmaceutical reps was "found to impact the prescribing practice of residents and physicians in terms of prescribing cost, non-rational prescribing, awareness, preference and rapid prescribing of new drugs, and decreased prescribing of generic drugs."

In December 2013, British drug maker GlaxoSmithKline announced it would no longer reward its reps on the number of drugs they sold, doing away with targets the following year. But they are not going far enough, and it remains to be seen whether other pharmaceutical companies will follow suit.

This is key, because, no matter how principled we believe we are as doctors, we are only human, and the dark side of Big Pharma casts a long shadow. There can be no doubt that when a charming drug rep visits a practice and introduces a physician to the latest product, it's likely to be at the top of the physician's mind when reaching for the Rx pad. In their busy practices, doctors often take the easy way, in the form of a shiny new prescription medication. But the easy way isn't always the best way.

Skills, Not Pills

Children and adults with ADHD, and many without the trait, have been caught up in a perfect storm of Big Pharma influence, a quick-fix mentality and poor training among physicians and mental health professionals. Often the so-called experts prescribe stimulants because they simply don't know any better. According to a survey of one thousand mental health professionals cited in a recent *Scientific American* article on ADHD overdiagnosis, 17 percent misdiagnosed hypothetical ADHD cases that fell short of the *DSM* diagnostic criteria. Thus raising "the specter of medicalizing largely normal behavior and relying too heavily on pills rather than skills—such as teaching children better ways of coping with stress."

Even in those rare instances with symptoms that are severe and where pills may be warranted, keep in mind that stimulants are naturally going to take a physical and mental toll. They pump up the heart rate and stimulate the nervous system, which puts a strain on the system over the long term. There are also side effects, such as sleeplessness, loss of appetite, mood swings and dry mouth, which, according to at least one study, affect almost half of those taking the drugs.

Since the trend now is for long-term use well into adulthood, there's growing concern about the effects of extended stimulant use on both the brain and the body. Another article in *Scientific American* compiled some of the most recent studies, and it seems we are only just beginning to understand the toll these meds are taking. Animal studies suggest that these drugs could alter the whole structure and function of the brain, increasing anxiety, causing depression and, despite the short-term gains of better focus, ultimately eroding cognitive powers.

Side Effects

Here is a quick summary of the *potential* long-term effects presented in the *Scientific American* article—and these are just the possibilities we know about. Stay tuned as science uncovers yet more pitfalls to popping these pills:

- **Stunted Growth**. There's strong evidence that shows ADHD drugs stunt growth in children. This may be because, according to studies on mice, elevated levels of the dopamine neurotransmitter produced by taking ADHD meds can reach the pituitary gland, which controls human growth. Researchers at the National Institute on Drug Abuse analyzed a National Institute of Mental Health study of ADHD treatments for 579 children and found that those ages seven through ten who took the meds over three years had a lower growth rate than those who were not on meds, growing an average two centimeters less in height, and 2.7 kilograms [6 pounds] less in weight. Incidentally, data from that same study also found that ADHD meds did not have the same level of effectiveness in children after three years, because they develop a tolerance, raising the question of the appropriateness of long-term drug treatment in both children and adults.

• **Mood-Killers**. Stimulant use can lead to depression and anxiety disorders later in life. As Edmund Higgins, a clinical professor of family medicine and psychiatry at the Medical University of South Carolina in Charleston, explains, "Stimulants activate the brain's reward pathways, which are part of the neural circuitry that controls mood under normal conditions." Animal studies found that when rats were injected with ADHD stimulant doses similar to what would be given to a child, they became less responsive to natural stimuli such as "sugar, sex, fun and novel environments." They were also more easily stressed. In fact, adult rats that had received stimulant treatment when they were young were so anxious that they would avoid crossing the open space of a new area, suggesting that adult humans could be especially prone to anxiety disorders. There needs to be more research to determine how, exactly, but clearly these drugs somehow change brain chemistry and function.

• **Addiction Risk**. ADHD stimulants are chemically similar to cocaine, and may even be as addictive, according to research at Rockefeller University in New York and compiled by Dr. Higgins. Stimulant use caused "cocaine-like structural and chemical alterations" in the brains of mice, and boosted levels of a type of protein that turns genes on and off even more than cocaine. It doesn't take much of a leap to conclude that, just as human cocaine users are more likely to crave more of it, ADHD stimulant users may also be more likely to seek out the rewarding effects of this and other stimulants. Equally, as many former cocaine addicts are prone to anxiety, depression and cognitive problems, long-term stimulant users may have "difficulty experiencing joy and excitement in life" many years after treatment.

• **Compromised Cognition**. Another study found that stimulants like Adderall caused hallucinations and cognitive impairments in rhesus monkeys. The animals also experienced problems with working memory—the system that can hold multiple pieces of information in the mind at once. These effects were found to last as long as three years after the monkeys were injected with increasing doses of stimulants over a period of six to twelve weeks. The problems were connected to lower levels of dopamine activity in the frontal cortex of the brain, a fact confirmed in a 2005 study in which researchers trained baboons and squirrel monkeys to self-administer oral doses of ADHD medications, much the way humans would. About a month later, they found signs of brain damage, with lower levels of dopamine.

With the exception of stunted growth, which is the best-researched and -documented effect of stimulant use in children, the negative effects of long-term stimulant use on the brain and mood that I've mentioned have yet to be proven conclusively in human studies. So taking ADHD meds as prescribed doesn't necessarily mean you will become a stimulant-addicted, brain-damaged, anxiety-ridden, hallucinating mess. But these early animal studies certainly raise enough red flags to warrant a rethink on how we use medication. In fact, with this new knowledge in mind, some more conscientious neurologists and psychiatrists have begun recommending only the lowest possible doses while keeping a cautious eye on blood levels with regular monitoring, so that they don't reach the levels that caused damage in the mammal studies.

When a Pill Is Appropriate

Let me be clear. These meds do work, up to a point. They help the executive functions of the brain, such as the ability to anticipate outcomes, make good decisions, suppress emotions, filter impulsive words and gestures and generally control urges. So, again, I am not saying never to ADHD medication. But I *am* saying far less often, and in a much more considered way. Even when meds are absolutely necessary, I also make a point of advising the lowest possible dosages, along with breaks, such as on weekends, holidays and in the summer, to give body and mind a chance to recover.

Mark Neeleman, whom you met in the previous chapter, has the right idea. He takes ADHD meds only periodically, when there are dull tasks he needs to focus on, things on his to-do list that absolutely must get done. He first discovered this approach when he was on his Mormon mission in Brazil. Part of progressing in his faith requires young people to memorize long passages of text, but after four months he still had not learned a single one of the six by heart, so he asked a family member to fill his Ritalin prescription in the United States and bring it to him. He took the pills for a week and successfully memorized all the passages. As soon as his task was complete, he couldn't wait to come off the stuff.

Since then, Mark has figured out that Adderall can be a useful tool, but only part-time. He takes it three days out of the week, and plows through all of the tedious tasks, like banking and payroll.

"When I am on it I am like a machine and can't stop working," he says.

Then he unleashes his ADHD brain and indulges in the free flow of thoughts, researching countless ideas on the Internet and seeing where that takes him. It's led to several ideas that have grown into successful businesses, but more on that later. Meanwhile, he's keeping ADHD meds in their place, as something he uses the minority of the time to help him with follow-through and execution.

"I have three days of work work, and four days of fun work," says Mark. "I couldn't do it otherwise."

I am glad Mark has figured out that stimulants are not a full-time necessity. Like many ADHD success stories, he has developed self-awareness, done the research and now uses all the tools at his disposal, custom-tailoring them to his own specific needs while never suppressing the natural strengths of the ADHD trait. Later on in this book, we will discuss the tools ADHDers can use to build success and become more focused and efficient without the aid of a pill.

The problem is, so many adults have been exposed to the aggressive marketing campaigns that lead them to believe they are somehow not reaching their potential without a prescription. It pains me when even those who are high-functioning and do not need meds are questioning themselves.

Recently, I was interviewing Durrell Hudson III, a highly successful jeweler, diamond merchant and importer who is an 8.5 on the continuum. He asked me at the end of the interview if he should be on medication. No, of course he shouldn't, and in fact, I would argue that his ADHD has given him an edge in his business, with an ability to hyperfocus on the diamonds and gemstones he cares about so passionately. Though he may procrastinate on the day-to-day tasks that are necessary to run a business or forget about an important staff meeting, he can tell you in amazing detail about any large diamond he has ever sold in his thirty years in business. In my opinion, if he took meds and his brain worked like everybody else's, he would lose that gift. But you can't get away from all the advertising for stimulant meds and their supposed benefits, and now he's feeling the pressure to conform.

Again, we must think of this as an allergy to boredom. The restlessness and inattention of the trait is often a result of being bored easily with routine. This is not a bad thing unless we insist on making a routine, structured life for everyone mandatory. Some of our greatest business leaders have embraced their ADHD and refused to medicate their uniqueness. Imagine the loss to our culture and economy if these extraordinary individuals had suppressed their restless energy with a pill!

THE TOOL KIT: TO MEDICATE OR NOT TO MEDICATE?

- Medication should be the last resort—not the first.
- Consider alternative schools, majors, jobs, or other circumstances that can help you make your lifestyle fit your traits.
- Have specific "target symptoms" and situations you need

medications for, such as writing reports, homework, paying attention in class, job interviews and meetings.

- Most experts agree symptoms lessen with age, even though adult ADHD has been widely acknowledged. Whatever your age, know that you don't have to be on meds forever.

- Before you think about medicating, be sure to get a proper diagnosis from a psychiatrist or psychologist who specializes in ADHD.

- Give yourself regular medication "holidays" such as weekends, vacations, calendar holidays.

- Monitor yourself for side effects insomnia, anxiety, etc. . . .

- At least once a year while working take a two-week break and see how you do and, again, monitor symptoms.

- Above all, trust yourself! If a diagnosis doesn't ring true, or you don't feel you need stimulants, do your own research and get a second opinion. As we've seen, physicians and mental health professionals are not infallible, especially with such subjective diagnostic criteria.

BREAKOUT II

You Are *Not* (Necessarily) What You Eat

By now you may be wondering, "If a stimulant doesn't work, can ADHD be treated with diet or nutrition? If there is no magic pill, can't there be some other way of ingesting a cure?"

This is a popular concept surrounding many areas of physical and mental health, and one that comes up on many of the websites dedicated to ADHD. Even some doctors are touting diet as an "alternative" ADHD treatment. But, sadly, the science does not adequately back these claims. When it comes to ADHD, you are *not* necessarily what you eat.

This is even true in the case of one of the biggest evils in the American diet: sugar. Numerous studies have looked at the relationship between refined sugar and ADHD. Most indicate sugar does not play a role, although mothers in the trenches with children bouncing off the walls often disagree.

Arguably, one of the most influential studies indicating that sugar plays no role in ADHD was published in 1985 by Dr. Mark Wolraich. The study looked at sixteen hyperactive boys over three days. On day one, learning was monitored in order to achieve a baseline. The boys were then either given a sucrose 1.75 mg/kg or a placebo drink at different times during the following two days. The test revealed no difference between the boys' behavioral or cognitive actions, whether they drank sucrose or placebo. However, critics emphasized the study was in an artificial setting, thus not representative of the real world.

But, in another study, children considered sensitive to sugar were given aspartame, a sugar substitute. Although all the children were given aspartame, half their mothers were told their children were given sugar, and the other half were told their children were given aspartame. The mothers who thought their children received sugar rated them as more hyperactive than the controls and were more critical of their behavior, compared to mothers who thought their children received aspartame. It's a popular belief that refined sugar causes ADHD or makes symptoms worse, and this bias is clearly indicated here.

The fact is that some ADHD (as well as non-ADHD) individuals may well become hyperactive after ingesting refined sugar, but this is not the norm. Perhaps some children are "sugar-sensitive," but these would be isolated cases, not reflective of the general population, or the ADHD population.

The Sugar Test

So sugar does not cause or worsen ADHD in general. But it's much more complicated than eating too many cupcakes or jelly beans. In order to rule sugar out as the culprit, you can always conduct a test to determine if it exacerbates ADHD symptoms. For a period of one week, allow yourself, or your child, to consume sugar and keep a written log to monitor behavior. Then remove the sugar from your diet, or your child's diet, for a week, and then repeat so you have a total of four weeks of data, and compare the results. This test is simple but effective and, unlike a research study, will give specific information on the impact of a sugary diet on an individual.

Whatever the result of this home test, it's worth remembering that, no matter the effect on behavior, ingesting refined sugar is not healthy. From getting cavities, to suppressing the immune system, to taking the place of healthy foods, to increasing the risk of diabetes, to obesity, it's well known that too much sugar can cause a range of health problems, even if ADHD is not an issue. Feeling physically well affects well-being, which in turn affects behavior, and that is true for everyone, regardless of their diagnosis.

Avoid Fads

There will always be scientific studies about the effects of certain vitamins or minerals. Less scrupulous doctors, holistic healers and nutritionists have been all too quick to tout the latest dietary "solutions" for a myriad of physical and mental health issues. But it's more complicated than that.

Take the iron study I mentioned in Chapter Two. That study found that iron, or specifically lower levels of it in the brain, may have potential value as a biomarker for ADHD. And yet in that study the iron levels in the blood in both the ADHD and non-ADHD study groups were normal. This finding highlights the fact that it's incredibly difficult and complex to determine causality with respect to mental health conditions. Not to mention dangerous. Too much iron can be toxic, so please don't rush out to load up on iron supplements at the health food store.

But I can understand the impulse. An earlier study from France, published in the December 2004 issue of the *Archives of Pediatrics & Adolescent Medicine*, also linked low iron to ADHD in children. Researchers measured levels of the protein ferritin—which allows us to store iron and is used as a measure of iron levels in body tissues—and found that 84 percent of children with ADHD appeared to have abnormally low ferritin levels, compared with 18 percent of children without ADHD. Those with the most severe iron deficiencies also displayed the most impulsivity and hyperactivity. But the researchers could not explain the reason for the low iron levels of these children. In fact, most of the experts interviewed about the study said there wasn't enough evidence to suggest iron supplements as a treatment for ADHD.

In fact, poor nutrition to the point of malnourishment can lead to symptoms often mistaken for ADHD. To complicate matters even further, malnutrition can lower iron levels. So drawing any conclusion is incredibly problematic, especially when the findings of various studies appear contradictory.

But maybe they are not; maybe there is indeed a difference between ferritin levels as an indirect measure of iron versus iron blood levels versus iron brain levels. We just don't know, and basing any conclusion on any of this would be foolish at this time.

Pediatrician and ADHD expert Dr. William Coleman told WebMD he has his doubts: "If it is involved, I believe iron deficiency is responsible for only a very small segment of the problems associated with ADHD."

The take-home message is that few of us in this country suffer from malnutrition, thus to suggest this would be a cause in the majority of ADHD cases is inappropriate. But if it makes you feel better, by all means have a steak for dinner. But tread cautiously when it comes to taking excessive amounts of certain vitamins and minerals to make up for perceived deficiencies without good science to back it up.

Micronutrients

The idea of "treating" ADHD with nutritional supplements has been heavily promoted on various parenting and ADHD websites. There's been a lot of buzz about micronutrients, which is a fancy word for vitamins and minerals such as iodine, copper, selenium, zinc and vitamins like A, C, D, E and the various B-complex entities, among others. They are called "micro" because they exist in small amounts in your food, unlike fat, protein and carbohydrates.

There is some evidence linking low levels of zinc, as well as vitamin D deficiencies, to depression, although it's too early to call this research conclusive. To my knowledge, using all these micronutrients together as a treatment for mental illness has never been formally considered in a double-blind fashion until now. A new study out of

New Zealand points to the possible benefits (and safety) of treating ADHD symptoms with vitamins and minerals.

The double-blind study consisted of eighty unmedicated ADHD adults; forty-two participants were given multivitamin and mineral supplements, while the remaining thirty-eight were given a placebo. After an eight-week period, their ADHD was evaluated. Hyperactivity, impulsivity and inattention were statistically improved in those receiving the supplements. As a plus, even depressive symptoms improved.

The lead author of the study, Professor Julia Rucklidge, claims those individuals taking the vitamins and minerals showed significantly better mood and focus than the placebo group, showing that micronutrients may be an effective way to treat ADHD and are an alternative for those who are unable to take standard medications.

Critics point out that the study was too short in duration to prove real-world efficacy, there were no children involved (in whom most ADHD is found), and that the fifteen capsules a day of vitamins and minerals is certainly not an easy regimen by any standard.

Of course, this data is only preliminary, and anything but definitive. More studies will be required with more patients over an extended period of time. But it's a start.

Good Fats

In addition to these small, preliminary studies, there is some speculation that omega-3 fatty acids from oily fish, nuts and olive oil—the so-called good fats—help with ADHD, although there is little hard science to back this up. What we do know is that these nutrients can help with memory and general cognitive function, according to a May 2012 study of six thousand women over the age of sixty-five that was published in the *Annals of Neurology*. But we don't know if these findings apply to the ADHD population.

Dr. Oren Mason has found that a small minority of the patients in his ADHD specialty practice do well with a diet high in protein, such as the Zone diet, and speculates this may be because these proteins are precursors for the neurotransmitters needed to improve executive function, but this is pure speculation. He has also found that "one or two percent" of patients do better with a gluten-free diet. But again, we don't have double-blind placebo studies to back up these anecdotal observations. The improvements may also be coincidence, he says. Patients who become more aware of their ADHD and how to manage and leverage the trait often become more intentional about their eating habits, as well as in other areas of their daily lives.

Look, I'd love to be able to say conclusively that a better diet will make a significant difference. Something simple that can improve certain aspects of cognitive function like short-term memory and focus, while not repressing the natural strengths of the ADHD trait, would be a gift. Because ADHD is so vastly overdiagnosed and overmedicated, anything that may slow down the prescription stimulant epidemic is welcome news. These preliminary studies and observations by medical professionals give parents of ADHD children, as well as adults with ADHD, at least some hope that there are more things they can do outside of getting a prescription.

That said, the best solutions for now are not as simple as ingesting vitamins and cutting out sugar.

"Nutrition is mostly a bust in the world of ADHD, which is disappointing," notes Dr. Mason. "But not enough of a bust that we don't at least talk about it."

As you will read in the coming chapters, there are other, more practical steps that can be taken to harness and leverage the ADHD strengths while lessening the potential problems of the trait, from behavior modification to mindfulness training to simple organizational tools.

Meanwhile, a healthy, balanced diet may not be the alternative "cure" that parents of ADHD children, as well as adults with ADHD, are hoping for, but it certainly can't hurt. We've known for a long time that eating well is integral to your sense of well-being. It makes you feel better both physically and mentally, so it stands to reason that nutritious, well-prepared food eaten consistently and in moderation could give your ADHD strengths that extra edge.

CHAPTER FOUR

The Explorer Gene

Looking out the window on a flight home to Washington, D.C., Trey Archer felt a creeping sense of panic. No, it wasn't fear of flying, nor was he claustrophobic. It was more like being trapped in a life in which he didn't belong, and it was enough to make him want to take a flying leap into the wild blue yonder.

My son, like many of his college classmates, had been interviewing for a job upon graduation, this time for a sales position with *Bloomberg Business News*, and a tour of their glass-and-steel New York City headquarters plunged him into a state of gloom. Sitting there, uncomfortable in his gray flannel suit, all Trey could think about were the endless rows of cubicles, where people were glued to their computer monitors like drones, occasionally stepping away to graze at a fully stocked snack bar, but almost never going outside.

Trey started imagining himself in their shoes, with their two weeks of vacation a year and their daily commutes to the suburbs of New Jersey or Long Island. The prospect nauseated him. Then he looked around the plane, which was full of business commuters looking somber, like him. It was at that moment he wondered if he could ever be happy with that life.

The fact that *Bloomberg* didn't offer him the job was a blessing, but at the time Trey was devastated by the rejection. "For years I thought that was my only option, so I had no clue what I was going to do," he said.

The next few months were particularly rough, as classmate after classmate found jobs but he didn't. It seemed as if everybody else's future was set. As it became apparent he would not be getting a job offer, Trey realized that the uncertainty of the vast unknown made him happy, happier than he had been in months, and that embarking on a path toward the unknown was exactly what he was meant to do.

His travels had taken him to South and Central America, Russia and Asia. Trey had always been interested in different cultures, religions and languages, majoring in international affairs in college. So during his junior year abroad, he opted to live in Argentina for six months, then Brazil for another six months. When the stint was over, he had two more months to kill before he had to return to the United States to finish his senior year, so he scrambled to find an internship that would keep him on the road.

He eventually found a project that would allow him to travel from Brazil to Mexico by land, covering thirteen countries in Latin America, communicating with locals to research their true feelings toward the United States. It was perfect, allowing him to "feed my addiction for travel and writing." Not to mention his curiosity, his desire to connect with people and his intense appetite for adventure. Having just watched *The Motorcycle Diaries*, about Che Guevara's journey up the continent from Argentina, Trey was especially inspired. The whole trip changed his life, getting him to think about what was possible.

"When it was over, I sat in the airport in Mexico thinking about what I wanted to do for the rest of my life," he recalls. "Whatever that was, it was pretty clear I wasn't going to be sitting in an office doing the nine-to-five deal."

Today, my son is in China, where he first taught English in Chengdu and did some freelance writing for local English-language publications and travel guides. He recently got his "dream job" in Beijing working for the Chinese equivalent of Lonely Planet—a start-up covering travel in China. It's been such a perfect fit that he was recently promoted to president of the company—Panda Guides. This way, he gets to delegate what he's less passionate about to other writers, copy editors and production assistants, leaving him free to roam from city to city, exploring new things and then writing about them.

In China there are enough challenges and new discoveries to keep his exploring nature engaged for a long time. But there are always other options. Adept at languages, he's fluent in Spanish, Portuguese and Mandarin, and gets by in Russian. As for now, he's happy traveling and writing throughout China. But as for the future, he's noncommittal, saying, "As long as I love this job, I'll stay here, but if it ever starts to get routine, then I'll be ready to move on."

Born to Explore

Trey scores very high on the ADHD continuum—a 9+. A true adventurer, he comes from a long line of restless souls who are curious about the world and eager to explore. It's an inherited trait he gets from me, and generations of our ancestors. And we are not alone.

In 1999, scientists at the University of California, Irvine, studied the genetic makeup of 2,320 individuals from thirty-nine different populations across the globe, including the Cheyenne tribe of North America, the Han of China and the Mbuti of Africa. After examining the migratory patterns of the ancestors of these groups in prehistoric times, they found that those groups with a long history of migration, and those who ended up at the far corners of the earth, had a predominance of what scientists refer to as the "long allele of the dopamine transporter gene"—a variant of the D4 receptor gene called 7R, which is linked with ADHD and is now commonly referred to as the "explorer gene."

Simply put, this is the genetic material that's associated with novelty-seeking, hyperactivity, curiosity and risk-taking, traits that have contributed to the survival of the species. Otherwise, so the argument goes, according to the rules of evolution and self-selection, this population would have died out millennia ago.

Some researchers have gone as far as to speculate that, from an evolutionary standpoint, the ADHD trait may have been lifesaving in prehistoric times, when we survived as hunter-gatherers, because being an explorer and always on the lookout for threats and opportunities are adaptive qualities.

Thom Hartmann, a radio host and former psychotherapist, popularized this idea in his book *Attention Deficit Disorder: A Different Perception*, coining the description of ADHD as being "a hunter in a farmer's world." He describes how we were all hunter-gatherers for centuries before we settled the land and stayed sedentary within one particular region or community. While the rest of the population adapted to farming culture, those with ADHD retained some of those nomadic hunter-gatherer tendencies, such as an ability to hyperfocus, take calculated risks and process different types of information at lightning speed.

During an age when food sources are scarce and threats of attacks by wild animals, for example, were all around us, these were the individuals who could lead the hunt or find safe places to set up camp, thus helping our ancestors to survive.

Subsequent scientific research lines up behind Thom Hartmann's theory. In 1997, researchers Peter S. Jensen, David Mrazek, Penelope K. Knapp, and others published a paper in the *Journal of American Child & Adolescent Psychiatry* calling ADHD a "disorder of adaptation." They concluded that ADHD exists for good reason. "Given the current estimated frequency of ADHD [11 percent], it is unlikely that such a 'disorder' could be as prevalent in the human species if not maintained within the species by selection forces that conveyed certain advantages to some ADHD characteristics or other associated traits."

In other words, the survival of a people depends on both the explorer and the settler. When times are good and the living is easy, the settler mentality carries the group. However, when resources are scarce and the village is threatened by war, famine or natural disasters, it's the adventurers who go forth to discover new lands, opportunities and resources. It's why there is a predominance of these genes in far-flung locations such as Australia, Polynesia and Tierra del Fuego—places that were so far off the grid there was nowhere left to go. It's also why the trait is often seen in nomadic populations, whose very existence depended on their ability to wander thousands of miles in search of food, water and lands to graze their livestock.

Forward Motion

Of course, it would be reductive and overreaching to say this one gene mutation drives all human exploration, and not everyone who has it can say they also have ADHD, so don't run out and get genetically tested. But the fact that 7R's positive traits persist in about 20 percent of the population and are so closely aligned with ADHD reinforces our argument about its strengths. A recent *National Geographic* series on explorers of the world draws heavily on this gene research, and perfectly sums up how the variant drives people in a constant forward motion:

> Dozens of human studies have found that 7R makes people more likely to take risks, explore new places, ideas, foods, relationships, drugs or sexual opportunities; and generally embrace movement, change, and adventure. Studies in animals simulating 7R's actions suggest it increases their taste for both movement and novelty.

A handful of recent studies take the idea of the explorer gene further, demonstrating how this exploratory ADHD trait drives curiosity and creativity and leads to an exploration of what is possible, through the mind. According to Bill Allsopp of Project Lab, for example, schoolchildren who excel in hands-on science and technology class displayed all the classic characteristics of the explorer, taking apart old equipment and machinery and, without any available instructions, putting them back together in inventive and unconventional ways that pushed boundaries. They were true inventors who, unconstrained by the limits of a manual, became totally absorbed in the task of finding solutions to a problem. Think Thomas Edison or Alexander Graham Bell.

"Over the years we had come to the stark realization that the youth that were successful in Project Lab were somehow different from their peer group," he says, realizing only after working with these kids for a few years that the list of common characteristics were in line with much of the general diagnostic criteria for ADHD.

Calling them "hunters" in reference to Thom Hartmann's theory, he goes on to describe the eye movements of the children in Project Lab:

> I have had a lot of fun watching kids' eyes in restaurants. The hunters are the ones who are constantly looking up and down, to the left and to the right, not furtively as a thief might, but openly and inquisitively as they look at the light fixtures, the rollers on the chairs, the people going by, the fire fixtures in the ceiling, the rug patterns and everything else that there is to look at. When asked what they were just looking at, they are usually totally unaware that they had been studying anything in particular, but it was evident from their scrutinizing appearance that something was taking place.

In all likelihood, they were members of the ADHD tribe—a group of young nomads, mentally exploring their environment, ever curious and stimulated by their new surroundings, assessing the situation and taking in every detail, ready and excited for whatever comes next.

Restless Soul

Without a doubt, international chef and restaurateur Bobby Chinn could have been one of those kids. His curiosity and wandering nature was evident early on in school, where being sent to the principal's office was an almost daily occurrence. His typical report card read, "Bobby is a very capable student. Unfortunately he spends most of the time playing the class fool (something he succeeds at). I hope he comes back with a determination to learn."

The issue wasn't a lack of smarts. As Bobby puts it, "My brain was always active, but I was bored out of my mind." He just couldn't sit still, and was often made to stand up at the front of the class, where he would wiggle his ears to amuse everyone. "I took being a clown very seriously."

Bobby didn't know where he fit, and his Egyptian/Chinese heritage was such an unusual combination back then, it didn't even make sense for him to try. Doing the interracial busing to school in the early seventies solidified his self-image as someone who did not belong.

"It was always black kids in the back, white kids in the front, and Asian and Hispanic kids in the middle. I had no idea where to sit," he recalls.

Eternal Misfit

The older he got, the more rebellious he became, whether he was attending inner-city schools in San Francisco, private schools in Cairo—where his family sent him in the hope he'd learn more discipline—or, finally, a top English boarding school, where he'd earned a sports scholarship to play rugby on one of the top teams in the country.

Bobby pressed on with his education. Boarding school, as well as a progressive high school in San Francisco, were turning points, motivating him enough to take his studies further despite the challenges. Unable to score high enough on his SATs, he went to junior college to get his grades up, made the dean's list, then attended three colleges in two years, dropping out to work as a busboy and invest his earnings in the stock market until he earned enough money to take a vacation and travel the world.

"I needed that extended European vacation to figure out what I was going to do with my life," says Bobby.

Continuing pressure from his family led him to finally complete a degree in economics and finance at a college in London, from which point he bounced between jobs as a research analyst in Boca Raton, a hedge fund trader in San Francisco and various positions in New

York, including working on the floor of the stock exchange, all the while confirming his hatred of everything to do with a desk, a chair and nine-to-five hours.

"Deciding what I wanted to do became like an algebra problem. I had to get rid of all the other variables that didn't make sense in the equations and whittle it down."

Process of Elimination

He tried comedian, waiter and, finally, chef. Bobby saw an opportunity to open a high-end restaurant in Vietnam, where, in 1993, the economy was opening up and creating more wealth. That potential made him even more determined to learn this new craft, so he returned to San Francisco, where he discovered that Vietnamese food had been largely overlooked, confirming his hunch that this was unexplored territory in the world of high cuisine. He tried to find work as an assistant chef at several restaurants and got the same reply: "But you're a waiter." He persisted, convincing Hubert Keller, who owned the renowned Fleur de Lys restaurant in San Francisco, to take a chance on him by offering to work for free.

After learning everything he could about creating and prepping food by shadowing a chef he admired while also keeping his waiting job, Bobby saved enough to make his move to Vietnam, moving from Saigon to Hanoi, where he found an investor and opened his first restaurant—one of four he would establish in both Hanoi and Saigon over the next decade, relishing the challenges of training local staff, establishing international standards of food preparation and dealing with the vicissitudes of the local economy and bureaucracy. He wrote a book on Vietnamese cuisine, which he reinvented by combining the country's traditional recipes and exotic ingredients into a more contemporary fusion menu.

Inventing new dishes was another chance to explore. "As a kid I used to love watching Julia Child take raw materials and create a perfect final product—it appealed to me, like building models without instructions." Being a chef in Vietnam gave him a chance to play with new ingredients and build dishes without a manual, trying things that hadn't been done before.

But here's the thing about explorers—conquering and exploring one territory is never enough. Bobby needed to keep moving. He found a gig hosting a show on the Discovery Channel called *World Café: Asia*, going from country to country to explore new foods and cultures. It was his dream job! Being itinerant led him to more opportunities, and in addition to his television show, which is now syndicated around the world, he wrote a book and opened a restaurant in London—House of Ho—earning himself international recognition from top food critics in food blogs and publications like *Time Out*, *GQ* and *Gourmet*, as well as appearances on top UK food shows. He is currently franchising his London restaurant and working on additional restaurant and hotel projects in Singapore.

To watch Bobby work in his restaurant is exhausting for anyone without ADHD. He zigzags from table to table, making friends with all the diners, cracking jokes, finding things they have in common and recommending dishes and wines to match. He clearly loves meeting new people, driven by his innate sense of curiosity about the world. He's also completely in tune with his external environment. His eyes dart everywhere, keeping an eye on staff, making sure presentation is just right, scanning the room to make sure customers are happy, in between visits to the kitchen to make sure his menu creations meet his exacting standards. He never stays in one spot for more than a couple of minutes at a time.

"I am like a shark—I have to keep moving forward to survive," explains Bobby. "If I stay still too long, I can't breathe."

Moments of Stillness

Of course, all this forward motion can be exhausting. Bobby burns out sometimes and struggles with slowing down his mind enough to focus for long on a single idea. Even sleeping through the night can be tough, as his mind races from one thought to another and never seems to shut down. So although his restless, adventurous nature is a strength and in many ways the source of his great success, this explorer would like to be able to stop once in a while to take in the landscape and get his bearings. Bobby doesn't want to change, but he does want to get better at what he is already good at, like so many others I talked to. He feels he still has untapped potential if he could just focus more often, but without medication. We have to acknowledge that life isn't necessarily always perfect with ADHD, which is why I am going to give you various methods throughout these next pages that can help. The point is not to suppress the explorer tendencies but to help make them less distracting.

The restless mind can be a problem that many in the explorer tribe face, and it's why they are turning to prescriptions, or self-medication in the form of alcohol or other narcotics. As I discussed in Chapter Three, while the ADHD trait is a tremendous advantage, and being explorers can lead us to new heights of success, we are not as good with certain executive functions of the brain that give us more control over where and when we can use these strengths. But we can actually have it both ways, without a pill. There are practices and exercises that can help slow down the mind and focus your wandering attention, creating enough calm and clarity to leverage your exploring tendencies and move in the right direction. Think of them as simple, practical tools to help you make the best of this strength, amping up your executive functions to help you better navigate your life while still preserving all that explorer energy that got you this far. After all, every great explorer needs a compass.

New research has found that it's possible to learn to focus the brain through mindfulness practices. Mindfulness exercises help build the mental muscles necessary for cognitive control, including filtering thoughts and emotions, impulse control, delaying gratification and the ability to pay attention—even when a task or information is boring! Mindfulness—which can take the form of meditation, yoga or even simple games and mental exercises that can be viewed on a video screen—has been shown to "flex the brain circuitry" for sustained mental focus, according to research at Emory University in Atlanta, Georgia.

According to a study published in July 2014 on mindfulness-based cognitive therapy (MBCT) published in *Clinical Neurophysiology*, adults with ADHD experienced significant improvements in mental focus, comparable with the immediate benefits of taking ADHD meds. While not a huge study—the researchers looked at fifty adults, giving twenty-six MBCT and assigning twenty-four to the control group—its findings show tremendous potential.

Another recent study, published in 2013 in *Frontiers in Human Neuroscience*, looked at brain images of twenty-seven meditators on a monthlong retreat while they went through the basic exercises of daily meditation practice, including focusing on a chosen point—whether that was the breath or an object—noticing when their minds wandered and then refocusing their attention on the target, sustaining their attention on the point of focus while simply observing, forgiving themselves and letting go whenever they were distracted by a stray thought. Over time, these brain movements appeared to improve concentration or what these researchers call "attentional performance."

The human brain retains its plasticity long after childhood, and we are seeing increasing evidence of its ability to build new cells in regions of the brain like the frontal lobes that are underperforming, through mental exercise. This has already been established for memory loss. It's why older people are encouraged to do crosswords, play Sudoku or learn a new language or skill. It's well known that those mental exercises help to strengthen the aging brain. But now we are seeing new technology that helps improve concentration when practiced regularly over a sustained period of time.

Dr. Adam Gazzaley, a neuroscientist who runs a cognitive neuroscience research lab at the University of California, San Francisco, developed video games that mimic the effects of cognitive control through meditation, enabling users to better self-regulate internal distractions. He created *NeuroRacer*, a three-dimensional video game for older people that challenges them to respond to the sudden appearance of traffic signs while driving on a winding road. The results of his study, which recorded the brain activity of the forty-six participants, found that regular use of the game helped improve their cognitive control.

Bobby the chef has also begun using technology prescribed to him by his neurologist to calm and focus his brain. In the morning and evening he pauses for about ten minutes to focus on a moving image or design he pulls up from an app on his iPhone—much the way a meditator would focus on an idea, breath or object. Any more time spent using this tool would be counterproductive, because too much sitting and staring in contemplation would drive him crazy.

"I think it's helping," says Bobby, whose only still moments of the day are when he's looking at those video images or playing his guitar.

Meanwhile, he'll do anything to avoid taking ADHD stimulants. "I don't want to be comatose all day with just one idea. Who wants that?"

Bobby is still all over the place, but biofeedback images recorded on weekly visits to his neurologist confirm that his cognitive control is improving. He is hoping that strengthening these executive functions will help him take his career to the next level. It would help, for example, if he could plan a little further ahead and stay in one location for long enough to beef up his media presence in the United Kingdom and the United States. He'd also like to be able to follow through on more projects so that they can be self-sustaining and more profitable. A good night's sleep would be another bonus of his mindfulness practice, and is something he is starting to get more of.

Bobby is one of a growing number of ADHDers who are adopting this technique to train their brains. The early results of many of these mental exercise studies represent promising news for our explorer tribe. It's a non-drug intervention that's long overdue. Unlike ADHD medications, which tend to flatten us out and kill our individual quirks, mindfulness practices in their various forms enable us to strengthen our areas of weakness while preserving our many gifts. The exploring mind must be free to wander if it's going to discover new places, things or ideas.

Makers of History

And why wouldn't we want to keep our explorer tendencies? We are in great company, after all. The explorer gene was embodied by the likes of Captain Cook, Amerigo Vespucci, Meriwether Lewis (of Lewis and Clark) and Ernest Shackleton, whose dexterity and imaginations, combined with their restless drive to push beyond the edges of known civilization, made history.

Of course, it's impossible to make a diagnosis on a dead person, so we'll never know for certain if any of these historical figures truly did have the explorer gene. But I, along with other psychiatrists, strongly suspect they did, and it's certainly fun to speculate. So let's keep going!

Take Sir Richard Francis Burton, another fascinating figure from history who fits the classic profile of the ADHD explorer. This nineteenth century Englishman, best known for his travels and discoveries in Asia, Africa and North and South America, traveled extensively not just from one far-flung place to another, he also flitted between his many interests and vocations as a translator, writer, soldier, orientalist, cartographer, ethnologist, spy, linguist, poet, Egyptologist, fencer and diplomat. He was also known for his extraordinary knowledge of cultures and his linguistic abilities, having spoken more than twenty-five languages. He traveled undercover in Mecca, translated *The Arabian Nights* and explored dangerously wild frontiers, having nearly died in his search for the source of the River Nile in the African Congo. Talk about restless! This was a man who simply could not sit still.

Others who likely had the explorer gene were Napoléon Bonaparte, General George Patton and Eddie Rickenbacker—the World War I flying ace. These were military leaders and adventurers who were unafraid to venture into danger, boldly covering large and hostile territories for the sake of military gains. They took calculated risks, and showed calm leadership and control under pressure. Their explorer genes were likely key ingredients in their exploits in the air and on the battlefield.

Literary explorers thought to have ADHD include Emily Dickinson, an eccentric figure whose eighteen hundred poems featured short lines and unconventional punctuation that defied the poetic rules of the time. Virginia Woolf, one of the greatest modernist novelists of the last century, broke new ground with her stream-of-consciousness prose—a classic example of the ADHDer's nonlinear thinking.

Eleanor Roosevelt is another woman in history who likely had the trait. Restless and energetic, she was compelled to be in constant forward motion. Never content just to play the role of first lady, she had to roam around the country pushing for reform, tending to wounded soldiers for the Red Cross and galvanizing the Democratic Party while her husband was handling matters of state. Her definition of happiness was to be of service to others:

"Usefulness, whatever form it may take, is the price we should pay for the air we breathe and the food we eat and the privilege of being alive."

This gene also accounts for historical figures like Benjamin Franklin, Albert Einstein and Thomas Edison, whose mental exploration pushed the frontiers of ideas and invention. And Amadeus Mozart, an avid explorer of musical frontiers, fits the bill perfectly. Prolific and impatient from an early age, he worked long and hard, writing his compositions at a rapid pace as each deadline approached. Restless and easily bored, he traveled from court to court throughout Europe as he explored every genre and invented new forms of music with his complex and passionate compositions.

Leonardo da Vinci was the ultimate mental explorer who may also have shared this trait. His boundless energy not only created the *Mona Lisa*, he was a musician, writer, sculptor, scientist, engineer, botanist, anatomist, geologist, cartographer and mathematician. He was the ultimate Renaissance man, whose curiosity about the world and mind brimming with ideas led him to invent and design flying machines centuries ahead of his time. Talk about a multitasker!

Although he was never formally diagnosed, the late Steve Jobs could be described as one of these modern-day explorers, pushing the frontiers of technology. His lack of a diagnosis hasn't stopped him from being a source of inspiration for ADHDers and, since his death, dozens of ADHD coaches and bloggers have cited him as a role model, and I can certainly see why. He embodied Apple's slogan, "Think different," a saying that perfectly sums up the minds of those with the ADHD trait. He went places no one else could or would in designing, building and packaging products, doing things in ways that were incomprehensible to other people, introducing extraordinary ideas that were often dismissed until they proved to be so perfect they revolutionized an industry. He carved out his own path, and in that sense, he too was an explorer.

Perhaps if these explorers had been alive today and diagnosed with ADHD, the trait would not be so stigmatized, and people wouldn't be in such a rush to suppress the impulses, ideas and desires that drive these adventurers. Perhaps the education system would find better ways to nurture and leverage their exploring tendencies from their earliest years. Perhaps there would be more incentive to develop non-drug interventions so that we don't lose the next generation's leaders, inventors and adventurers.

We could use more of this adventurous spirit today. Over a relatively short span of time in evolutionary history, our migratory ancestors settled down, farmed the land and built roads and cities. In short, they became sedentary, like the occupants of those cubicles at *Bloomberg*, and our adventurers and explorers became less in demand. But in these turbulent times of economic and social transition, we need the leadership and innovation that these ADHD adventurers can contribute. Their time has come again.

THE TOOL KIT

Some unscientific signs you may have the explorer gene:

- The thought of staying in one place for the rest of your life fills you with a sense of mind-numbing boredom.

- Two of your favorite classes in school were phys ed, and geography. If you are an explorer you are naturally going to be interested in the world. In my experience, kids with ADHD are fascinated by maps, and deeply curious about other cultures. I love maps, and so does my son, Trey!

- Given a choice of vacation, you'd take trekking in Nepal over lying on a beach in Hawaii any day.

- When you were on camping trips in the Boy Scouts or Girl Scouts, you were the first to go out and explore those unmarked forest trails.

- When you walk into an unfamiliar room or travel to a new place, you are brimming with curiosity, taking in every facet of your external environment.

- Your ideal job involves constant travel to distant lands, and almost no time sitting at an office desk.

- New places, people, experiences and challenges keep you motivated.

- You are most comfortable with the unfamiliar, while routine leaves you feeling dead inside.

- You love to start a new project, but once the challenging part is done you quickly become bored.

CHAPTER FIVE

Learning with ADHD

Small-town Texas doctor Mike Watson, was a lousy student. It's not that he wasn't bright. In fact, he's brilliant. But like the nuns at his strict Catholic school used to say, he had ants in his pants. Mike just couldn't sit still, and his mind would wander all over the place. It took him a long time to get the hang of reading, he could never sit down and do homework and, even if he did, he'd forget it at home.

"The nuns just about didn't let me graduate from Holy Ghost Grade School," Mike recalls with a chuckle, although his experiences were probably more painful than he lets on—because when you dismiss a child as stupid, wicked or incapable, it can scar him for life.

In college, when he was studying chemical engineering, he couldn't remember any of the math theorems he needed to solve equations, so he would redo the theory on a piece of paper to come up with the formula—basically figure it out from scratch. That's how brilliant, and scattered, he was.

And yet he graduated from that program and went on to medical school. Today he's a general practitioner and emergency room doctor who can perform anything from a C-section to an appendectomy, as well as treat sore throats or depression. He's a generalist, and a local hero in the small Texan town near Midland where he practices—a regular Marcus Welby, MD, and a rarity in an era when we could use a few more good men like him.

Luckily, Mike had the native intelligence, persistence and resilience to survive his education. As many bright people with ADHD find, it gets easier if you can make it into college, where you're more in control of your time and study methods, and you are able to major in subjects you are passionate about.

But, for millions of children with ADHD, the system has been set up for them to fail. It's the curriculum and classroom setting that is the problem, not the kid. Forcing these children to sit still for hours at a time to absorb information taught to classrooms with thirty or more students simply does not cater to the ADHD learning style, and it doesn't appear as if our public school system has the capacity or interest to develop a more progressive education model anytime soon.

Instead, exhausted parents and teachers, with the doctor's blessing, are dosing these kids with Ritalin, Vyvanse or Adderall. As I mentioned earlier, teachers are on the front lines, making the recommendations for diagnosis and putting pressure on families to medicate their children. I don't blame them entirely, because in overcrowded classrooms a few disruptive kids can make it next to impossible for them to do their jobs, and our public schools are so poorly funded and resourced that they are forced to cut corners whenever they can. But make no mistake, it's for the benefit of the majority, *not* the individual child being forced to take the medication. The fact that so many of these kids are on meds is a sad commentary on the state of our health-care system and a poor reflection on what has happened to education in this country.

As Dr. Allen Frances, one of the leading mental health experts in the world, puts it in his editorial "Treat the Classroom, Not the Kids," we are mislabeling kids with mental illness due to simple immaturity.

"The surest proof of misplaced diagnostic exuberance comes directly from the classroom. Research shows that the youngest kids in class are much more likely than the oldest to be diagnosed as having ADHD and to receive stimulant treatment. It is shameful . . ." he writes, referencing studies that suggest an alarming number of referrals for ADHD diagnosis that come from teachers.

Those children who are legitimately diagnosed may benefit from extra school attention, he goes on to say, "But the two-thirds or more of active kids who have been mislabeled with ADHD suffer unnecessary stigma, reduced expectations and harmful drug side effects."

Dr. Frances is right about the stigma. Often it is not the ADHD that holds back these children, or adults, it's the poor self-esteem that usually develops in the classroom, when they start to realize that the overly structured and regimented system, particularly in most public education settings, makes it next to impossible for them to learn, and they fall behind their peers.

But the good news is that there are multiple ways we can set these children up for success, both in the home and at school, including practical recommendations and concrete steps that we can take as parents and teachers that can motivate and encourage high performance. Again, being successful with ADHD is all about having the right context and support systems. Because it's not that we can't learn, it's just that we learn differently.

Some of the strategies being employed by progressive schools, enterprising individual teachers, parents and the students themselves have led to breakthroughs for many ADHD students. I've found that more associative learning styles, visual learning, certain methods of highlighting, writing down and physical note-taking, which vary according to what works for the individual, as well as more freedom during classroom and study time, can have a real impact. When they are passionate about a subject, ADHD students can hyperfocus and excel, but even when they are not, these kids can learn just as well as non-ADHD students. If they are allowed the scope to study in short increments, perhaps even while texting and listening to music, and if they get lots of outlets for their restless energy, they can ace any curriculum.

I'll delve more into specific methods later in this chapter, but the underlying theme is that ADHD kids thrive with the right balance of flexibility and boundaries. Like any child, they need a foundation of good parenting and caring teachers or mentors who are clear and consistent about what is expected of them. But they can't be boxed in or constrained by the traditional classroom setting. As in all things ADHD, it is never one-size-fits-all.

Many of the individuals interviewed for this book managed to figure out their own study methods and learning styles, and thrived academically despite the limitations of the typical classroom setting. Some possessed a high intelligence that allowed them to get good grades anyway, even ace tests despite their distractibility and inability to sit still with a textbook—although imagine what their grades could have been if they'd cracked their own study code. Others, like my son, Trey, began to flourish academically only when they got to college, where they could multitask, study at their own speed and take courses that were of genuine interest to them.

Leveraged Learning

Chicago native Tatiana, who was introduced in Chapter One, found that her impulsivity and short attention span became more of an impediment throughout grade school and middle school. As a preschooler, she'd been used to the less structured, more individually supportive environment of a Montessori school, and being forced to sit still in the standard classroom setting was a tough adjustment.

Tatiana struggled to focus. As soon as she was taught something, she'd forget it. There were too many other things to grab her attention, so if it wasn't inherently interesting to her, the lesson simply would not stick. But, as a gifted volleyball player and highly competitive by nature, she could not accept her mediocre performance and knew she could do much better if only she had the right tools.

"I needed to be the best, so I pushed myself," she told me.

Tatiana took matters into her own hands when she was thirteen and began to research learning techniques that she could tailor to her own needs. She began reading up on behavioral psychology, which taught her tricks like reading aloud under her breath, running her finger along the lines of text, and taking notes in margins. These visual, hands-on techniques helped her to focus on and process the exact words she was reading.

She also taught herself the art of association. Whenever there is new information to remember, she first takes the time to understand the why behind the concept. She then pairs the new concept up with what she already knows, making up an analogy, story or metaphor tailored to the meaning. A simple way to describe it is the picture/word association technique commonly used to learn a new language. By this method, the word and meaning "raconteur," for example, could be remembered through the image of a raccoon telling a story.

Tatiana also researched methods of long-term learning. She wasn't just interested in keeping it in her working memory—she wanted to be able to use the information later in life. Whenever she was in class, she would write down what the teacher was saying in her own words. If she had any questions, she would go back to the lecturer and ask him if that was what he really meant. The immediate feedback and instruction on how to interpret something properly helped her to store it into her long-term memory bank.

"That lecture feedback is something I applied both in school and the working world—it's made all the difference to my success," says Tatiana.

This tool worked particularly well for learning things we might put under the banner "boring but important." As ADHDers, if something does not fascinate us from the get-go, it often doesn't get past our short attention spans. But by trying to understand the value of it—the why—and its importance in helping her get to the next step, Tatiana was better able to retain the information, however uninteresting she found it, and apply it in her daily working life.

Making Connections

Hong Kong–based IT entrepreneur Gordon Sanders applied a similar method when he first moved to China and studied Mandarin. For much of his life, learning had been one of his biggest challenges. While he did well in school, the challenges of adolescence and being bullied caused his grades to slip toward the end of high school, resulting in a loss of focus on his studies. In 1981, Gordon made it into college, but he found he'd always rather be somewhere else besides the lecture hall or in front of his books—whether that was deejaying at parties or managing a doughnut shop.

"I became quite good at paying for classes, just not attending them," he told me. He got kicked out of university four or five times, and in 1988, after repeatedly changing his major to one that required a lower GPA, "They were on to me and I got kicked out for good."

So studying wasn't exactly his strong suit, especially when it came to learning to speak and write one of the most difficult languages ever invented by mankind! Unlike my son, Trey, Gordon didn't have a natural facility for foreign languages and had never attempted to learn one before. Even worse, his Chinese language teachers tried to get him to memorize the words and characters. Unless his passion for the subject can lead to hyperfocus, asking an ADHDer to learn something by rote is futile. It's just doesn't come naturally to us.

Yet Gordon was determined to learn. The Dallas native wanted to embrace his new home and connect with the people he met, and he knew that learning the language was a key to making this happen. But those first eleven months were pure torture.

"I would stand up in class trying to say something as simple as, 'I want to buy some fruit,' and after reciting the line eight times, I would break into the biggest sweat," Gordon recalls. "After thirty seconds it would look as if I had just stepped out of the shower."

He hit a wall multiple times before he realized there *had* to be a better way to learn the language. Then he researched alternative methods of learning and decided to use the fact that, as a written language, Mandarin is visual. The characters were originally designed as pictograms as well as ideograms, and were *intended* to have associations. The language is also made up of compounds, so that one part of the speech can have associations with multiple words and phrases.

"I would find a word, look at its character, learn it and figure out what other combinations existed, find it in other characters and build the lines for the relationships," he says.

He also found online games to reinforce the word associations. It was as if the language were made for the bingo brain! As a nonlinear thinker, Gordon was able to gain a working knowledge of Mandarin within months, and was making good progress in his conversational language skills. And he's applied that interactive learning method to other subjects ever since, including his project management certification exam, which he subsequently aced.

Entirely on his own, Gordon stumbled upon a study method that works for him. Now imagine how much heartache and disappointment he might have saved himself if he'd had the opportunity to explore these different learning methods while he was still in school.

Finding the Right Software

Don't be afraid to experiment. You have to be willing to try different things. But if your child is not able to do so well in a traditional classroom setting, do not assume it means she is any less capable of learning. In fact, when our ADHD minds lock in on something that we are passionate about, we're able to hyperfocus, retain an extraordinary amount of detail and go beyond what you will find in any school curriculum.

"There's nothing wrong with these children," says Jane Beckley, a UK-based teacher who specializes in ADHD. "Traditional schools run on Microsoft, but these kids are Macs. Their software is not compatible. Put them on Apple software and they will fly."

Jane, who has ADHD herself, became interested in different methods of teaching ADHD children when her son was diagnosed in middle school. Searching for answers, she came across a book, *The Gift of Dyslexia*, by Ronald Davis, who was dyslexic and a functional illiterate until the age of thirty-eight, when he taught himself to read by other, more visual learning methods. Jane was so impressed by the book that she started taking training programs from Davis Dyslexia Association International, which encompasses ADHD, and got qualified to teach the Davis method in schools around England. The experience opened her mind to alternative approaches to helping a child learn.

Today, her own son, Sam, is excelling as he works as an accountant at a top music label in London. Her students are realizing their potential as well. And she continues to have a positive impact on children like Sam—ADHDers who've been left behind by the school system despite their enormous potential. Jane discovered the scope of their talents when she brought a group of these kids to Stafford University, which has a special program to encourage middle school children to consider a future in engineering. The unit encourages them to create robots out of different computer and machinery parts. Each time, they excel at the tasks they are given, often outshining their peers who do well in the standard school exams.

"These children are the inventors and entrepreneurs of our future who will change our world," she says. "Imagine how Einstein or Edison would have done if they had to go through today's education system or, worse, taken medication."

So it's well worth taking the time to explore different approaches to teaching, however unconventional they may seem, because you never know the kind of creativity you will unleash in a child. In fact, by doing less, we may be shortchanging ourselves of the extraordinary contributions these unique brains could make to our collective future.

A Teacher Who Gets It

It goes without saying that every child could use a mentor early on who recognizes their potential and can give them insight into their strengths. But this is particularly true for ADHD children, who need that early boost to their confidence to get them started. They need a caring and wise educator, like Tichelle Harris, an ADHDer who decided to switch careers from finance to become a county middle school teacher in Winfall, North Carolina.

Tichelle, who, like Jane, became aware that she had ADHD when her own son was diagnosed in the fourth grade, was inspired to get into teaching full-time when she started doing financial presentations in public schools for the credit union where she was working. Visiting these classrooms, it struck her that students like her son faced even more of a struggle in school than when she was his age, and she wanted to be that teacher who made a difference in their lives.

Tichelle's own school experience had been positive.

"Early on I had awesome teachers," she recalls. "Times have changed."

Tichelle began researching ADHD to help her son, and quickly realized they shared similar styles of learning. She took that knowledge into the classroom, where she teaches business, entrepreneurship and computer application systems.

That first semester, adjusting to the standard classroom methods was rough. A lot of the students questioned the relevance of what was being taught on the school syllabus, and so did she. So she tried to come up with a curriculum that was more engaging and interactive for her students, four of whom had been diagnosed with ADHD. She found that doing more visual presentations, like PowerPoints, and having her students lead those presentations, was particularly effective. She also gave a little extra attention to the ADHD kids in her class, to make sure their wandering minds didn't miss anything crucial in that day's lesson. By the end of that first semester, her different approach had an impact on all her students whether or not they had ADHD, and many of them asked to come back into her class.

Another method she uses to engage her students and figure out what sparks their interest is to talk with them each Monday about everything from a topic in the news to what they did that weekend. She also has them keep a journal. This way, "I can figure out what they like and don't like, and implement what they are more passionate about into my lesson plan." As a result, the ADHD students who used to "zone out" during class time have become more active, raising their hands and participating in the conversations or debates with enthusiasm. Since the ADHD brain works best when activated, she made it her goal to provide that activation.

"I get excited when I can give them new insight and focus on a topic," she says.

These discussion topics can come from various articles Tichelle has read, sourced from publications like *Newsweek*, *Time*, the *Wall Street Journal* and *Forbes*. In fact, she got in touch with me after reading one of my *Forbes* blog posts, "ADHD: The Entrepreneur's Superpower."

"As we started talking about it, and all the strengths you have with ADHD, I could see it started changing their minds on what it is and how it affects people," says Tichelle. "A few of my students were in shock, and it's already reshaping their thinking process on many things."

It was almost as if a light switched on in the eyes of one of her ADHD students who had been struggling with self-esteem issues. The boy had been openly wondering if he would ever be able to reach his full potential and make something of his life. Reading examples of businesspeople with ADHD who've done extraordinarily well because and not in spite of their ADHD was a huge boost to his self-esteem. He has been walking taller and focusing on his schoolwork, especially his entrepreneurship studies, ever since.

"Effective teaching is all about challenging their belief systems and stimulating their curiosity to help open doorways . . . to change," says Tichelle.

Tichelle also teaches the way she, as an ADHDer, would have wanted to be taught when she was in school. She dislikes too much structure, as do most of her students, so instead she flows quickly from topic to topic, and often meanders through the class discussion.

"When we do get off topic, my students will ask something that reminds me to relate it back to what we were originally talking about."

This mission to educate and engage her ADHD students is personal. When he was in grade school she noticed that reading was hard for her son, and his teachers took that to mean his reading skills were below grade. However, the problem was not that he couldn't read but that he wasn't interested in the fiction books they assigned in class. He preferred nonfiction, especially books about animals, because he aspired to become a zoologist. That discovery of his interests kept improving his reading by inspiring him to read something, even though it wasn't class-related, and helped him pass.

By zeroing in on her students' individual interests, Tichelle finds information and digs up research that challenges them about the particular topic they are focused on. They open up when she starts presenting different points of views and ideas about their favorite subjects, and from that point on she has their attention.

"It's a way of finding the place they are in and getting them to learn where they are," says Tichelle.

The takeaway here is that ADHD students do especially well when they come across a teacher or mentor who gives them more individual attention. By tapping into their passions and being sensitive to their responses in the classroom, these educators are able to build the confidence of these students and help them to lock in on their ADHD strengths.

A Better Blueprint

We could use a few more gems like Tichelle in the public school system, and they do exist. But these outstanding educators are usually forced to work within the huge constraints of large classrooms, limited budgets and standardized teaching and testing requirements. What our public education system needs is general reform that can address the different learning needs of millions of children. We need to do away with restrictive policies and programs that leave so many kids out in the cold.

That seems a long way off. But a handful of private schools and summer programs that specialize in teaching kids with ADHD and other so-called learning disabilities are leading the way and providing blueprints for the rest of the nation. These more progressive schools are moving away from the traditional classroom setting, with an emphasis on diversity in learning styles, in the steadfast belief that these kids have an individual genius that just needs to be leveraged in the right way. There's a recognition, for example, that their students learn best when there's plenty of variety in the curriculum, so classes tend to be taught in shorter increments. (Fifteen minutes is ideal for an ADHD child's attention span.)

It's worth noting that students from many of these schools have high acceptance rates at top colleges and universities, with a sizable portion of the students earning merit scholarships. So the proof is in the results. Accepting and enabling individual learning styles is the path to academic success for ADHD children, who have a particularly hard time adapting to the conventional classroom.

"Ad Hocracy"

The one thing these alternative schools have in common is that they almost never mention the term "learning disabilities." In fact, Eagle Hill School, based in Massachusetts, does not regard ADHD as a disability at all. Instead, administrators at the school, where approximately 70 percent of its students have the diagnosis, believe in leveraging individual strengths with smaller classes, custom-designed curricula and greater flexibility in its teaching programs.

The school, admittedly an exclusive private institution, is redefining the conventional wisdom regarding the education of students with learning disabilities, preferring the term "learning diversity." The school's philosophy is grounded in the belief that its students are not disabled at all, and that their poor academic performance in the past has more to do with the constraints of the traditional classroom.

I was so impressed by what the school had to say about learning diversity on its website that we reached out to the headmaster, P. J. McDonald, and Michael Riendeau, assistant headmaster for academic affairs, at the prep school to learn more. What struck home was how focused they were on the individual student, whose curriculum is custom-tailored to his or her preferred learning style and needs.

"It's not about determining which kind of kid we have in front of us and applying a standard practice from some menu, but working with each student in developing a program that works for her or him," Michael explains.

For example, students get to have a say in what courses are taught and what the curriculum should include.

"They come into that process in a very significant way," says P.J.

He uses the term "ad hocracy." So instead of the rigid bureaucratic system that overtakes most schools, Eagle Hill adapts and adjusts regularly, according to the individual student's needs and development. Teachers at the school may start with all the previous school reports, cognitive testing and psychological assessments of the student, but they acknowledge that until they get the students into their own classroom, they don't really understand them as individuals. And that's exactly the point. These kids are individuals, not diagnoses, and what works for one student with ADHD may not always work with another.

Education Ownership

The school has put a lot of thought into this individualized learning approach. Students are empowered to voice their own preferences through a course the school offers called Seminar on Learning. It gives them a chance to explore their own strengths and needs, and the language to express these needs to their teachers.

"So they can take some ownership of their own learning," says Michael.

Eagle Hill has built flexibility into its programs, enabling it to customize learning to each student's strengths, interests and weaknesses, by restructuring the entire school term system. Each school year has nine one-month terms. Depending on the student, some courses will last one term, while others will last all nine terms. So if a student is interested in studying the Vietnam War, for example, she can take such a class for one or two months, and then move on to something else.

It's ideal for the ADHD student to dabble in different subjects until something clicks. This also introduces a more collegiate style of learning where a student can take electives, which is why ADHD kids tend to do better in college. They have more control over their own schedules. Eagle Hill, which is primarily a boarding school, has a team of full-time resident counselors, certified life coaches who work from 3:00 to 11:00 p.m. each day helping students with organization and time management. It's a way to help them prepare for a college setting, where they have even more academic freedom.

That aspect of the program appears to be working, since 96 percent of their students have gone on to college, and 71 percent have graduated with a degree within six years of leaving Eagle Hill, compared with the national average of 60 percent overall, and 15 to 20 percent for those with learning differences—a phenomenal increase of triple the national average.

Finding Their Own Level

Another innovation at Eagle Hill is in its grade system. Students are put in classes based on their own performance, not by grade. If a ninth-grader is at an eleventh-grade level in math, for example, he'll be more challenged and at less risk of getting bored and disengaged. But if his reading and writing levels are closer to a seventh-grade level, he'll still get the foundational skills he needs, while not being held back in areas of strength.

Teachers are trusted to make the best choices together with their students, and best practices aren't imposed from on high. So if an ADHD child has a hard time focusing during a fifty-four-minute class, the teacher can break down the lesson into increments, or give distracted students some discrete activities on the side, in order to enable them to shift gears.

Eagle Hill is also leveraging mobile technology like smart phones and tablets to do what Michael and P.J. call the "flipped classroom model." So instead of talking at students for an hour in class and sending them home with hours' worth of homework, teachers have the option of uploading videos of themselves giving ten minutes of instruction, using class time to coach the students during the actual assignment.

The technology "is an asset for students who have trouble attending to a teacher's voice for thirty-five minutes straight," says P.J.

It's also helpful to use as many different types of media as possible, other than a blackboard, to engage a student's attention. Hands-on learning is an important aspect of the curriculum. The school has a cultural center where students put on theater and musical productions, and get to explore creative interests outside the academic curriculum. Students don't just perform. They get involved in production work, working as sound and lighting engineers. They even get to experience professional events at the venue, such as music concerts. Students handled much of the production at a recent Livingston Taylor concert.

Giving Back

By now you may be thinking, "This is all very well, but what about the rest of us?" It takes money to place your child at Eagle Hill, a private school with the kind of resources that the rest of the education system simply does not have. It's a lot easier to custom-tailor an academic program with 55 teachers for only 210 students. (The average national student-teacher ratio in public schools is just over fifteen-to-one, and much higher in urban settings.)

But Eagle Hill has been giving back for the past decade, having trained about a hundred urban public school teachers in Massachusetts. In fact, when we spoke with them, they were in the middle of one of these training weeks, which has yielded impressive results in terms of teacher retention rates. About 90 percent of teachers who have gone through the program have remained in their public systems, when the usual retention rate is about 50 percent. This is important, because a host of research suggests that teachers with more tenure are more effective. It also gives the students and teachers time to build up a relationship, and trust, during the course of a child's school career.

Among the things these public school teachers learn at Eagle Hill is that they can be more flexible even without the additional resources of a private school. Instead of viewing mobile technology as a distraction and banning it from the classroom, for example, they are taught through the example of the flipped classroom model mentioned earlier that smart phones can be an asset. Since over 80 percent of students in even the poorest schools have smart phones these days, schools could apportion some of their budget for computers to mobile technology, so that every student can take home instructional videos from teachers. This is also a way to enhance the multisensory learning that's so helpful for kids with ADHD.

Even if these schools can't break up classes into shorter increments, teachers can help ADHD students who struggle to stay in their seats for forty-five minutes at a stretch by making them the class managers when project work is under way, allowing them to move from group to group and get involved in problem solving.

These are just a few of the simple but effective and doable adjustments that are being passed on through the Eagle Hill training, which P.J. and Michael hope to take nationwide through "training the trainer" programs in Chicago, Houston and Los Angeles.

"A lot of the stuff we are talking about is completely applicable to a regular classroom setting; we just have to get the word out," says Michael.

What Parents Can Do

Even parents who don't have the means for or access to top-notch private academies can create a supportive environment for their ADHD prodigies at home. There is plenty they can do to bolster their children's self-esteem and give them opportunities to find something they excel at and enjoy.

Dr. Oren Mason, the family doctor and ADHDer you met in Chapter Two, discovered that the eldest of his two sons had the trait when he was in second grade and his grades started declining, not because of his ability, but because of his performance.

The diagnosis led Dr. Mason to study and specialize in ADHD. It also inspired him to be more present as a father.

"I'd set high goals for myself and accomplished a lot, but when it came to parenting I was hitting a brick wall," he told me.

He was away so much, whether it was to run his practice or indulge his many interests—including running marathons around the country—that he was failing to provide the right kind of structure for his children. This is true for all kids, but particularly so for children with ADHD, who need a stable foundation at home as they navigate countless social and academic challenges. They are already dealing with an "unstructured" brain, so external structure becomes even more important.

"Kids with ADHD need things to be laid out, clear and reliable, so that they have a safety net," says Dr. Mason. "You need to come home when you say you are going to come home. As a parent, you need to be consistent."

This reliability is key both for helping ADHD children develop their self-esteem and for giving them a strong foundation, so they'll have the confidence to go out and explore new things.

"I encourage parents to give their kids every opportunity and a wide-ranging variety of experiences that can help them learn what their passions and gifts are," he says.

So if a child shows any kind of athletic prowess, don't just focus on one sport. Let him try different activities. But if he gravitates to one thing, let him go for it.

This goes for any type of pursuit. Get out there and take your ADHD child to museums and parks. Encourage her to watch Animal Planet or the History Channel. If it captures their fancy, indulge them in it until they are ready to drop it and move on to something else.

"Instead of steering kids into what we think they need to do, give them a chance to find something that surprises you," says Dr. Mason.

He speaks from experience with his own son, whom they assumed to have no musical talent. He signed up for French horn in sixth grade and surprised them by practicing loudly every day. Before they finished paying for that instrument, he asked to switch to trumpet. At first Dr. Oren and his wife refused, reasoning that he had committed to the French horn and had to see it through. But then his wife chanced on a coronet in a garage sale and picked it up. His son started playing, switching to trumpet in his school band. But each year it was something else: a guitar, a drum set. Finally he asked for software that would help him put musical tracks together.

Today, Dr. Mason's son is finishing his bachelor's degree in business and public relations, and has a music studio on the side. He does beats and backups for hip-hop artists and has been in several bands. He has been able to stay on the dean's list in part because he can see how music and business will work together as he opts to expand his studio or perhaps run his own record label someday.

"Passion drives the desire to practice, which instills the discipline and structure necessary to see things through," Dr. Mason says. "But that motivation provides the fuel for the discipline, which otherwise is very unnatural for someone with ADHD."

Unfortunately, Toronto-based Andrew Ryan didn't get that kind of encouragement. He struggled in school, and yet he was able to teach himself music, had an "insatiable" interest in art, read voraciously—particularly about history—and got into cooking. Anything that was a creative outlet captivated Andrew's imagination. The problem was, he lived in a small, remote town in Ontario—Sault Sainte Marie—and if he'd pursued any of these interests as a career, "I don't think my parents would have accepted that."

Andrew eventually went on to become a successful project manager and engineer, but not until his late twenties, after years of frustration and depression as he tried to conform to the expectations of parents and teachers. He wouldn't have been such a late bloomer if someone had recognized and nurtured his passions as a child. It's an all-too-common story.

Unusual Study Habits

Parents also need to understand, and accept, that the best ways for their child to learn may seem contradictory to their set notions of good study habits. My son, Trey, for example, needed to have the television or radio blasting, with several online messaging conversations often in multiple languages, while he would study. He was an A student in college precisely because he had the freedom to do it his way. But at boarding school, he struggled. Those two-hour mandatory study hall sessions every evening were about as horrifying to him as being shackled in a prison cell.

Dr. Kashinath Yadalam, a psychiatrist who runs a successful research site conducting clinical trials for pharmaceutical companies in Louisiana, was fortunate enough to have a mother who, while unaware that he had ADHD at the time, knew that her son learned differently, and was willing to do whatever it took to help him retain the information necessary to pass his exams. Dr. Yadalam, a man in his fifties who grew up in India, would never have made it through that rigid colonial school system if it weren't for her.

In primary school, Dr. Yadalam, then known as "Kashi," remembers constantly being made to sit on the floor of his classroom as a kind of public shaming for always chatting with the person sitting next to him. He was so distracted and bored in school that he didn't even write notes from the lessons, which put him at a huge disadvantage when much of the education was based on the memorization of facts. To get around this problem, his mother would ask to borrow the notes from a classmate, copy them and sit Kashi down in front of her, making sure he read them through several times. The result was a dramatic improvement in his grades.

What's crucial to note here is that Mrs. Yadalam didn't feel the need to punish her son. While she knew he was slightly mischievous, she innately understood that his brain worked differently than most, and this served her son well throughout the rest of his education. In fact, it got him into medical school, which is so competitive in India that only 25 percent of the class graduates by the fourth year, and it takes many eight years to get their degree. Knowing he had to try harder than most, Dr. Yadalam would read most of the course material five or six times, methodically underlining the important parts in pencil upon the first read, then in red ballpoint, then highlighter pen, then margin notes. Depending on the color, he would know how many times he had already read something, and whether the information was likely to have sunk in.

His mother taught him well, because he passed each year. Again, unconventional study habits can suit the ADHD brain's different pathways to learning. It's a matter of patiently experimenting to find out what works.

Trial and Error

It's amazing how even some of the smallest tweaks and changes can impact a child. Fusion Academy, which started in 1989 as a one-on-one tutoring service out of its founder's garage in Solana Beach, California, and has since expanded to locations all over the country, was designed specifically for children who don't thrive in the traditional classroom setting. It works particularly well for ADHDers, who make up more than 30 percent of the student body. Some of the little things they do to adapt to these students' needs include:

- Permitting a student to multitask in class, listening to music through an earbud in one ear and the teacher's instructions at the same time.
- Letting a kid who is getting antsy take a break from the hour's lesson by going to the pull-up bar in the hallway.
- Providing yoga balls for fidgety students.
- Providing a PE room, if needed, before each lesson.
- Allowing teaching and assignment sessions to be broken up into ten- and fifteen-minute increments within the scheduled hour.

Although it's a day program, no one gets homework. The name Homework Café notwithstanding, all the assignments are done on site, with a teacher present and available to answer any questions in case a child gets stuck. The result is that homework gets done, and these children go on to get college degrees and jobs in fields they are passionate about.

"One of the things we love most about our school is that we take a student-centered approach, with no preconceived notion about what works," explains Francisco Ayala, head of the school in Manhattan, New York. "We are adjusting constantly to their needs."

As a result of this student-centered, easygoing and adaptable environment, Francisco reports that many of the kids on ADHD meds manage to come off the medications within this new context. Without the rigid structure of a traditional classroom setting, they tend to thrive, and are better able to focus on their own terms. The fact that many are able to do away with meds, or at least lower their dosages, is a testament to the fact that this style of learning works for ADHD kids.

Exercise to Learn

A common thread for all of the best ADHD schools is the emphasis on exercise. Dr. John Ratey, author of *Spark: The Revolutionary New Science of Exercise and the Brain*, and associate clinical professor of psychiatry at Harvard Medical School, cites one school in Colorado that begins the day with twenty minutes of aerobic exercise to increase alertness. If kids act up in class, they are given ten minutes of activity on a stationary bike or an elliptical trainer.

It's an idea that's being wholly embraced by Eagle Hill, where Dr. Ratey has collaborated in a $15 million athletic facility to house one of the nation's first Spark programs. All Eagle Hill students are required to either participate in a team sport or do some kind of intense exercise for an hour and fifteen minutes before their dinner and evening study hall. It could be any activity, and it can be a different thing every night, from swimming to martial arts. The point is to allow ADHD kids to recalibrate before being asked to focus on their studies again.

As Ratey explains, exercise, even relatively small amounts, helps raise dopamine levels, improving focus and lessening impulsivity and the need for other forms of stimulation. (I'll delve more into the many ways in which exercise can help all ADHDers, whether school-age or adult, in Chapter Eleven.) It can make all the difference in how children learn, and how much information they are able to absorb. "The result is that kids realize they can regulate their mood and attention through exercise," Dr. Ratey told *ADDitude* magazine. "On a practical level, it causes kids to be less impulsive, which makes them more primed to learn."

The physical activity also helps build an ADHD child's natural resilience, says Dr. Ratey. "The refrain of many ADHD kids is, 'No matter what I do, I'm going to fail,'" he says. "Rat studies show that exercise reduces learned helplessness. In fact, if you're aerobically fit, the less likely you are to learn helplessness."

Pump the Blood

As an ADHDer herself, educator Lisa Castaneda knew instinctively that physical activity could help the children in the school where she taught. Lisa, who is now CEO of Foundry10, an educational not-for-profit dedicated to exploring nontraditional methods of learning, always tried to give her students the flexibility to walk around when trying to solve math problems. Another child in her class found it helped to do a quick lap around the campus before starting each class.

"Even as an adult there are times I am not able to sit still and focus," says Lisa.

The most progressive schools recognize that children with ADHD thrive when there are periods throughout the day when they can burn off that excess energy. It calms them down and focuses their minds, so that distraction and boredom are less of an issue.

It's important to note that many schools across the United States have curtailed phys ed classes. As budgets get cut, these are the programs that are among the first to go. A May 2013 report by the Institute of Medicine finds that 44 percent of this country's school administrators have cut back on PE, recess and arts classes—all the interactive programs that help give the ADHDer a chance to press the reset button and focus.

This trend hurts ADHD kids the most. I can tell you from personal experience that exercise is the tool that enhances every aspect of the ADHDer's life, especially learning. I used to go for a hard bike ride when my attention faded while studying for medical school tests and Dr. Mike Watson hit the water for a vigorous session of canoeing. We passed with flying colors.

And these are good habits you can pick up from your school years that carry through to the rest of your life. Lisa, who works at a standing desk to help her stay focused, has learned that some brisk exercise, even if it's just a few minutes of running up the stairs of her office building, helps her to transition to her next task or meeting.

"Kids need something physical to move into the next mental space after they've been hyperfocusing or frenetically multitasking," says Lisa. "Exercise, even splashing water on your face, can help."

It sounds simple, and it should be. But ADHD children need an environment that's flexible enough to support their diverse and different needs. The most important thing to take away from this whole discussion on education for ADHD students is that they do not learn like the average kid. We have built a one-size-fits-all education system and these are the children who lose out. So why not experiment? Trial and error, exercise, short increments of coursework or homework, taking the trouble to find out what an individual child is passionate about—these are the small steps that could make a profound difference in ADHD children's lives. And we owe it to them to do just that.

"When I was teaching I always did my best to acknowledge the amazing creativity, enthusiasm and skills of my ADHD students," Lisa told me. "I truly think they were some of the brightest most innovative thinkers I had."

So why not do all we can to bring out the best in these kids? Yes, public education needs to invest in more teachers and resources for these kids in order to be more inclusive of different styles of learning.

They also need to consider changing policies that give individual teachers more control over what they can do in the classroom to adapt to their students' needs. But this is a drop in the bucket for a nation that spends billions on prescription ADHD medications that may not even be necessary if we make a few changes to the classroom setting and curriculum. These children are our future—the next generation of Neelemans, Bransons, Mozarts and Dickinsons. Aren't they worth the investment?

The key is not to write these kids off as destined to fail by the time they hit middle school. That is simply not the case. It's all about understanding what works and what doesn't. When children with ADHD can't do their homework, forget to do their chores or run around with restless energy, it's not that they're trying to be bad kids. It's just their adventurous spirit, which can be a strength when channeled in the right way. Sitting quietly in a room for long periods of time is simply not for ADHD children, but that doesn't mean they are any less capable of learning. In fact, given the right start in life, they have the potential to soar.

THE TOOL KIT

A few learning tips to help fast minds include:

- Teach in short increments, so there is no time to be bored or distracted.

- Split homework up into fifteen minutes per subject and then move to another subject, even if it's right in the middle of a problem or reading—keep repeating until done.

- Multitasking is okay if it works. Some students actually do better when they can study two or three different subjects at once. Some work best in short bursts of concentration, or a combination of both.

- Don't get stuck on traditional quiet study hall methods for your child or student. Some learn better in an environment with multiple stimuli. Allow them to study with music or TV on if it works for them. Again, be flexible and experiment!

- Incorporate multimedia, from PowerPoints to videos. All learning doesn't have to happen from a blackboard. Although there is no hard science to suggest ADHDers are more visual learners, anecdotally ADHD educators note that more stimulating visual components to learning can be particularly useful.

- Do something hands-on. Many ADHD kids learn better by doing.

- Encourage study after exercise.

- Go with whatever works, and adjust and tweak along the way. With ADHD, nothing is static. Sometimes it's helpful to change up strategies, just as you may need to change up everything else with ADHD.

- During study time, suggest that your child try standing up or moving when bored. Even walking around while studying is okay.

- Ask students directly what works for them.

PART II

Discovering Your Strengths

CHAPTER SIX

Resilience

David Neeleman knows all about hard knocks. Like many entre-preneurs, he failed multiple times before he went on to transform an entire industry.

The crushing disappointments began in school, as is often the case for ADHDers. David somehow scraped through, landing at the University of Utah before leaving just short of graduation to start up his first business—a tour company based in Salt Lake City. David had formed a partnership with a small airline that was taking his travel clients by charter to Hawaii, and had handed over most of his working capital to the airline partner to pay for the tickets. One day he got a phone call from someone at the airline, who told him they wouldn't be flying anymore because they'd gone out of business.

David was suddenly faced with the realization that he had dropped out of college and had nothing to show for it. He was in his early twenties and it seemed as if his career had ended before it had even started. But he wasn't done yet. Soon after, he was asked to partner with June Morris to found Morris Air, a lowcost charter airline company. He'd learned about capitalization from the first failure and to "never again let an external event affect me, to never let the action of one company, cause me to go out of business."

His second venture was so successful that it was sold nine years later to Southwest Airlines for $130 million. As the second largest shareholder, David got $25 million for the buyout, and went to work for Southwest. With all that money in his pocket and a brand-new adventure, thirty-two-year-old David was on top of the world. But within five months he was terminated.

"I didn't fit; we were driving each other crazy," he says. "I had all this money and I was miserable because I had sold my little baby and thought things were going to be different."

It was another devastating blow, because David had signed a five-year noncompete with Southwest, and he had four and a half more years to go before he could start another airline in the United States. Young, ambitious and impatient, "You might as well have told me I'd be out of business for a hundred years."

Disheartened as he was, David used the time not only to dream up his vision for his next airline, JetBlue, but also to become the CEO of Open Skies, an innovative touch-screen airline reservation and check-in systems company, and helped to found the Canadian airline WestJet. So, instead of just sitting still and allowing boredom and misery to take over, he launched two more successful start-ups, finding new ways to leverage technology in the airline business (which wasn't being done at the time) and improve the customer experience.

He founded JetBlue in early 1999 under the original name "NewAir." His mission was to redefine the air travel experience for consumers, providing comfortable seats, better amenities and reasonable prices to budget-conscious travelers, and he took the airline industry by storm.

Time and again throughout his career, David would have to start over. In 2007 he was replaced as CEO of JetBlue, and a year later started Azul in Brazil, which, with more than $5 billion in sales and 107 destinations, stands as the third-largest airline in that country— even bigger than JetBlue!

"Sometimes things happen in your career and in your life that you think at the time is devastating," he says, "and you wonder how you can recover, and you wonder how you are ever going to be able to turn it around. And a lot of times it is not what happens to you in life, it is how you react to it. I really believe that."

The Comeback Kids

All that David has accomplished in his life and career is a result of a little-known strength that I have seen repeatedly among the many ADHDers who have come through my practice or whom I have met: resilience.

David, like me, is convinced that his own reaction to disappointment, which is to pick himself up, dust himself off, learn from the experience and try again, stems from his ADHD.

Anecdotally and instinctively, I've always known that those with ADHD possess an innate resilience. When you think about it, these are folks who have to deal with crises hour to hour, day to day, as they struggle to conform to expectations in a non-ADHD world. We get so much practice with failure. We are always having to deal with the consequences of our own forgetfulness, procrastination or our inability to finish things. Things those who don't have ADHD take for granted, like remembering to gas up the car, making it to an important meeting on time or focusing on what the boss is saying. Instead, we get so distracted by that thing on his face that we don't hear the words and can only watch helplessly as his lips move . . . you get the picture. On a regular day, there are a lot of ups and downs, some more serious and earth-shattering than others. Just to be able to survive, we often need to muster all the resilience we can.

So it was quite the eureka moment when I first learned about a small but highly significant study of resilience in college students with ADHD versus those without. The study, which took place at Elon University in North Carolina, looked at seventeen undergraduate students with ADHD (not on medication), versus nineteen students without ADHD, the control group. Of the thirty students, ages eighteen through twenty, those with the ADHD diagnosis were found to be overwhelmingly more adaptive and resilient in the face of significant odds, contrary to past assumptions—findings that surely merit further research.

When you think about it, the results of that study make perfect sense. Everything is new in college. A lot of students are away from home and their support networks for the first time. They are meeting new people, in a new place that may be thousands of miles away from the place where they grew up, and are experiencing the unfamiliar, pulled completely out of their comfort zone. Nothing is routine, which can be tough on the average young adult. But, by the time they get to college, kids with ADHD have already lived through many variations on these challenges. Theirs has already been a lifetime of adapting, finding their own path and dealing with change. As ADHDers, these students also embrace the change and newness of college.

This is a small study sample, and there are many variables, depending on how much family support each individual student had, their demographics, whether they are male or female, and their overall self-esteem and academic success. But there can be no doubt that resilience is indeed one of the most life-enhancing traits of ADHD. No matter how many obstacles, disappointments and catastrophes life has thrown our way, we possess an enduring optimism and ability to bounce back.

Of course, failure to learn from mistakes and instead repeating them is a potential downside of rebounding too quickly. When something goes wrong, it's important to press the pause button, however briefly, to analyze what caused the failure. You will grow and progress when you remind yourself to take a moment to reflect. But your particular strength is that you never let setbacks hold you back for long. Something is continually driving you forward. This, combined with adaptability, a sense of purpose, self-awareness and resourcefulness, is among the key ingredients in the secret sauce of resilience that so many of ADHD's most prominent success stories possess.

Cultivating Grit

Resilience is an innate sense of hope and optimism about the future, so it stands to reason that many with ADHD have the ability to dust themselves off after a setback and start thinking about what comes next. In my clinical experience, while many patients have issues with self-esteem and depression, that depression is often circumstantial and usually temporary. This ability to rebound is due to the combination of faith, hope, love and gratitude that is also essential in resilience. People who have this strength tend to maintain a positive outlook on life and rise to the occasion during times of crisis, always asking, "What can I do to help myself?" These are the internal factors that determine who is a victim and who is a survivor—an ADHD trait that may well be our greatest gift.

It's not clear which comes first. Are ADHDers born with innate resilience, or is it something that develops under the often stressful conditions of trying to conform in a structured environment like school? Resilience is one of those traits in the mental health field that we would like to see more of in our patients, but it has so many elements and variables it's hard to fully understand and define. One thing we do know is that the more that resilience muscle gets tested, the stronger it gets.

So how do we tap into this resilience? It doesn't just flick on and off like a light switch, and it can fail us if we don't cultivate and build upon this strength. Although severe depression among ADHDers is not the norm, certain conditions can put us on the wrong track. It's already well known that the sense of stigma and low self-esteem that ADHDers suffer from when they don't have supportive teachers or family members in their developing years can lead to problems such as addiction, alcoholism, unstable relationships, even incarceration. And yet I've also seen remarkable endurance, tenacity and optimism—also ingredients of resilience—in the face of relentless hardships.

It's already there in your tool kit. But, just like everyone else, we need encouragement to learn how to use it. A stable and loving family, or a great teacher or mentor, can be crucial in helping ADHDers cultivate that natural grit and take it further. David was fortunate to have a strong faith and tight-knit family—a foundation that gave him enough confidence to tap into the inner reserves of resilience he already possessed. But all it takes is one person in a position of authority to remind us that we are already capable. Even as adults we can benefit from a friend or a family member to highlight our strengths.

The Turnaround Agent

Resilience is the light at the end of a tunnel of pain and self-doubt that can plague ADHDers well into adulthood. But encouraging children by helping them recognize their own strengths and talents will help them develop resilience much earlier in life.

It's worth noting here that, as adults with ADHD, many of us have been forced to find our own way. There were no voices of reason or blueprints for how to harness strengths like resilience. Those of us who've had success have had to do some soul-searching, and we figured it out the hard way. But that's no reason for the next generation to suffer, and fortunately resilience is a burgeoning area of study in the mental health field.

In their book *Raising Resilient Children: Fostering Strength, Hope, and Optimism in Your Child*, Robert Brooks and Sam Goldstein discuss specific steps parents can take to bring out the innate resilience in their ADHD children. Brooks, the staff psychologist at Harvard Medical School, also urges parents and caregivers to give ADHD children more credit for their successes, since many ADHD kids exaggerate their flaws:

"By focusing on your child's strengths—or what I call 'islands of competence'—you're not letting ADHD define your child," he says. He goes on to explain that helping children cultivate an awareness of weaknesses as well as strengths will help give them the perspective they need to help build on their innate resilience. "The key is working on our weaknesses while exercising the things we're good at," he says.

Dr. Paul Yellin, director of the Yellin Center for Mind, Brain, and Education, and an associate professor of pediatrics at the New York University School of Medicine, also suggests encouraging interests and passions, which can bring comfort during times of struggle at school. He also recommends finding mentors or "turnaround people," including teachers, to help ADHD children recognize their own strengths, including resilience, and to help them put the challenges they face into a larger, more positive context.

Aaron Smith, thirty-one, greatly benefited from having mentors as a teenager. Diagnosed at seven with ADHD, he was labeled "learning-disabled," and could have easily become a statistic. When he was attending public school in Aurora, Colorado, he always felt "less than" or "not smart enough." His distractibility and struggles with reading kept him behind his peers. He avoided doing homework, procrastinating on anything he felt was too hard to successfully complete, attracting all kinds of negative attention from the adults in his life

His grades suffered and he was defiant, talking back and questioning teachers as well as his parents, constantly challenging the status quo. He also was bullied at school, and regularly got into fights with other students. In sixth grade he was almost expelled for multiple behavioral incidents and more than twelve referrals to the dean in six months.

As a teen, Aaron's "delinquency and risk-taking behavior" went to another level. He stole from stores and other students, as well as from his old elementary school. At fifteen, Aaron got arrested for trespassing on school property and could have received a felony charge if he'd already had his sixteenth birthday, which was only six months away. But the punishment was bad enough: a year's probation and thousands of dollars in fines.

The stress at home was exacerbating his impulsivity, which was his ADHD version of a cry for help. At five, he was drawn into a long and involved custody battle after his parents had divorced. To make matters worse, his stepfather was physically and emotionally abusive. He didn't fully comprehend the scope of his actions or consider them stealing.

"I didn't realize there could be real consequences for my behavior. I naively thought that it was just part of an adrenaline rush."

There was a lot to endure at home, as well as at school. Because he had always been pegged as someone who was going to fail, he didn't see the point in trying harder. There was no worse feeling than sitting through those school tests, answering questions in a fog and being the last to put down his pen and walk out of the exam room. In fact, the experience was crushing to his self-esteem.

"As I look back at the trajectory of my experience, it definitely wasn't easy," says Aaron. "I could have ended up in prison, or an alcoholic or addicted to drugs. I could have become a statistic."

But a teacher saw something in him. In sixth grade a dean recognized that, despite his grades and the behavioral concerns, he was naturally bright. Instead of scolding Aaron and pointing out to him where he was going wrong, she told him she knew he was capable of much more. Another educator, an English teacher in high school, reached through by telling him he had a gifted mind. A high school psychologist also took an interest, noticing Aaron's insights and compassion for others. At critical junctures in Aaron's life, these three adults showed they cared and asked him how he was doing instead of judging and constantly telling him what he was doing wrong and what he should do. Once those authority figures recognized the positives in Aaron, an internal shift happened, and he was able to see it himself as a light came on in his mind. At first it was just a dim glimmer, but by reaching down inside he was able to leverage his resilience, and started applying himself. He graduated from high school and made it into the University of Colorado.

College was still a struggle. By his second semester, Aaron got distracted by all the campus activism, social scene and "all the other stuff," causing his grade-point average to slip to a 1.5. He almost dropped out. But then he remembered what those teachers had seen. He pulled back up and started slogging through challenge after challenge to complete his BA. For his second degree, a bachelor of science, he excelled, pulling his average up high enough to qualify for entry to Columbia University, where he completed a master's in social work.

Even with the breakthrough realization that he was capable, getting through his courses was still more difficult for Aaron than for most. He had to work twice as hard, reading assignments took two to three times as long and he was still always the last person to turn in a test. Two undergraduate degrees were a lot of time and work to qualify for graduate school, but the more he persisted, the more successful he became. He also realized that if he could overcome all the obstacles in his life to that point, he could overcome anything.

"It was always hard; it was always there. I just got better at managing it," he says.

Today, Aaron is a successful motivational coach specializing in ADHD, with his own practice, Potential Within Reach. He spends much of his professional life trying to be that "turnaround person" for others as he helps his young ADHD clients cultivate their own resilience.

The Gift of Setbacks

As difficult as his experiences were growing up, Aaron wouldn't change a thing. Like many successful ADHDers I spoke with, he is grateful for the challenges that ADHD has thrown in his path—experiences that made him who he is today.

"Resilience is really persistence, a kind of stubbornness and strong will, and I think the kids who have the biggest trouble growing up have that," he notes.

They grow accustomed to failure, and constantly having to course-correct and adapt to situations not native to their natural style of learning. They fail, and try again, and again, hoping to learn from their mistakes, adjusting and doing a little better the next time around.

"Knowing how to fail is half the battle of succeeding," says Aaron. David Neeleman concurs.

"We don't usually ace the standardized tests and do law at Harvard; we get chucked out of the boat and forced to swim. We have to get creative and find our own way," he told me.

Each challenge has spurred David on to the next big thing. It also makes him less afraid to fail, and more willing to take calculated risks when everyone is telling him no. So each setback has led to something great, whether it's televisions at airplane seats, lower airfares or at-home online reservation systems.

"You don't stop having ideas just because you have a failure," he says. "Obviously, once I had successes, I had more confidence and was more willing to persevere. But this is the way I have always done it."

Early on, Aaron and David understood the gift of their diagnosis—something that leading experts on human development are only just beginning to discover. In his recent book *David and Goliath: Underdogs, Misfits, and the Art of Battling Giants*, Malcolm Gladwell refers to learning disabilities, including ADHD and dyslexia, as a "strategic disadvantage," and maintains that these traits can be instrumental to future success because, exactly as in the case of David, Aaron and the many other ADHDers we have been describing in this book, we have to learn strategies to get past obstacles and overcome setbacks from childhood, or what he calls "compensation learning." He cites entrepreneurs who can successfully navigate the many hurdles that get thrown up in the day-to-day running of their business, and excel at problem-solving because, at this point in their lives, it has become second nature.

Speaking at the 2014 World Business Forum, the best-selling author gave the example of dyslexic business owners who learn business skills just to survive their school years: passing off reading assignments to a friend, fast-talking their way out of handing a paper in late and gathering friends who are willing to help out in areas of weakness.

"So you take this group of people, this small group of successful compensators, and they emerge out of high school or college if they get that far, and they want to start a business, and they have been practicing the four skills that are absolutely essential for entrepreneurship," he explains. "Delegation, leadership, oral communication, problem-solving. They've taken a graduate-level course in the four most important traits by virtue of the fact that life dealt them one of its most grievous disadvantages."

On the Rebound

Even if we don't have the benefit of a turnaround person in our lives, we have other gifts that we can use to fuel our resilience. Part of the reason many ADHDers come through events that could stop others in their tracks may be the ability to hyperfocus. A crisis gives us the stimulation our brains crave, it gets the dopamine pumping, and that's when we can be at our best. We get so involved in solving problems and putting out fires that we forget about everything else. We don't have time to be victims!

California real estate developer and entrepreneur Joseph is a case in point. In the early 2000s, his business was booming. He had all kinds of venture capital and commercial deals flowing, and was bouncing from one location to another, closing on the next subdivision or building, funding new high-tech ventures, hiring contractors, buying, developing and selling almost anything. As someone who ranks about a 9 on the continuum, his career was the perfect way to leverage his ADHD strengths. But he was so busy that he overextended himself, and when the financial crisis hit, he found he was juggling it all to keep from crashing. As the dust of the 2007–2008 financial crisis began to settle, he realized the worst was over and that he had made it through—or so he thought.

Joseph had been working with a group of investors in the small community where he lived to help them develop a commercial business park. But zoning regulations were holding up the work, so he turned his attention to another project until all the red tape could be sorted out. The investors, antsy to get a return on their money, accused him of putting their money into something else, and some influential members of the group used their connections to call in a favor. The next thing Joseph knew, he was being arrested and handcuffed outside his office for everyone to see by a sheriff from three counties away.

He was released on bond that day, and the trumped-up charges were dropped in less than a week. At worst, it should have been a civil case that never would have led to him being treated like a criminal, and in such a public way. But the damage was done. Everyone heard about what had happened, and no matter what the facts of the case were, there's always going to be that lingering doubt. In the venture capital world of Southern California, his reputation was ruined.

As a result, none of his contractors or subcontractors would work for him on credit anymore, fearing they would not get paid. Joseph, who can't reveal his real name due to pending litigation, had plenty of contracts on the move, and it was as if everyone, from the plumbing contractors to the roofers, were on strike. So he lost the deals and went into bankruptcy. He's spent the last few years digging himself out of this debt hole, and has just about succeeded in becoming solvent again, taking back control of as many properties as he can.

Joseph was railroaded, publicly humiliated and thrown in jail. But here's the thing. Every time I spoke with Joseph, he was remarkably upbeat. If anything, he seems happy and thriving. So I had to ask what it is that drives him to come back from such a loss.

"I don't even think about coming back," Joseph told me. "I am just able to hyperfocus on one project at a time and that is what saves me."

Joseph doesn't dwell on what happened or how it affects him. He's so obsessed with his next project that it's "my medication; my therapy."

"As long as I can focus on the next deal, I'm happy, and that's that," he told me.

This is true for so many ADHDers. Their need for stimulation compels them to move forward, because dwelling on the failures and disappointments of the past is just too boring! It's not that Joseph didn't learn from his mistakes. He'll be a lot more careful about who he does business with next time, and he won't allow himself to be as financially leveraged or exposed. But he's not letting fear of failure get in the way of his future.

Laugh It Off

Joseph's sense of humor helps him to rebound. The ability to face the truth and not take it too seriously, with clear-eyed, self-deprecating wit, is another ingredient in the resilience recipe, and one that I have noticed in many ADHDers. Put simply, we can laugh at ourselves—a powerful adaptive tool that fosters resilience and helps manage what can often be painful setbacks.

Howie Mandel's ability to rebound after many humiliations and flops, ever hopeful and plotting the next great gag, is a case in point. The setbacks that would make most people pack their bags were fuel for Howie. Success is never a straight line to the top, and this actor, producer, comic and game show host has bombed onstage many times. He thinks nothing of crossing the line if there's the possibility of getting a laugh, or venturing off into the land of the absurd where no one else can speak or understand his language.

"When something bombs, it just bombs. We are all human. But I've gotta try it," he told me.

A last-minute request to appear on *The Tonight Show with Johnny Carson* ended in disaster when Howie decided to borrow a giant plaster saber-toothed tiger from the set of a movie he was acting in. He strapped a giant carrot to the back of it, and then shipped it to the Carson studio in Burbank. He dragged the thing onstage, and when Johnny asked him about it, Howie's response was, "I don't want to talk about it." There were a few more awkward exchanges about his daughter's potty-training, but the audience was eerily quiet and Johnny did not look amused. The YouTube clip of that moment is almost painful to watch. A favorite after twenty-one appearances, Howie was never invited back while Johnny was doing the show. Apparently his absurdist theater made the late-night host feel uncomfortable.

For any young comic, being shunned by Carson would have been soul-destroying. This was an example of Howie's impulsivity going horribly wrong. It was like being banished to stand-up Siberia, and most comics would curl up in despair, or change their approach and lose their edge. It was a brutal experience, and for a moment he felt the sting of such a public flop. Yet even the most devastating career setback couldn't keep Howie down.

"Winston Churchill said, 'Success is the ability to go from one failure to another with the same vim and vigor as the last one.' That's me," Howie said.

Interestingly, Howie always expects to succeed, and each time he falls flat on his face he is surprised.

"My wife says, 'What, are you an idiot?' But if I thought about it too much I wouldn't do it, and that would be far worse."

Again, it's not that Howie doesn't learn from his past. Throughout his career, he has continued to take risks in his comedy, but is always tweaking and refining to become more seasoned as an entertainer. There is a difference between learning from your mistakes and being paralyzed with the fear of failing yet again, and the comedian lives that every day. Although he feels his share of self-doubt and disillusionment, Howie is incapable of staying in that place for long. Like Joseph, David and the thousands of other ADHDers I've talked with, his trait won't allow him to, because that need for stimulation drives him onward as he looks for the next great gag.

Paying It Forward

There's another tool Howie, Aaron and David share that inspires them to persevere: compassion. The desire to help others is a common theme for the many ADHDers interviewed for this book. So many who have struggled have made it a goal to inspire others who face similar obstacles. These acts of compassion have the dual benefit of improving the lives of those who are less fortunate, and enhancing their own self-esteem, which in turn builds resilience. Nothing is more gratifying than giving back and having a positive impact on those in need. It creates a sense of purpose that can help you endure a multitude of setbacks.

While Aaron practices compassion directly as a life coach, Howie and David use their platforms as a celebrity and high-profile business leader to raise awareness about the many positives of ADHD. Living through their challenges has given them a deeper understanding of what it is like for others with the trait—a sense of empathy. Knowing they have the power to better their own lives sparks the desire to work toward easing the path for the next generation.

"Since ADHD'ers know what it feels like to be marginalized, they are deeply compassionate people," writes ADHD coach Carol Gignoux on her blog *Live ADHD Free*. "They know what it's like to be rejected and ignored, and so often they are ready to stop that sort of injustice from happening to anyone else."

This may explain the extraordinary numbers of high-profile people with ADHD who are starting to embrace the trait and talk about it publicly.

A recent example is Channing Tatum, whose success today belies some deep frustrations and crushing setbacks in his earlier years. The actor, who was diagnosed with a combination of ADHD and dyslexia, suffered severe depression and anxiety as he struggled through school, and he shared this experience on a recent episode of the show *Running Wild with Bear Grylls*.

"It gets really, really discouraging when you are the last person up from the test every single time," he told his host on a precipitous cliff ledge in the middle of Yosemite, in between bites of barbecued rattlesnake.

But watching Channing rappel up and down sheer rock faces, negotiating obstacles in the wilderness while showing nothing but grace and good humor, joking and laughing in the face of discomfort and danger, it struck me that he was the epitome of the ADHD spirit. Not once did he complain. In fact, he seemed to be relishing the challenges Bear threw at him. The more terrifying, the better.

Channing's battle with focus and dyslexia still make it harder for him than most. He admitted it takes him three times as long as others to read through scripts and remember his lines. But his innate resilience explains how he's making it through the rejections, criticisms and scrutiny of an even more hostile wilderness: Hollywood.

So as hard as it was to grow up with ADHD, he wouldn't change a thing.

"Looking back, I am grateful for it," he says. "It gave me the fight."

THE TOOL KIT:
HOW TO RECOGNIZE YOUR OWN RESILIENCE

By living with ADHD, you have developed a strength you never knew you had, and here's why:

- Your whole life you've dealt with a mind that has to wander, yet somehow you've still managed to survive your education and learn. Example: you have a test and scant notes to study from, so you collate that material with notes from a friend and pass the test. It is par for the course, but imagine if things are off-kilter for a more linear thinker, and due to an illness they miss two weeks of classes. For them, it's a crisis of epic proportions.

- You've gone above and beyond the average person to be successful. Most people have no clue how hard you have worked to get there, because this is your reality—something you have accepted and deal with on a daily basis.

- You are constantly fighting against procrastination, beating yourself up for it. And yet your down-to-the-wire homework assignments have taught you how to pull an all-nighter on a project and still get to work on time.

- This allows you to function at a high level in times of crisis, multitasking, putting out fires and hyperfocusing on whatever needs to be done to save the day.

- You've had to live with and fix the consequences of impulsivity, rebounding back from failure again and again.

- This does not mean you should not pause to consider what caused the failures and learn from past mistakes. That's the potential downside of rebounding quickly. But you will grow and progress when you remind yourself to take a moment to reflect.

- Despite the low self-esteem that often results from these challenges, your self-deprecating sense of humor and faith in the universe keeps you moving forward.

- Remind yourself of these facts daily. Be your own turnaround agent, and surround yourself with people who celebrate your successes and strengths.

- Practice compassion, toward yourself and others. It will enhance your self-esteem, which will, in turn, build resilience.

CHAPTER SEVEN

Bingo Brain

Have you ever noticed how the balls in a bingo machine jumble around together before coming up with a number sequence? The balls ricochet off one another and the sides of the cage, popping up out of nowhere and making seemingly random connections in rapid fire.

That, according to Perry Sanders, is how his brain works. The ADHDer, whom you first met in Chapter One, is a highly successful plaintiff attorney who represented Michael Jackson's mother in the estate litigation. Perry attributes many of his case wins to his nonlinear thinking, which enables him to come up with ideas that may at first seem completely crazy to anyone but him, but in retrospect are elegant and creative solutions. When those balls, or thoughts, hit off one another, they spark different ideas. It doesn't occur to him that he has to go from A to B. In fact, it's more productive to skip around and shake things up a bit. It gives him the capacity to come at a seemingly unsolvable problem from a completely fresh angle.

In a recent issue of *Psychology Today*, one of my colleagues described the ADHD brain as the "quintessential supercomputer" because it has enough bandwidth to run hundreds of programs all at once, processing colossal amounts of data at the speed of light, and it never switches off. That's about right.

We are at an embryonic stage when it comes to brain mapping

and research on the neuroscience of ADHD, but in my clinical practice it is clear there is something nonlinear in how the ADHD brain functions—a kind of lateral thinking that opens things up to big ideas, albeit in jumbled succession. It's an uncanny ability to be in the moment, think on your feet and put ideas together in startling new ways. While creativity is not necessarily an inherent strength of ADHD, this nonlinear thinking can open the door to brand-new concepts as well as fresh and surprising ways of seeing the world, thus lending itself to creativity, which may well be why so many artists, from Leonardo da Vinci to Vincent van Gogh, are believed to have had ADHD.

A Different Lens

Perry, whose other accomplishments include songwriting, investing in restaurants and a hotel, property design and development, mass tort litigation and practicing environmental law, is convinced that his unconventional way of thinking is his greatest strength. He told me linear thinkers may never understand the exhilaration of topic-hopping in one's own head—at least not at the pace of an ADHDer. As far as he is concerned, those bingo balls aren't a random mess of ideas. Inside his head, they're in perfect working order, even if they come across as nonsequiturs when he verbalizes his thoughts. But he's not being flighty. In fact, he's keeping a running inventory of ideas, and when he gets distracted, he has no problem going away for a while and then coming right back to the issue, knowing exactly where he left off.

"It's like I have panoramic vision, while others have a more narrow focus," he says. "The more things I have going on, the more they are interconnected. Even when they seem like stand-alones, they are all part of a master plan that is going on in my head."

Whereas most people want to finish one project and move on to the next, that sequential thinking puts blinders on, Perry says. Linear thinkers tend to get so caught up in accomplishing one thing on its own that they lose their peripheral vision and miss out on ideas that can come from tangential activities.

"People assume it's a tangent, but in reality it's the tangent that's the answer," Perry says.

This played out in the year 2000, when Perry was asked to serve as lead counsel on a potential class action suit on behalf of a large group of homeowners who had pollution underneath their homes. The law in Colorado was such that you could get a class certified with enough commonality. The courts had held that individuals in a similar class action suit did not know what they had in common, so it could not be certified. The main lawyer who'd asked Perry to help him represent the case was stumped. It seemed like there was no way of getting around it.

But then Perry's bingo brain sprang into action. He came to the conclusion that what the potential class action suit folks actually did have in common was the fact that they "did not know what they had in common."

"When I called him to share what I'd come up with, he had to pull off to the side of the road so I could explain it to him—three times," Perry recalls.

The case was certified at the district court level over hard-fought objections by the defendants, and ultimately was upheld at the Tenth Circuit Court of appeals. By bringing in the testing necessary to determine with certainty exactly what level of pollution crept into each home, Perry and his team won the entire class action suit and were able to get all homes tested so that the home owners would always know if their properties had environmental issues. It set a legal precedent, something that's happened many times over in his extraordinary career.

Too Much at Once

Of course, as with many of ADHD's strengths, there's always a flip side. That jumbled thought process can be overwhelming and confusing to others, and with so many thoughts going on all at once, ADHDers can get so distracted with their ideas that there's either no follow-through, or those flashes of brilliance get quickly forgotten. And those more linear thinkers who are witness to this seemingly jumbled thought process might be forgiven for thinking we've lost our minds! In a professional or workplace context, this can be a liability. Others can't necessarily see that we are going somewhere in our thought process, however circuitous the route, or routes, we are taking.

Brian Scudamore, CEO and founder of 1-800-GOT-JUNK?, realized his bingo brain was becoming a problem in meetings with his staff. He couldn't switch off his brain, was constantly coming up with new ideas, and in the moment each idea seemed more brilliant to him than the next. A decade ago, his mercurial approach had been so frustrating to his best people that some of them were on the brink of leaving his organization

"It got to the point where my team would say, 'Watch out—here comes Scudamore,'" he recalls. "'Let's see what his flavor of the month is!'"

Brian's description of how his thought process works is remarkably similar to that of numerous other ADHDers I have treated or spoken with.

"I have all these ideas and things going on all at once, almost like a constant flowing of thoughts. They are going, going and going, in random order, although they start to make sense over time," Brian told me. "I don't think too much about them or try to solve anything, I just let them flow."

Except when he is in meetings, or trying to attend to some pressing issue at his business. Timing is everything. While Brian's bingo brain was the gift that gave him the idea for his many innovative businesses, his challenge has been knowing when to put the blinders on, because he would get so carried away he would forget to attend to the more important problems at hand.

It was reaching the point where he needed a self-intervention. He felt the need to control his steady stream of consciousness, or at least leverage his bingo brain for the greater good of his company, so he created a system to set up company priorities each quarter and then publicly committed to them.

"This meant that *no* new ideas would be pursued," recalls Brian. "It required great discipline for me to contain my ideas and let them marinate."

He dumped all of his new ideas into a folder in Outlook. Ever since, he has noted each new idea in an email message, which he sends to himself with the words "new idea" in the subject line. The message then goes straight into his ideas folder for later review, which turns out to be a great filtering system.

"What I've found is that at least a third of my 'great ideas' don't look so great at second glance. Now there are thirty-three percent fewer distractions for me and my team," he says.

Brian also makes a point of reviewing his ideas once or twice each quarter, allowing him to pick and choose the best ideas to present to his team during their quarterly strategy meetings. And, of course, other ideas are welcome. Everyone else on the team writes ideas on Post-it notes, which go on a wall under various headings, and are edited down during the course of the discussion. This ensures that Brian hears everyone and it's not just his own bingo balls that are dominating the discussion. In the work setting, he's also learned skills to help him focus. If someone is presenting important information to him, he makes a point of writing down what they are saying, to keep his mind focused on the conversation.

Not that Brian is overly rigid about controlling the roiling waters of his thought process. Besides, sometimes there is a crackerjack of an idea that cannot wait ninety days.

"Yes, sometimes you have to go with the flow. The primary objective of my systems is to create a pause in which one can weigh the benefits, costs and timing of any idea," Brian explains. But he's pressing the pause button, not delete.

Brian also builds in enough time and space for himself to let those bingo balls bounce freely, allowing new ideas, thoughts and creative opportunities to enter his brain freely. He doesn't beat himself up for being distracted by all these ideas. He has long since recognized that there is no point in trying to fight the ricocheting thoughts in his head that, over time, can add up to a complete and detailed picture of his next big project.

In fact, within the right context (that is, not a meeting), he welcomes the flood of ideas, which he also likens to popcorn kernels popping in the popcorn maker. It's how he's managed to come up with ten different brands and companies over the years, "and many more popcorn kernels in the air." In fact, many of his business concepts lend themselves to multiple branding opportunities, franchises and spinoffs—a direct result of the bingo brain!

Brain Dump

Many ADHDers lament the fact that they can't focus. The easy distractibility of their bingo brains is one of the biggest complaints I hear from ADHDers everywhere. They can be so overwhelmed by the onslaught of ideas it's paralyzing. Interior design entrepreneur Anita Erickson calls it her "tornado of ideas," which was stopping her from being as productive as she would have liked at her previous job at Dell, where she managed the computer giant's email program. Anita was responsible for testing all the links and formatting to make sure they worked. But between the time she clicked on the link and when the landing page came up—a matter of seconds—she had so many thoughts running through her head she would forget what page she was supposed to be looking at.

"It took me forever to proof these emails, my brain would wander off that fast," she recalls.

Today, at her home office, Anita has become a consummate list maker. She writes her ideas down on Post-it notes, scraps of paper, anywhere, and by the end of the day her house is littered with this storm of thoughts, but through the act of physically writing—not typing—it down, she is able to empty out some of what's in her head so that she can focus on that day's priorities. "I make so many lists, and some of the ideas are so random that people would laugh at them," she says.

Ninety percent of what she writes down many not be important, but getting it on paper lessens the wind speed and flying objects in her mental tornado. And when she reviews what's on the list, she often finds a few gems.

Anita's most important list is written out on Monday mornings, "to help me feel more structured." She also uses a file folder system, keeping all of them closed except the one she is currently working on. It doesn't stay that way, but it's another one of her tricks for controlling the bingo brain, "because with too many folders open in your brain you feel overwhelmed."

Juicy Goals

Another way to leverage your bingo brain is to set goals. An enticing plan—something that you would love to see made into a reality—can help ensure that those bingo balls will evolve from sparks of ideas into actions and accomplishments. By deliberately putting the ideas that relate to these goals into action, you can also avoid getting stuck in the quicksand of too many disparate thoughts that go nowhere.

"When you are not implementing, the brain goes wild with a million new ideas," explains Shanna Pearson, the Toronto-based ADHD coach whom you met in Chapter Two. She recommends making your life and career goals "juicy" to keep you motivated.

One of the potential hazards of the bingo brain, says Shanna, is that it can create a false sense of achievement. When the brain is in overdrive, things aren't getting done, although all that mental activity makes it feel as if we are moving forward. But, once in implementation mode, the bingo brain slows down enough to focus on a few of those brilliant ideas and bring them to fruition.

There's a time and place for these thought streams, she says. During down time, even on a lunch break, it's productive to let your nonlinear mind roam free, "but if you had a hundred ideas last month and did not take action on any of them, then it's time to put some thought into what makes the list and why."

In other words, letting your mind roam can be productive and less draining as long as you give yourself a time limit. Designate moments when your bingo brain can pop all over the place, then be conscious about when it's appropriate to rein in all those meandering thoughts.

Jumping Ahead

Another concern is social. It's not unusual for our nonlinear thinking to take us several steps at once, seeing the whole picture before more linear thinkers can catch up. Frankly, when we try to communicate these thoughts, ideas or visions to colleagues or friends, we can sound a little crazy—like mad scientists. We can also come across as a little rude as we overtalk our peers when we get caught up in the excitement of each new idea.

"You end up finishing people's sentences," says Emily Anhalt, an ADHDer who, at the time of this writing, was completing her doctoral dissertation titled "ADHD and Success Without the Use of Medication" at the Wright Institute in Berkeley.

Emily also sees the nonlinear thinking of ADHD as a strength, but one that needs to be used wisely. "Socially, if you don't put filters on, especially when you have above-average intelligence, you can unintentionally cause offense," she says. "Not everyone appreciates that type of energy and some can get overwhelmed. You need to be patient, communicate clearly and find like-minded people."

As head of the German Pirate Party, a popular left-of-center political movement comprised of "techies and activists," Berliner Christopher Lauer lives almost permanently on "the other side" and struggles at times with the perception among his peers that his decisions aren't rational.

"I know that from the outside I am looking a little bit mad," he says. "My decisions seem like bold moves at an institutional level, but for me they make perfect sense."

Christopher, a trained physicist and amateur actor who spent a year studying the political climate in China, is described in Germany's media as the party's "intellectual force," and his ability to rattle off complex, obscure facts and numbers leaves many of his listeners breathless. A typical Christopher statement goes like this:

> Internet smashes all paradigms and the political status quo across the spectrum—right-center-left-green—is still mainly providing timed-out concepts, outdated solutions and irrelevant answers which no longer fit today's world and certainly not the aspirations of the digital generation.

There's a lot going on in that sentence, although that isn't but a fraction of what is happening in the narrative inside Christopher's head. He computes information quickly, perceiving things and where they fit into the whole picture, and recognizes that his ADHD brain is the gift that enables him to do so. But he struggles with explaining himself and often comes across as abrupt or impatient as he tries to bring what he calls more "neurotypical" people up to speed. The result is that taking other people with him is one of his biggest challenges, and an essential skill even in the world of radical German politics.

"I know I have all these advantages, but it frustrates everyone else," he says.

Finding Balance

To be sure, our bingo brains can be distracting. They can also cause us to be misunderstood, unless we are communicating with fellow ADHDers who have no problem following the intricate paths and byways where our thoughts lead us. But suppressing this gift in order to be more normal, as many try to do through medication, or by relentlessly trying to force our minds back on that metaphorical landing page, is a mistake. We *can* have it both ways by being more conscious, and by using a few simple organizational and filtering tools we can leverage our bingo brains in ways that can break new ground in countless ways. It's just a question of being more conscious of how we use our gifts.

Mark Neeleman, who was first introduced in Chapter Two, dedicates three days out of his working week to indulge his free-roaming mind. Monday and Tuesday are for routine "got-to-do-it stuff." Then on Wednesday he comes off his ADHD medications, allowing himself to dart from one project location to another. He also sets aside plenty of time to sit in his garden in São Paulo, Brazil, and Google ideas on his computer, getting lost inside his bingo brain for hours.

It was during one of those extended free-association sessions that Mark came upon an idea for his newest business—a sustainable construction-grade bamboo plywood. This is one of six businesses he's created or cofounded, in addition to working alongside his brother David at Azul Airlines. It took Mark thirty hours to come up with the idea, from concept, to the remote jungles of Brazil where he had to source the bamboo, to the patents he would need, to the logistics on manufacturing, to the marketing for the product—all in a day's work for an ADHDer. He then enlisted the support of his team—a technique he learned from his brother—to bring his idea to fruition.

Inspired by the deforestation taking place not just in Brazil but all over the world, he wanted to come up with a solution, and started linking ideas in that classic bingo-ball fashion. Azul Airlines has a carbon-free policy that uses its carbon emission tax to plant bamboo forests, which burn carbon dioxide. From offsetting carbon emissions, Mark's mind made the leap that he could do more by creating materials to replace the hardwoods used in the construction industry in Brazil—one of the biggest culprits for deforestation in the Amazon. He also founded a nonprofit dedicated to reforestation in Brazil. Mark took a circuitous route to his business concept, but each piece of it fits perfectly into a larger vision, which is what can happen when you let those balls bounce.

Making Connections

Lisa Castenada, the educational not-for-profit head whom you met in Chapter Five, comes up with equally inspired ideas that connect seemingly unrelated things. Her solution for leveraging her bingo brain was to find a career that requires innovative, out-of-the-box thinking, so she founded an educational nonprofit that looks for alternative ways of reaching kids through their passions.

An avid video gamer, for example, Lisa's nonlinear thought process hit upon a way to connect video games with learning, and she has several projects for kids that link one of their favorite pastimes to an assortment of educational subjects. She's also developing arts programs with a difference by working with deejays, hip-hop dancers and skateboarders. But, sitting and speaking with all of these different people, gathering ideas and sharing them with university professors and educators, Lisa is able to find and weave connective threads between seemingly disparate subjects. She noticed, for example, that a deejay mentoring a student and a professor teaching college students each made a strikingly similar point about how a novice becomes an expert, which led to another innovative learning program.

"It may seem odd that a deejay would have something to say that's on a level with a university professor, but I am always connecting random dots and seeing a pattern," Lisa told me. "All that jumping I do puts me in places and gets me talking to people from all walks of life who can really inspire."

It's exactly why the nonprofit hired her. They wanted someone who could see things through a different lens.

Seeing What Others Don't

Spanish photographer Guadalupe has an equally surprising and unusual take on what she sees through her camera lens, and she's come to recognize that it's her nonlinear approach to her craft that makes her photographs so distinctive.

"I try to see something exciting, something that will astonish me," she says. "And then I get to that spot and try to get deeper, to really see what is happening there."

An in-demand photojournalist who works freelance for a number of magazines in her hometown of Madrid, Guadalupe manages to find unusual beauty in any subject. Most of her bread-and-butter jobs come through taking portraits and photographing interview subjects.

"I tell people to look one way or another, to do mechanical things, but in that movement the light will strike them, or they will get a certain look when they smile, and there is something fresh there," she explains. "It's something metaphysical, as if they were being made there in that moment for me, and I am seeing them newly."

Guadalupe can find magic even in the mundane. When she shoots interviews, observing the interviewers speaking with their subjects, she notices how people talk with their whole bodies, and how their feet, hands, watches, rings will "suddenly come alive." By simply "following my natural flow," she creates striking and memorable images that celebrate the unexpected.

She's seen the world this way ever since she was a child and first picked up the camera as a hobby. "I had this perception of things being alive, not just lying there inanimate," she recalls.

As a girl, Guadalupe remembers seeing faces in things, but not in the way you would think. "It wasn't like chairs had eyes and smiles, or that lamps were talking to me," she says, recalling how her mother was always slightly concerned about her daughter's unusual sensibilities. Instead, she would notice a small detail that no one else had noticed that would create a presence.

"It's just how I see things," Guadalupe says.

She never tried to force it. It would simply happen through her nonlinear thinking process—something she recognized was a gift even before her recent diagnosis. Allowing her mind to roam free heightened her visual awareness, and she made some startling and beautiful connections with the objects she was looking at through her viewfinder. Taking up photography full-time has become the perfect vehicle for her bingo brain, as well as a glimpse into the fresh and often eccentric way Guadalupe sees the world as an ADHDer.

Of course, she still gets distracted. Her mind jumps so quickly from thing to thing that she avoids going back to edit photos she shot just two weeks before. Typical for an ADHDer, she's most excited by what's new, but in order to meet her deadlines she always felt she should work on the oldest pictures first. But she's recently learned how to leverage her bingo brain to work for her not just behind the lens but also on the computer in the editing phase. She works on the newest first, and the pleasure she takes from her new work fuels the momentum and helps her complete the task quickly. Stimulated by her sense of accomplishment, her bingo brain is eager to bounce to the next thing on her to-do list, so then she starts in on the older photos, which by then have become fresh and new again.

Flipping the order of the work was a way of allowing herself to follow her natural flow and better leverage her bingo brain, along with her many other ADHD strengths.

Brain Burnout

Successful ADHDers work with what they have, gently guiding their superpowers in a direction that leads them to where they want to go. But it does take a certain conscious control to leverage your bingo brain.

Zoë Kessler, an author and ADHD blogger, writes about how her bingo brain can take her in either a positive or a negative direction, depending on her state of mind and how self-aware and on guard she must always be. If she is feeling tired, overwhelmed or stressed, it can work against her.

She gives the example of sitting down on her deck on a beautiful summer evening in a lousy mood. "Instead of feeling uplifted I found myself fixated on the thick ferns growing along the fence in my back-yard," she says.

The ferns reminded of her of prehistoric times and dinosaurs, which got her thinking about violent times in prehistory, which then led her to all the news of destruction and war in the present day, and finally to a postapocalyptic version of the future. Unleashed, those nonlinear thoughts took her down a dark path. But then Zoë came to the realization that she had a choice about where her free-range mind could go. By catching herself in the act, she could turn it around.

"Instead of catastrophizing, we can use our creative thinking to build ourselves up and support our dreams and goals," she says.

That's exactly my point. Your nonlinear thinking is an ADHD superpower. Use it wisely, and all those bingo balls in your brain can bounce you along the road to greatness.

THE TOOL KIT

- Set aside a time and place for your bingo brain to roam free. A meeting may not be the place, unless it's a brainstorming session, and even then you may need to edit some of those ideas.

- Write it down, write it down, write it down! When you have to go through the act of physically writing down your ideas, or sending yourself emails with subject headings to go in a bingo brain ideas file, this process works as a natural filter. You can always go back to it, and this way you can empty or close just enough of the folders in your head to weed out the weak ideas.

- Remember, the next and newest thing isn't necessarily the best thing, or the most important thing, it's just where your mind is taking you at the moment.

- Give your bingo brain the space to roam until it builds a whole picture. We make connections and build these to surprising, out-of-the-box conclusions, but it's not a direct route to get there. Be patient and see where that nonlinear thinking takes you.

- Be conscious of the fact that others may not be able to follow your train of thought. You might be miles ahead of your more linear-thinking colleagues and friends in your perceptiveness. Or you may be so off-topic they have no idea what you are saying. So try to be patient. Yes, it's hard. But often you'll have better results if you can take people with you.

- Resist the temptation to blurt out these ideas and talk over others. You don't necessarily intend to cut them off or dismiss what they have to say, but in your excitement it's all too easy to unintentionally alienate your peers.

- Find a profession or a career that encourages out-of-the-box thinking and values your ability to bring a different perspective.

- Set "juicy goals." A great way to get your bingo brain working in your favor is to set it in the direction of something concrete that you want to accomplish. If the onslaught of ideas starts to overwhelm, bring yourself back to the excitement you feel about reaching that milestone. This will help you filter and prioritize.

- Catch yourself in the act. Your bingo brain can take you in all kinds of directions, but you have a choice about where you go. All it takes is a little extra consciousness, or mindfulness, to set your mental GPS to a positive destination.

CHAPTER EIGHT

Juggling Act

B radley, the specialist truck driver introduced in Chapter One, is a
man in constant motion, and I am not just referring to the fact that
he makes his living on the road. His job requires the unique combination
of mental agility and hyperfocus that makes him a great multitasker—a
trait that is particularly prevalent in folks who have ADHD.

Someone who transports oversized loads—typically those mas-
sive electrical control "buildings" used at oil refineries, gas compres-
sor plants and other heavy industrial sites—must be able to manage
many moving parts for sustained periods of time. These are loads that
can be 150 feet long, 20 feet wide, 17 feet tall and 140,000 pounds,
which means there are only certain roads they can clear, with potentially huge hazards literally at every turn.

Traffic lights, overhead signs, bridges, telephone poles and every
other piece of a highway or Interstate can pose a huge problem, so
Bradley, has to plan out every inch of his journey, anticipate each obstacle and have eyes in the back of his head as he makes decisions
about when to move forward, where to start a turn and how to get
that colossal piece of equipment safely from point A to point B without causing an accident, knocking over a tree, scuffing up his load or
creating some minor environmental disaster.

Adding to the logistical challenges is the fact that he must have a police escort, a scout who drives ahead to verify the height and width of an obstacle, since the state department of transportation bureaucrats aren't always accurate, and his wife, who brings up the rear in a pickup truck, to let him know what's happening behind him. Bradley is responsible for the safety of a whole group of people, as well as the other pedestrians and traffic on and around the road.

It is quite the juggling act. But Bradley loves what he does. Among the many jobs he's held over the years, he tried regular long-haul trucking and was bored out of his mind. Bradley, whose other multitasking pursuits include professional drag racing and poker playing, needs to have many things happening at once to be sufficiently engaged and able to focus. Managing the chaos and jumping from one thing to the next is how he thrives.

A New Level

There is no scientific research that directly supports my contention that those with ADHD are particularly good at multitasking, only my clinical observations over the last twenty-seven years. In various studies involving subjects who were given several things to do, it was found that those with the diagnosis were no better or worse at multitasking than the general population. Yet, in my experience the big difference is that those with ADHD *enjoy* the multitasking so much more.

But here's the thing: someone with ADHD can put a huge amount of intensity and focus into something for a short period of time before getting bored and moving on to the next thing. Again, it's that hyperfocus that helps bring multitasking to a whole new level. It's how they naturally operate to keep that dopamine pumping. So it stands to reason that ADHDers enjoy multitasking much more than the average person, who tends to get overwhelmed and stressed from juggling tasks. And because they multitask so much more often than the average person, they get good at it.

It is why, in this technology age, many successful IT entrepreneurs have ADHD. What the average person finds distracting—an on-slaught of data in the form of text messages, tweets, online messaging and the buzzes and alerts of multiple devices—can be highly stimulating to those with ADHD. Facing a new situation and doing many things at once increases stress and that raises dopamine tone. So for someone with ADHD, multitasking is almost like meditation. That swirl of activity that confuses and exhausts the non-ADHDers of the world actually relaxes us. The effect can be addictive, but in a good way when leveraged correctly, because we can get things done quickly.

"Multitasking is paramount in my brain," says Chester "Lee" Mallett, fifty-six, a highly successful serial entrepreneur based in southwest Louisiana and a major fund-raiser for Governor Bobby Jindal. "My brain works in such a way that I take care of business, staying a step ahead. I focus and perform much better when I am multitasking, and I do not find it hard to deal with all the problems that come up in my businesses," he adds.

Lee, who owns and operates numerous widely different businesses, including a privately run halfway house for former prison inmates, a grain salvaging company, a housing and commercial property development company and a truss manufacturing plant, is constantly buzzing from one thing to the next. Somehow, with dozens of ongoing projects at any given time, he manages to stay on top of his businesses through apps on his iPhone and iPad.

"Technology is great because it enables me to do even more," says Lee, who is another example of the many ADHDers who seem to thrive in the age of technology, when most of us are required to use our devices for managing multiple tasks at once.

High-Tech Roaming

Washington, D.C.–based social media consultant Stephen Anfield has found the perfect context for his multitasking strength through Facebook, Twitter, Pinterest, Instagram and just about every other Internet platform that allows him to be creative in short bursts. He enjoys the variety and speed of this form of communication, which keeps him moving from one open computer window to the next.

"I love the fact that it's always changing, it's never the same," Stephen told me. "The platforms themselves are always evolving. Whenever there is something new, I am the first to sign up for it."

Stephen doesn't enjoy writing long pieces but excels at the quick sound bites that work best online, which encourages roaming from topic to topic. The platform, which has trained him to think and write in a more concise manner, is ideal for his fast mind and restless nature. And the inherent multitasking of social media, which requires posting, uploading, creating and sharing content simultaneously, keeps him fully engaged. The combination of many different physical actions, combined with the mental process of researching and developing new content, stimulates his ADHD brain just enough.

Stephen also enjoys the challenge of making his comments and statements more attention-grabbing and interesting, usually against the busy backdrop of a coffee shop, or in his home office with music from Spotify playing softly in the background "for the white noise." He's normally not a numbers man, but the analytics of social media "tell me a story about how well I am doing, and how I can improve content," he says. These quantifiable results—the views, the "likes" and the retweets—give him a sense of accomplishment and spur him on to do even more with social media. His current favorite mediums are Facebook and Twitter for breaking news. He's a pro at navigating his way through that constant flow of information, and every time his iPhone pings with an alert it gives him a thrill.

Stephen, thirty-three, recognized he needed a career that involved multitasking when he started his first desk job. "I just wasn't used to sitting still."

Being sedentary felt wrong. At the end of the workday, he couldn't sleep. At the office he was miserable, wondering how everyone else was able to sit quietly with their heads down while he was climbing out of his skin. He finally went to a neurology center in Virginia to get himself checked out. When he was first diagnosed with ADHD, he cried, wondering how it was going to affect him. But as he looked back on his life it all began to make sense.

He did well in school, but only because he was in advanced classes that challenged him and kept him busy. In college, he moved from major to major, switching from the music department, where he was on scholarship as a bassoon player, to biology, then political science and communications studies. He was constantly on the go, working as a campus tour guide, interacting with new people, talking, leading and rarely having to spend much time in class.

When he graduated he joined City Year, an AmeriCorps national service program for young adults. In that role he led a team of nine people, traveling to all the schools in Washington, D.C.'s school district, hitting all four quadrants in a day. That constant movement, rushing from school to school and meeting with students and teachers, was exhausting, but fulfilling.

Out in the workforce, Stephen was equally restless, working in computer sales, doing media for car dealerships and serving as an intern at PR giant FleishmanHillard. On the side he's worked as a contractor for several nonprofits and social entrepreneurship organizations in the D.C. area, which have limited resources and require that people juggle many tasks at once. The more he does this kind of work using his creativity in social media and leading teams, the more Stephen is able to leverage his multitasking and feel fulfilled.

But he also needs to be free to walk around and work at his own pace. Stephen's ability to multitask through leading, talking, coming up with ideas and creating media content is the perfect antidote for his restlessness and high energy. Like many ADHDers, he needs to be in constant motion, both mentally and physically, so a rigid office setting won't work for this multitasker.

"I work best on a team, in a flexible environment," says Stephen, who at the time of this writing was interviewing for a tech start-up in Silicon Valley.

High Concept

High-level multitasking, is not to be confused with mundane busy-work. Those of us with ADHD need to be passionate about what we are doing. It's not that all tasks need to be inherently fascinating or challenging, although that certainly helps. But they do need to be part of an overall goal, or in an area of interest that we truly care about.

One of Stephen's worst moments was when he was assigned to a desk next to his boss's office in a high-traffic area and was asked to answer the phone while working on the company's social media platform. It was at a car dealership, "and I couldn't care less about cars," he says. The constant drudge work he was being asked to do, along with the number of people stopping by his desk to talk over him to his boss or ask for favors was distracting, and he couldn't get his work done. It was such a disaster, one of his supervisors asked him why he couldn't multitask.

"When I am not interested in something it becomes a chore and slows me down," explains Stephen.

But it wasn't that he couldn't multitask. Within the context of social media, Stephen juggles long lists of challenging tasks for hours throughout the day. It was just that his ADHD brain was not being stimulated, and he couldn't handle the tedium. But when he combines passion with the strengths of this trait, multitasking included, there is no stopping us.

A Born New Yorker

Kelly Dooley, founder and CEO of the fashion company BodyRock Sport, is a case in point. Another high-concept multitasker, the entrepreneur is a one-woman whirlwind of activity from the moment she wakes up until it's time to go to bed at the end of many long and frenetic hours at work.

Kelly's typical day starts with waking up early to answer emails before breakfast, during breakfast and on her way to the gym. By 8:30 a.m.

she's on a conference call while answering emails and sending texts, and preparing for the first of "a zillion meetings" on everything from working on design concepts to PR and marketing campaigns, manufacturing and operations. Because hers is a small and lean operation, she must handle every facet of the business herself.

"I am running around all the time," she says. "A lot of people do that, especially in New York City, but this is not a normal level of functioning. This is much more intense."

Kelly can't help herself. From the time she was seven years old, when the California native came to New York City on a family vacation, "I just knew I had to live here." Because she was always an active tomboy who moved at warp speed, the sight of so many New Yorkers rushing around on the streets, eating their lunch and making phone calls on the run while hailing taxis or hopping on the subway was fascinating and perfect for her in every way.

"I loved the pace and diversity, so much was always happening."

The city gave context to her ADHD. It was where she fit. Her restless nature and constant need for activity wasn't so out of place in that hyperactive city. Her next step was to find a career that could keep her there. So after getting a degree in journalism at Boston University, it was on to New York University, where she majored in media, culture and communications, attending classes in between running marathons and competing in triathlons.

Like so many ADHD entrepreneurs, Kelly switched gears, spotting her big idea for a business before she even graduated. In 2009, when she was about to run a marathon, she was looking for a sports bra with a discreet pocket for her iPod, and found they didn't exist. Then and there sprang the idea for a new business: selling funky yet functional sportswear for women that was about "rocking a body with confidence."

Kelly did it all, launching a successful business, throwing her family inheritance into the company at the height of the recession, building a $10 million fashion sportswear business with a cult following of celebrities like Kim Kardashian and Lady Gaga. She handled the design, marketing and manufacturing, as well as the financing, "which is the hardest part," doing what many start-up business owners do by running operations on a shoestring and doing most of the work herself. She even warehoused and shipped the sports bras from her apartment.

"I have a hard time delegating," says Kelly. "I felt that if I wanted to get something done I had to get it done myself."

Part of the intense pressure comes from the fickle and highly competitive nature of the fashion business. The fashion void Kelly discovered has since been filled by dozens of competitors.

"I've gotten knocked off so many times," says Kelly, who is continually running between Manhattan's Garment District and Brooklyn, working with contract manufacturers to come up with fresh new designs for her customers.

"The line is about fierce women who know who they are and are not apologetic," says Kelly. "I've built a community of badass women who are confident in the product."

Kelly might as well be describing herself. The intensity of her life continues even when she is home in the evening, sitting next to her triathlete husband as he unwinds in front of the television and she continues to multitask.

"Even when I am asleep I am so awake in a way. My brain is always in overdrive, solving problems in my head. It's like I am never not working."

Vacations are equally as active. Kelly's ideal getaway also involves multitasking, whether it's climbing a mountain or, preferably, roaming around a new city in Europe, shopping, eating, going to museums and walking everywhere. Sitting down and relaxing in a lounger is out of the question:

"I get antsy. I feel more relaxed when I am busy."

Striking a Balance

Kelly's found the perfect context for her ADHD strength. Every day is different, so she can't get bored. Her restless energy needs the outlet of multitasking, which she also supplements with plenty of physical activity and exercise alongside her equally athletic husband. But, as is often the case with ADHDers, the trick is finding a balance. Kelly is the first to admit she does too much . . . of everything.

"For years I've been totally overextended," she says. "There's only twenty-four hours in a day, and aside from running a company and having a life, I have to be a good wife and get dinner on the table. It's a lot to handle."

Looking back, Kelly would have delegated more and appointed a CFO. Her recent ADHD diagnosis has helped her to realize that she's been spreading herself too thin.

"Self-awareness would have helped me understand the importance of putting structures in place," says Kelly. "It also would have given me the confidence necessary that I was the creative one, and needed to focus my energy on that side of the business instead of trying to do it all."

Kelly is already planning her next business venture and hoping to sell BodyRock. She has a few ideas, so far nothing concrete, although she is hoping to do something in the health and wellness field next. But she does know that next time she'll do things a little differently. She'll always be a multitasker, but next time she'll be more focused and selective about which facets of the business benefit from the whirlwind of her intense energy.

Tasmanian Devils

Of course, you don't have to own a business to leverage your multitasking strength. Waitress and housecleaner Eileen is known for starting a task, only to drop it and move on to something else that "catches my eye and needs tending to." It's not unusual for Eileen to get halfway through dusting a shelf, to start polishing silver and defrosting the refrigerator, only to pick up the dusting again hours later. She operates the same way at a Louisiana barbecue joint where she works part-time, prepping coleslaw one minute before busing a table the next.

Finishing or following through on tasks can be an issue for many ADHDers. It can help to set small reminders to go back to tasks already started before they are completely forgotten. But the key is not to fight the desire to multitask. Allowing herself the freedom to buzz from task to task instead of forcing herself to complete one thing in a single session may not look efficient to a more linear thinker, and it can be exhausting to watch, but somehow she always gets the job, or jobs, done by the end of her shift.

"If I see it needs doing, I just do it; I just can't help myself," says Eileen.

Lifestyle can be just as much of an outlet for your high energy. As a homemaker at her off-the-grid Northern Californian homestead, sixty-year-old Ruth Joy Burnell does everything from gardening to canning, cooking, crafting, helping her husband build a drip irrigation system and maintain their solar-paneled house. She also swims regularly and does yoga. Anything to burn off that excess energy.

"My friends say I am the busiest nonworking person they know," says Ruth. "I have so many balls simultaneously in the air."

After years of drifting around the world and dabbling in multiple careers and interests, including working as a curatorial assistant at a museum in Chicago, adventure traveling in Papua New Guinea and running a bakery in Hawaii, Ruth met the love of her life and settled down on the West Coast, where she and her husband had their home built using wood cut and milled on their land.

Because they live so far away from the rest of civilization, about twenty miles from Mendocino in the middle of eighty acres of redwood and Douglas fir forests, Ruth elected to homeschool her children up until the eighth grade.

"When you have two kids three years apart in age, that's definitely multitasking," she jokes.

Again, it was another great outlet for her strength. Ruth got creative, using toy cars lined up down the hallway to teach her son the multiplication tables, and put on Gilbert and Sullivan operettas to teach them about music and culture. It meant there was constant movement, "and I think better when I am moving," says Ruth.

Whether by accident or design, Ruth has made choices throughout her life that helped her to adapt beautifully, aiming all that Tasmanian devil energy into positive goals like building an eco-friendly home and raising a happy family.

"I do think my life here has allowed me to learn so many different things, and do so much with my hands."

Ruth didn't get diagnosed until much later in life. But she never tried to fight who she was—a consummate multitasker. In fact, she embraced it, which is why she is happy, healthy and fulfilled today. Yet another ADHD success story.

So determine whether or not one of your ADHD strengths is multitasking by taking the quiz on the next page. And if you recognize yourself in some of the stories in this chapter, be proud, because your tendency to get bored quickly and move from task to task is not just about lack of follow-through or a short attention span, as you've probably been told many times by teachers, bosses, parents, colleagues . . . Channeled the right way, it is another gift, because even though you are working in shorter increments, you can achieve a great deal in your life and career.

Whether those with ADHD are better than average at multitasking during those windows of time contained by the studies, the simple fact that they enjoy it more and are going to choose to do five things at once in their everyday lives suggests that multitasking is a *significant* advantage of ADHD. It's also a huge factor in the accomplishments of so many ADHD entrepreneurs and CEOs, but more on that later.

THE TOOL KIT

How to tell if you are cut out for multitasking:

- Do you find yourself texting while carrying on a conversation, picking up your dry cleaning while thinking about a business plan for a new app?

- Do you tend to work best in short bursts of attention?

- Do you prefer to move, or pace, while thinking or talking on the phone?

- Do you work better in a noisy Starbucks, with the murmur of crowds and the blast of the cappuccino machine, versus the quiet of your own office?

- Do you see social media and technology as a distraction, or as a relief because it gives you more to do and look at while you are working on company's business plan for the next year?

- When you get bored with a project, is the best course for you to drop it and move on to something that seems more interesting at the time?

- Would you rather work on several things at once than see one thing at a time through to completion?

- Are electronic reminder alerts and Post-it notes how you get through your working day?

- Are you watching television, posting on Facebook and making a pot of gumbo as you read this?

CHAPTER NINE

Cool in a Crisis

In my younger years I was an avid sailor, and nothing was more thrilling to me than the challenge of sailing solo around the Caribbean or across the Gulf of Mexico. On one of these trips I was about two hundred miles offshore when water started flooding into the boat from God knows where, overwhelming the bilge pumps and threatening to sink the vessel. There are numerous through-hull attachments on a boat, any one of which could have failed. There was also the possibility of a cracked hull. I had about three minutes to find the problem and fix it, or I would be calling a mayday to the Coast Guard. So the question was, what to do first?

A big joke among family and friends is how inept I am when it comes to doing jobs around the house like plumbing, electrical wiring or general maintenance—I am clueless. But when I am on a sailboat out on the ocean and something breaks or leaks, or the engine shorts, I suddenly become the world's most proficient general contractor. Somehow I can repair anything, quickly and efficiently, anywhere, anytime. I go into hyperfocus mode, discovering talents that neither I nor my sailing buddies knew I had.

This is because when something goes wrong on the high seas there is no one to call. If the problem doesn't get fixed right away you may be forced to call the Coast Guard at best, or end up in a life raft hoping for help at worst. Luckily, I discovered that the valve for the water maker had sprung a leak, and swiftly fixed the problem, avoiding both outcomes. It could have been much worse, and if it had been, I am certain I would have dealt with it. Because crisis mode is when I am at my best. Do-or-die puts me in the zone. Under those conditions, I thrive, because something about the pressure makes me calm and focused. It brings out the best in me.

And this is true for many ADHDers. We are cool in a crisis. The restless, high-energy natures of those with ADHD often seem out of place in the normal world of predictability and routine. As we spin around at warp speed, we must appear completely out of sync with the daily pace of life. But give us a crisis situation, a deadline or a sense of urgency, and the world finally catches up to us. These are our moments, our times for redemption, because we are never more comfortable and at home than when we are surrounded by chaos.

A crisis gives us the stimulation we crave. We spend our lives pushing up against deadlines and creating intense, high-pressure situations because they help us produce the dopamine and adrenaline levels necessary to feed the reward centers in our brains. It's not exactly that people with ADHD are adrenaline junkies. It is simply the level of excitement we need for balance, to even out our neurochemistry and help us function at a high level. It's just the trigger that the executive functions of our brain needs.

It's why we procrastinate. There is nothing wrong with putting off something until the last minute if that creates the crisis condition that brings out your best performance, as long as you beat that deadline. Mozart, who in all likelihood was at the far end of the ADHD continuum, was a constant procrastinator. In fact, he wrote the overture to *Don Giovanni*—one of the most iconic pieces of music in history—the very morning the opera premiered!

Our need for the stimulation of crisis mode is also why people with ADHD tend to thrive in high-pressure jobs, whether a trader doing deals worth hundreds of millions of dollars, the police chasing bad guys, or firefighters putting out dangerous blazes. Even a Silicon

Valley CEO at the helm of a fast-growing businesses in a rapidly evolving industry could use an ADHD brain to solve problems and put out fires on a daily basis.

Thrill of the Chase

Those tense moments are all in a day's work for private investigator Brennan Benglis. Plenty of things about this career get his dopamine pumping. First, there's the risk.

"I've been threatened a few times; it doesn't bother me," says Brennan.

Most of his clients are insurance companies looking to bust people making fraudulent claims, and that's where Brennan comes in. He follows people, goes undercover and tracks down the evidence that proves the subject he's following is a liar and a criminal. These people are desperate, and will go to great lengths to avoid being found out, so situations can become chaotic, hectic and even dangerous in an instant.

"I can be sitting in my car on a stakeout for hours and all of a sudden, boom, I'm on the interstate in a ninety-mile-an-hour car chase."

That thrill of the chase and allure of risk can be found in a multitude of professions. Although technically you're not supposed to have been diagnosed with a "disorder" when you join the military, particularly special ops, ADHD is tailor-made for jumping out of airplanes and thriving in situations of extreme duress, such as combat. Recent descriptions of the anonymous SEAL who pulled the trigger on Osama bin Laden make him sound like so many ADHDers I know: unable to relax with downtime and always amped up for the next mission.

It's no wonder that so many with ADHD are drawn to some of the most physically challenging and dangerous units of the military. I'd wager that if the armed forces were to ever allow a study, they'd find a much greater prevalence of this trait than in the general population, particularly among those in special ops. And that's a good thing. These are the folks we want on that wall, ready to jump into action in a split second when needed.

Driven by Emergencies

I should add emergency room doctor to the list of ideal professions, because Dr. Mike Watson, whom we discussed in Chapter Five, thrives in intense situations, such as performing an emergency C-section or treating a near-death patient on a gurney in his ER. He's the guy who is perfectly calm while everyone else is going crazy. He likes it best when his waiting room is full and someone is going into labor. But ask him to go through the mountains of paperwork required on his patient charts, and he runs away. There's nothing that sends him into a panic more than having to sit down and update patient history files. According to Mike, he'd rather stick pins in his eyes! That's why he waits until the absolute last minute to get it done, then plows through the paperwork in hyperfocus mode.

He was the same way in med school, which Mike hated. He attended far fewer classes than most, struggling to read the texts and review his class notes. But when it came to exam time, his study method was to stay up all night to cram for the test, paddle a canoe in the morning hours right before it was time, write the exam and then hit a favorite bar, have a few drinks and then do it all over again. He was creating a crisis situation to get focused on the task, and it must have worked, because he passed!

"I work too many hours, drive too fast and always run late—I have to be late," explains Mike. "A crisis is how I like it best."

A Happy Place

Being up against the wire is the happy place of many with ADHD, especially the entrepreneurs.

Chicago-based business owner Kenneth "Bucky" Buckman finds

joy in the chaos and pressure he bumps up against on a daily basis. The CEO of TradeTec Skyline, a $13 million business that does installations for trade expos and conventions around the globe, and Rainy Investments, a $25 million business that owns and develops commercial and residential property throughout the Chicago area, it's as if Bucky were born to run several hectic and high-risk businesses at once.

"I run two companies with multiple divisions and nonstop chaos," he told me.

Looking back, Bucky figures there must be a reason he was drawn to the exhibit/event industry, or, as he puts it, "what is truly one of the most chaotic, f&#*ed-up industries on the planet." Each show is run like triage in a trauma center and "Murphy's Law" was written on the trade show floor. "You never know what's going to come through the double doors on a stretcher next," says Bucky, whose daily interactions involve negotiating with unions, coordinating with dozens of tradespeople and "transforming bare concrete into a beautiful functioning city."

Bucky thrives on the unpredictability of his work, which gives him an opportunity to think on his feet and problem-solve on the fly.

"I could write an encyclopedia and update chapters weekly on crap I didn't see coming," he jokes.

But having to react quickly and figure out solutions to complex problems within seconds keeps him stimulated and engaged. In fact, when things are calm and running smoothly, alarm bells go off and Bucky panics, expecting something bad to happen.

"People think it is a joke but it really isn't," says Bucky. "All the ADHD people I know are like me. We are not calm unless there is chaos."

That may be why, just after the recession hit, combined with his two top sales reps quitting and suing him for their noncompetes, his 50 percent partner asking to be bought out and the state of Illinois deciding to do a detailed tax audit, Bucky was at his best. Just as everyone around him was predicting disaster, he convinced a banker friend to give him a $2 million loan to do a buyout of his partner and fund the business. Stimulated and hyperfocused, he then presented his case at the tax court hearing with a comedic twist, using a stick-figure PowerPoint presentation. He ended up paying a small penalty instead of the crushing $486,000 they originally sought, and grew his sales force to take back his business, all within six months. Fifteen months later, the company doubled in revenues.

Seeking the Unsafe

Members of our ADHD tribe tend to be drawn to challenges, and the more extreme, the better. After medical school, Dr. Kashinath Yada-lam, whom you met in Chapter Five, headed to Zambia "in the thick of a civil war and a lot of people were being robbed for a carton of milk" to take his exams. Most people would have gone to any other English-speaking country, like the Philippines or the United King-dom, but Dr. Yadalam wanted—in fact, needed—an adventure.

"I guess it was impulsive," he says. "I had very little information to go on about that country."

Once he passed, Dr. Yadalam and a couple of med school friends headed to Zimbabwe, known as Rhodesia at the time—a country that was undergoing a struggle for independence, and where he narrowly escaped gunfire and bombings.

"I thought it was fun," he told me. "But looking back, it was fool-ish."

So after six days he left, seeking more "uncharted territory" in Nebraska, the first of many stops, teaching and working in private practice all over the country before finally moving his wife and family to Louisiana. Through his entire career he had opportunities to take the safer option, but chose the riskier path with his eyes wide-open. He had a job at a top clinic in Austin, Texas, but resigned before he had a job to go to, even as his wife was pregnant with their second child. He took a risk by giving up private practice and saw his income level drop precipitously for two years.

"People thought I had presenile dementia," Dr. Yadalam jokes.

No, he had ADHD, and the trait's need for risk and uncertainty to stimulate him and engage his passion for the work. And these decisions have paid off. Today Dr. Yadalam has founded and is the CEO of a successful drug-testing clinic that now has eighteen employees. If Big Pharma needs a psychiatric drug tested in human trials for FDA approval, Dr. Yadalam is the guy. He took risk after risk, and the pressure to perform and support his family helped him to focus and calmly make all the right moves, giving up the headaches of a group clinical practice and its onerous requirements for the freedom and financial success of running a company on his own terms.

"I might be a big fish in a small pond here, but I call all the shots in my company," he says.

Of course, his enterprise has its own pressures. Running a complex business like a testing lab can require some tough calls, especially when dealing with the high stakes of drug companies and strict FDA regulations. A single business decision can have fifty different possible outcomes, and the wrong decisions can be costly. But his clear thinking and focus under the gun enables him to navigate through the toughest issues quickly, and it's usually the right move.

"Fear of failure has never stopped me," says Dr. Yadalam.

I would argue that is exactly what propels him forward.

Manufacturing a Crisis

When that high pressure doesn't occur naturally, we ADHDers tend to manufacture a crisis, whether it's procrastinating until we are flush up against a deadline, taking on high-risk ventures or juggling multiple things at once. Consciously or unconsciously, we want that gun to our heads. Again, it's what gets that dopamine pumping to our brains, and that isn't necessarily a bad thing. You probably noticed this about yourself in school. Bucky Buckman was hardly ever in class, but he crammed for exams and did just fine. Middle school teacher Tichelle Harris, from Chapter Five, had to do all of her teacher licensing courses up against a deadline, otherwise she felt completely disengaged.

"I'd have these surges of high energy, but as it dragged on, I'd slack off," she says. "I'm just not interested in sitting at a teacher's conference all day."

Doctoral candidate Emily Anhalt, from Chapter Seven, already knew this procrastinating tendency in herself, so she embraced it. She found an academic career that allows her a certain freedom in how she works, without the frustrations of being micromanaged and checked up on before an assignment is due.

"I rely upon doing things at the last minute," she told me. "Deadlines raise the anxiety that allows me to get it done."

In his blog, psychiatrist and ADHD expert Dr. Kenny Handelman, who also has ADHD, recently wrote about two days of incredible productivity he experienced just before he was due to get on a plane.

"I felt like every moment mattered. I used my time wisely. I made lists and checked them repeatedly throughout the day to make sure that I was on track," he writes. "My productivity was at an all-time high. I got more done in 2 days than I would normally have in 5 days."

Self-Imposed Pressure

The deadline was circumstantial, but it doesn't have to be. You can set deadlines regularly for anything that needs to get done, whether it's homework or a big project at work. This is especially effective for ADHDers because of the way we think of time. For us, there is only "now" and "not now," so if you need to be somewhere by, say 5:00 p.m., you don't even think about getting ready to walk out the door more than a few minutes before the hour. It's why so many of us are chronically late. If something is due in a week, it's "not now." But if it's due the next morning, that's a whole different story, and that's when we can spring into action.

The key is not to fight procrastination, which is a natural impulse for ADHDers. Insurance entrepreneur Louis M. Todd is successful largely because of the high-pressure situations he creates for himself, and yet, he says, "I battle my tendencies to put everything off until the last minute."

Calm in Chaos

Louis, who owns a small commercial insurance agency, leaps into projects at the worst possible time in his life, taking on what would be far too much stress for the average person, and executing to perfection. One thing he doesn't procrastinate on is giving his customers quotes for renewal policies. He has the system and, more important, the support personnel in place to get this information to them thirty days in advance, although he sets early deadlines to ensure it gets done.

As for the rest of his life, the more chaos, the better. In the middle of taking care of a sick wife and daughter, each of whom coincidentally needed major surgery, he took it upon himself to buy a commercial office building, which he spent several weeks refurbishing, working with multiple contractors on everything from what color paint to put on the walls to which flowers to plant in the landscaping. He did all this while running his insurance business and without the typical help of his recovering wife, who does "whatever needs to be done" at his office.

His need for the stimulation of chaos and uncertainty may seem somehow counterintuitive for a man who runs an insurance agency, but that's another major reason why Louis decided to go on his own at forty-nine, after years of taking a secure salary at a large national insurance company.

Today, he revels in the freedom of doing things on his own terms, away from "safe harbor" that was leaving him unfulfilled.

"I can't even describe the feeling," says Louis. "Here I am making it; I almost want to cry."

Staying Awake

Anesthetist Frank Stuart also adapted his career midstream because the tedium and predictability of what he was doing was becoming unbearable.

Frank's profession requires hours in an operating room, monitoring patients for vital signs and administering just the right amount of drugs to keep them sedated or unconscious.

"It was just the same thing over and over again," Frank told me. "I didn't know some doctors and surgeons could be so slow with such routine procedures."

It got to the point where Frank would only work either the fast cases, like colonoscopies, or the extremely complex surgeries where a patient's life was on the line.

"I can do heart surgeries or long trauma cases—something that is going to take all my time and energy, and where I am really going to have to work to keep the patient alive," says Frank. But if it's a four-hour routine case, "I go crazy with boredom, stuck in a room with no windows."

So Frank decided to wake himself up by establishing more businesses. Unwilling to give up the money that comes from being so good at his field, he started four different anesthesia practices, where other nurse anesthetists who work under him take the most boring and time-consuming cases. Frank also started dabbling in real estate, buying up distressed properties, fixing them up and flipping them. He first bought condos in Florida at the bottom of the market in 1999, riding the bubble all the way up, then switching his energy to New Orleans after Hurricane Katrina.

Frank has discovered his true passion in real estate, where he chases down deals at cents on the dollar, and the wild ride of turbulent markets keeps his mind stimulated and engaged. It helps that making and executing deals, renovating and decorating involve juggling many tasks. Multitasking can be inherently chaotic, and requires quick thinking and problem-solving, which is another reason why Frank loves what he does.

"Being insanely busy calms me and helps me focus," he says. "Multitasking triggers something in my brain and helps me get through the day."

Warp Speed

Members of our tribe also thrive when they take on physical risks—another form of pressure that stimulates dopamine production and has a calming effect on the ADHD brain. Dozens of the success stories I met with are daredevils in their spare time. Hong Kong–based IT consultant Gordon Sanders, whom you first met in Chapter Five, found his Zen through in-line skating. The athletic Texan fell in love with the sport and the inner calm it gave him to move along at high speeds, anticipating bumps and turns in a state of hyperawareness, knowing precisely when to move and shift his body without ever needing to slow his pace.

"Skaters have a different attitude to life. One of the premises of skating is that you have to learn to release control . . . You really have to let go and let the skates roll."

Gordon discovered in-line skating, which he calls his "meditation," about twenty years ago and became an instructor, and it was then that he started accomplishing more in his life and career. There was something about the extreme clarity that being in the moment of the sport gave him that produced insights into other areas of his life, such as completing his university degree twenty years after being kicked out of college, and passing various certification exams. It taught him the different between reacting to something without thinking, and responding to something that he had already anticipated. It also gave him insight into his ADHD strengths, and his ability to see things others don't.

"With skating, you are already moving fast, and the brakes don't act immediately, so panic is useless. But if you harness that energy you can slow it down and think it through."

In other words, Gordon was able to realize that one of his strengths is his calm and focus as the road speeds beneath him. Under those conditions, when cars are whizzing by and he has to hyperfocus on everything that's around him, Gordon is able to mentally slow things down and make the best possible decisions.

Road risk has become such an important part of Gordon's daily life that during a recent stint in Vietnam, where "road rules do not support skating," he took up riding a motorbike. Anyone who has been to that part of the world knows that it's rife with street accidents, and driving conditions are utter chaos, so you could argue that this was another extreme sport to help fulfill Gordon's need for risk.

"Most people have to have some level of predictability, but I loved, loved driving a motorbike there," he says.

Risk Rewards

Throughout my years of clinical practice, it has struck me how many ADHDers had such dangerous taste in past times. Plenty has been written about the impulsivity and risk-taking behavior associated with the trait, most of it negative. But here's the thing—it can actually be a *positive*, especially if it's calculated risk, or contained within the framework of a sport, which takes training and expertise.

The ADHDers in this book like to mountain-climb, solo-sail, ski and surf. Bradley the truck driver drag races in his spare time. Shane Jordan, owner of a successful chain of computer repair stores in Southern California, is learning how to ride a motorcycle and fly a plane. These activities actually help him relax and recharge after a day of multitasking and thinking on his feet in his computer repair shop.

"I am constantly looking for things that force me to concentrate so hard that I don't think about anything else," says Shane. "I am so focused on not dying, on the art of riding a motorcycle proficiently, that it's my escape from being mentally all over the place."

But as he gets better and more confident on his bike, that effect wears off, so he's finding his ultimate escape as he pursues his pilot's license. The intense concentration and pressure is like therapy for

Shane, who finds an afternoon of flying as mentally refreshing and calming as a week on the beach for the rest of the world.

"It's such an extreme challenge for me that it clears my head," says Shane.

But the best moment, Shane's nirvana, is those thirty seconds it takes to land the plane.

"That moment when you are setting yourself up for final, lining up with the runway, is golden. You have to concentrate or you will crash and die, and in that immediacy I am not thinking about work or relationships or anything. It's the one time everything goes perfectly still and nothing else exists. How awesome is that?"

THE TOOL KIT

How to positively channel your need for heightened pressure without going off the rails:

- It's okay to leave things until the last minute or pull an all-nighter if that's what brings about your best work. That's your ADHD guiding you toward your best performance. Don't change!

- Leverage procrastination. With the right controls in place to make sure you don't miss those deadlines, it can be a useful tool.

- Realize that what makes you calm drives other people crazy. You need a little controlled mayhem in your life to stimulate that hyperfocus dopamine release.

- Any career can work if you tailor it to your need for crisis and resolution. Classic examples include police officer, firefighter or paramedic. But as you've seen in this book, even insurance brokers, computer nerds, truck drivers and doctors can create the right context for being cool in a crisis.

- Of course there needs to be a balance. Creating that pressure to stimulate the brain and put you into hyperfocus can distract you from other priorities if you are constantly putting out those fires, so when you manufacture that crisis to stimulate your brain and get yourself focused on a task, make sure it propels you toward a higher goal.

- Keep it moving. Once the stimulation of a crisis or high-pressure situation is over, there's a danger of crashing down to earth. Stay on a physical routine and focus on the next task at hand—even if it's simply planning your next vacation. This will help minimize the sense of deflation when the period of hyperfocus has passed.

- Be that hero who steps into a crisis, fixes the problem and enables normal life to resume. It's a role you were made for, so embrace it.

- When possible, avoid jobs with a fixed daily routine.

- At the risk of repeating myself, exercise, exercise, exercise. Nothing is more calming and focusing for an ADHDer.

- It's okay to run late as long as people understand when you say five you mean five fifteen. Just take the time to fill people in on how you operate.

Your Antidote to Boredom

By now you've probably noticed a common theme throughout these chapters: hyperfocus. While it has not been highlighted as a strength, hyperfocus is nevertheless a key tool—perhaps *the* key tool—in your ADHD tool kit. It's the agent that makes it all happen. Unfortunately, being able to switch it on and off at will is difficult and elusive. Yet it can make all the difference between successfully leveraging your strengths and letting them run away into dysfunction.

Our successful ADHDers have placed themselves in contexts and careers that engage their interest and stimulate their ADHD brains, kicking their focus into high gear. With that focus, they can accomplish a great deal—more than most non-ADHDers—often forgetting to eat and sleep, and oblivious to the hours that are passing. Nothing can distract them when they are in hyperfocus mode, which they use to creatively solve problems and complete projects. Hyperfocus helps them research intriguing topics while absorbing information like a sponge and assimilating it in ways that often lead to groundbreaking advances in their chosen fields. But hyperfocus needs to be used wisely in conjunction with your other strengths. There are times when hyperfocus can get you stuck on activities or topics that may not be to your benefit. Be aware that you have this gift so that you can switch gears and hyperfocus on the *right* things—passions and interests that will bring you positive outcomes in life.

Of course, anyone can hyperfocus. It is not a skill particular to those with ADHD. But here is the key: as ADHDers, we need hyperfocus to compensate for our *lack* of focus. Our brains naturally seek stimulation, and when something isn't interesting to us we become highly distractible and our attention wanders. The problem is, what is interesting to non-ADHDers often isn't exciting for those with the trait, who chafe at the routine and predictability of daily life. It's why ADHDers often seem restless, impulsive and, at times, self-destructive. Without hyperfocus, we may even seek stimulation in the form of risk-taking behavior like drinking, driving too fast, gambling . . . We can't sustain our interest in school or a typical desk job because we are novelty seekers. What's new and interesting to the average person isn't enough to feed our brain reward circuits.

A recent *New York Times* editorial by Richard Friedman, a professor of clinical psychiatry at Weill Cornell Medical College, points out what I've always known anecdotally to be true, that "if you have 'the illness,' the real problem is that, to your brain, the world that you live in essentially feels not very interesting." He cites new research, based on PET scans that compared the number of dopamine receptors in the reward region of the brain deep beneath the cortex, and found that adults with ADHD had far fewer than those without ADHD. The lower the number of these receptors, the lower their level of attention. So ADHD truly is a diagnosis of boredom!

"These findings suggest that people with ADHD are walking around with reward circuits that are less sensitive at baseline than those of the rest of us," notes Dr. Friedman.

It's therefore no surprise that these "symptoms" disappear the more interested and engaged the ADHDer becomes. It's become a cliché to say, "Do what you love," but for those of us with the trait it is crucial. The ability to hyperfocus could even be seen as evidence of a potential career for you. There is no better method for activating hyperfocus than doing something that you are passionate about.

That's when the focus takes care of itself. It is also why, when you finished public school and started in college, where you could choose your concentration, you likely found that you began to do better.

But what if you are still searching for that context? What if you need to hyperfocus on something now? How can we kick into hyperfocus at will—or at least have some conscious control over the process? Here are some methods to try:

- **Procrastination.** There is nothing like a looming deadline to trigger hyperfocus. Running late will put you on high alert. A little danger goes a long way. But be precise in your timing. There is a very fine line here—don't leave it so late that you'll fail to meet the deadline and jeopardize your project, your grades or the success of your team. Creating an artificial deadline before the real deadline is a good strategy that will allow a buffer if you feel you need it.

- **Fear.** Procrastination ties in with fear—it produces that emotion when you face the consequences of missing a deadline. You can help fan the flames of fear by exaggerating the potential consequences. For example, you can tell yourself, "If I don't turn this project in on time I will get fired," or, "If I don't ace this test I will fail the course." Neither outcome may be accurate, but there is nothing like the adrenaline rush of fear itself to sharpen your focus like a laser. It's why Shane can learn to land a plane, Gordon can in-line skate at warp speed through the worst Hong Kong traffic and I can plug a leak on a sailboat in the middle of the high seas. Use your imagination to manufacture and exaggerate situations of danger when you know you need to focus.

- **Exercise.** I cannot state this enough. Physical activity just before you need to concentrate on something—be it homework, an important conference call or thinking through a complex problem—will increase dopamine tone and help trigger hyperfocus. That's why many ADHDers prefer to walk around when having a phone conversation or when thinking about a project. Try to incorporate brief periods of exercise—even if it is just a quick walk in the morning before work, at lunch or in the evening before homework.

Of course, if you find that you are forcing your attention on daily pursuits more often than not, you may need to consider other, more global changes to your career or lifestyle. ADHDers often find that when they change their environments to something more stimulating—going from a desk job in a bank to a sales position that requires travel, for example—they suddenly find themselves able to pay attention with laserlike focus, and their careers take off. They move from a work situation that's static to a vocation that's more dynamic, with a steady stream of variety and challenges that feed the reward center of a brain that is "hardwired for novelty-seeking."

If you still haven't found your fit, take heart. There is plenty of variety in what the best career for you might be. There are countless ways to ignite your passion and constructively flick that hyperfocus switch. But more on that in these next chapters.

PART III

Finding Success

CHAPTER TEN

The Entrepreneur's Superpower

After spending the day at one of his six computer repair stores, Shane Jordan noticed a slight security breach. But when he went back to review the store's security footage, the minor incident wasn't what caught his attention. Instead, Shane, whom you met in the previous chapter, couldn't help but notice that, while the rest of his staff were staying in one place, working with their heads down throughout most of the five-hour tape, he was the only one moving in fast-forward. Watching himself buzzing endlessly from task to task, never sitting still for more than thirty seconds, was a lightbulb moment.

"I thought, 'Holy crap! I really *am* different from everyone else,'" he recalls. "Just watching myself was exhausting!"

For years, Shane had felt his high energy was a curse. But today he views it as a blessing, because his low boredom threshold, ability to hyperfocus, calculated risk-taking, resilience, bingo brain and restlessness—that continual desire to be moving from one thing to the next—are qualities he sees as his entrepreneurial strengths. He now believes these tendencies are precisely why he has already become a successful entrepreneur, with a thriving and ever-expanding business while still just in his twenties. (Shane turned thirty in 2014.) He's absolutely right. ADHD was his superpower.

Of course, growing up, Shane didn't see his ADHD as an advantage. Until a few years ago, when he noticed more media chatter about business leaders having this trait, Shane had always assumed that something was wrong with him. It was the usual story. He didn't finally get diagnosed until he was a teenager, and even though he scored high on IQ tests, school was a struggle. He was never a troublemaker, but the idea of sitting in a classroom all day still gives him nightmares.

"I wanted desperately to be able to sit down in class, study and do my homework like everybody else. I was unable to conform and could never understand why," recalls Shane, who spent most of his childhood battling who he was, with the help of plenty of authority figures. "My teachers told me I would never succeed."

Shane soon proved them wrong. College, where he studied prelaw and got his BA, was better, but he had the insight to know that the career track he was on—sitting in a law office for hours poring over contracts—was not for him. Luckily, he had a fallback, as a "computer nerd" who'd been making extra money since his teens helping folks out with their technical difficulties. In fact, the one thing he was able to sit still for was tinkering on computers. He could spend hours taking apart and putting together electronic devices, relishing the challenge of solving a problem and finding ways to make something broken work again. So he started a small business on the side fixing iPods in New York City, where he'd been living and working since he graduated, eventually growing it into Repairs World, the tech repair company that fixes everything from shattered iPhone screens to Xbox 360s.

The business allows him to leverage all of his ADHD strengths. Unless he is in hyperfocus mode, Shane gets bored if he has to stay on one job for too long, but having six shops actually requires him to be constantly multitasking. Shane accomplishes a lot in one day, "maybe not sequentially," he admits, but his high energy not only gets things done, it helps him to cope:

"Working on a whole bunch of things constantly throughout the day is exhausting, but I would not have it any other way."

The variety of challenges in his work also keep Shane engaged. No single computer or iPad glitch is identical, and when customers come in for help, he has to come up with a diagnosis and prescription on the fly. With technology constantly evolving, his work is never routine, and that suits him fine. When he is hyperfocusing, he will spend hours researching and "vacuuming up" information to develop new ideas, like advertising slogans and franchise plans. As his business grows, he is also continually tweaking his business model, coming up with solutions to make sure systems and procedures are in place to help him delegate and keep things running smoothly.

Shane's resilience is also custom-fit to his career path as an entrepreneur. He readily admits to making mistakes, especially early on in his business, when he tried to do it all. At times the adversity was so overwhelming, many others would have walked away, but Shane bounced back and learned from his failures. He's also not afraid to fail.

"To start my business I risked everything I had. I gave up my day job and put in all my savings," he explains. "Okay, it's not cheating death. The consequences of failing would have been moving back in with my parents, which was kind of scary."

He took a calculated risk, and the subsequent pressure he felt galvanized him into action. It wasn't a foolish risk: "I wasn't throwing $50,000 on red at the casino." But it was nevertheless a throw of the dice that many others, especially those without ADHD, would be less likely to take.

The Entrepreneurial Gene

Shane has plenty in common with the dozens of other successful entrepreneurs and CEOs I interviewed for this book. Studies have shown that a tendency to be self-employed and an entrepreneur is dominant in individuals with ADHD. One study of twins in particular, out of the United Kingdom, found that the gene variation associated with ADHD, what we defined as the "explorer gene" in Chapter Four, has a huge influence on business ownership.

It makes sense. Those with ADHD in prehistoric times were constantly looking for fresh hunting grounds, water supplies and sites for a new place to settle. Village life made them restless, so they felt the urge to keep moving.

Sensation-seeking is also more common among entrepreneurs than in the general population. Several anecdotal reports bolster this point, saying that people with ADHD are three times more likely to own their own business. It takes an adventurous spirit to strike out on your own. Entrepreneurship fits perfectly with the ADHDer's need for stimulation and a willingness to take risks. The greatest success stories in business took a leap based on what they saw in the marketplace at a particular moment in time. Rejecting solutions that seemed to be "normal," they instead trusted their instincts and forged ahead with something new and unproven while their more risk-averse peers shook their heads and insisted it would never work.

These ADHD entrepreneurs are also creative, with high energy and an ability to hyperfocus on something they find innately interesting. This gives them the ability to spend limitless amounts of time accomplishing any task necessary to take their business to the next level. They thrive under pressure, or, as ADHD entrepreneur and career coach Laurie Dupar puts it, the ADHDer "eats chaos for breakfast." In addition to being easily bored with routine and the status quo, those with the ADHD trait tend to thrive in times of crisis.

A recent study by Johan Wiklund, an entrepreneurship professor at Syracuse University in New York, bolsters the case. Johan, who partnered with the Stockholm School of Economics in Sweden for the soon-to-be published research, noticed an unusually high number of people in his field with traits such as ADHD who are entrepreneurs, and a surprising dearth of academic research on the topic. He notes a 1993 *JAMA Psychiatry* study that found elevated rates of self-employment and a 2013 Dutch study that touches on higher entrepreneurial intentions among people with ADHD, but little research that examines a causal link between these tendencies and the diagnosis, and certainly nothing that looks at these qualities in a positive light.

"I find it remarkable that research on the potential benefits of ADHD is virtually nonexistent in scholarly journals," he shared with me. "For example, no articles mention hyperfocus. I think it is obvious to anybody who hangs around with people who have ADHD that they actually have the ability to be very focused on the tasks that interest them."

CEO Strengths

I could not agree more. Johan went on to list the strengths he sees as specific to entrepreneurship and ADHD:

> My initial and preliminary findings suggest that the actual ADHD symptoms can be positive. Impulsivity drives them to act despite uncertainty (uncertainty deters most others from action). They act intuitively and not planned or rationally. Entrepreneurs who have a hyperfocus within an area crucial to their business can be very effective and successful.

Johan decided it was time to focus on some of the psychological drivers for entrepreneurial action, delving more deeply into the many potentially positive iterations of the ADHD trait through the study of fourteen business owners with diagnoses of ADHD, including:

- Resilience and coping skills developed early in life can be "highly valuable in subsequent entrepreneurial endeavors." Successfully overcoming the challenges of having ADHD in a traditional classroom setting, for example, can build up the resilience needed to persevere through the many challenges and setbacks that can occur when building up a business.

- Impulsivity, acting without thinking or, as Johan puts it, "rapid decision making in situations that would, for most, require extensive analysis and deliberation," can be an advantage when hesitating and getting mired in all the complexities and uncertainties of a situation can result in a missed opportunity. Of course, it can lead to failure, but in a fast-paced, ever-evolving business landscape, little is certain, so going with your gut may be the best way forward.

• An ability to hyperfocus. Although ADHDers have difficulty focusing on tasks that do not interest them, they can get so absorbed in subjects and tasks they find pleasurable that they will even forget to eat and sleep. When they are in the "zone," they can become extremely productive and develop expertise, provided their area of business or industry mirrors their true passions.

• "Productive action under uncertainty." In other words, someone who is cool in a crisis and who thrives in chaos. As Johan puts it, "These characteristics lead to higher propensity for taking action despite high uncertainty." The combination of these kinds of proactive, intuitive and risk-relishing characteristics with expertise can lead to successful decision making in business.

• High energy. Several respondents in Johan's study said they had a higher work capacity and energy, and less need for sleep, than their non-ADHD associates—a useful quality when starting and running your own business or businesses, and something we've noticed about a large number of the ADHD success stories we've interviewed. He notes how a mother of three children in his study who works full-time and studies at university part-time routinely wakes up several hours before her family to work on her business while simultaneously developing other business concepts.

Of course, energy levels vary throughout the day, and many ADHDers are either night owls or, like me, routinely awake at 4:00 a.m., when they do their best work. Johan speculates this may be another reason why many opt to be self-employed. They aren't constrained by the typical nine-to-five office schedule. "Everyone I ask who has started their own business has this issue," he says. "They have all this energy in the middle of the night—that's often when they get their best ideas. But if they work in a regular job they can't start their day at ten a.m." It's often about being able to adapt their energy levels in a way that the situation requires.

The few researchers who have studied the personality types that tend toward entrepreneurship list many potential positives that overlap with ADHD's strengths. One 2013 United Kingdom study about the general entrepreneurship population found that these self-starters possess an abundance of traits associated with entrepreneurship, including extraversion, openness to experience and agreeableness. It takes an innate sense of optimism and self-belief, as well as an adventurous spirit, to strike out on your own—qualities that perfectly describe so many of the ADHD entrepreneurs interviewed here.

Entrepreneur = Multitasker

But I would add one other thing to this list of traits that many of these studies have missed: a desire to multitask. This strength lends itself perfectly to entrepreneurship because that's what owners of start-ups do: juggle many tasks at one time, from sales to research and development (R & D), admin and payroll. When you start something from nothing, you have no choice but to dart from task to task—like Shane in his computer repair business—doing everything for yourself until you can afford enough extra staff and infrastructure to delegate. It's a role tailor-made for people like us!

The entrepreneurs who have publicly embraced their ADHD are all very different, but their ability to leverage their ADHD traits as strengths is the common thread, and it's why so many high-profile CEOs are beginning to publicly embrace their diagnoses.

There's an ADHD pride movement emerging as the trait is embraced by prominent entrepreneurs in a multitude of industries. Paul Orfalea, the founder of Kinko's, couldn't write letters or fix photocopy machines, but his wandering nature lent itself perfectly to moving from store to store, observing and interacting with customers and understanding the big picture of what he needed to do, and who he needed to hire, to keep his service-based business competitive.

Consider also Sir Richard Branson, whose tongue-in-cheek ads for Virgin mobile say it all. Even as a red-bearded toddler, the airline, entertainment and media mogul was extremely busy: pulling phone wires out of walls, doing a brisk trade in lemonade out of his parents' hothouse, playing records at a children's garden party, delivering newspapers with laserlike precision from his bicycle and predicting a high-speed digital future to his disbelieving college buddies and an even less impressed girlfriend. In the ad, he's always rushing on to the next thing, a point driven home in a spicier version, in which he's seen leaving the bed of a woman, boasting about how fast he was. Both ads end with him in first class on his spaceship sipping champagne, a woman's red stiletto floating suggestively by.

The commercial is about how fast, innovative and forward-thinking Virgin Mobile's services are, but it might as well be a vignette of Sir Richard's ADHD, and the tremendous success that this business mogul's multitasking ways has brought him over the years. He is perhaps the archetype of entrepreneurs who launch business after business, driven by their curiosity, distractibility and short attention spans to create entirely new industries and business models.

The list of ADHD entrepreneurial success stories is a long one. Alan Meckler, Chairman and CEO of WebMediaBrands, has a famously short attention span. But it enables him to listen for the most important details and digest complex information, to grasp the big picture and spot the most relevant trends before his competition. It's a lightning-quick reaction time that's typical of many of the IT industries leading innovators. I've already speculated on the likelihood that the late Steve Jobs had ADHD. Other late, great business leaders with the trait may include Walt Disney, Andrew Carnegie and Malcolm Forbes.

Desk-Free

But a little self-awareness can help anyone unleash their entrepreneurial superpowers. During his fourth year of LSU's mechanical engineering program, Benjamin Blanchard, the twenty-seven-year-old serial entrepreneur from Louisiana whom you first met in Chapter One, began to realize that most engineers are less social and more analytical than he was, and seem content to sit at a cubical and crunch numbers. That wasn't him. Ben can do math with the best of them, but what he loves most is schmoozing with other people.

One summer, in between academic years, he became a property leasing agent, because a friend of his had a business. It was just something to earn a little extra cash, but his sales ability was so great that he ended up setting a record for the most leases in Baton Rouge. While at the leasing company, he met someone who turns over properties for the next occupant in an apartment complex—cleaning, painting and repairing.

Seeing Ben's sales abilities and contacts with property owners throughout the area, the guy suggested they team up to start what became a flourishing business. After the painting company, Ben started a janitorial company, to maintain all those properties they were contracting services to. The serial multitasker then started a transportation company, a medical sales company and is in the R & D phase of a nutritional supplement business, all based on ideas that popped into his head through random conversations with people.

Business Triage

Chicago-based business owner Bucky Buckman, who was first introduced in Chapter Nine, is another serial entrepreneur who figured out his superpowers early on.

Bucky, now forty-four, was one of those kids who was always busy. While "never much of an overachiever" in school, he managed to get B's and C's, but his real passion was numbers, especially those with dollar signs next to them.

It's not that Bucky set out to get rich, he was just naturally enterprising. A regular in his high school's "Breakfast Club," Bucky was able to get out of that punishment—sitting quietly in a classroom for the day with only two bathroom passes—by bribing his favorite chemistry teacher—the crazy scientist who used to appear regularly on David Letterman's show. Bucky would offer to tune up his bicycle for free in exchange for a pass out of what his school called the "Behavioral Adjustment Center," or BAC room. He told his teacher, who rode his bike every day to the school, to leave it in the wood shop, where Bucky did the repairs.

"It was then that I realized I had a gift for sales."

At sixteen, Bucky had a part-time job assembling and repairing Schwinn bicycles for $3.33 an hour. But what he loved to do even more was sell to the customers, and he got his first taste one day when none of the sales staff showed up. Bucky sold bikes to a whole family—the mother, the father and their son—and got such an adrenaline rush from the experience that "it was my cocaine." His father, a doctor, wanted Bucky to follow the same path, but when he got home that night, Bucky said, "Sorry, Dad. I don't know what I am going to sell, but I am absolutely going to be in sales."

Back then, "Schwinn was the shit," recalls Bucky, who got his first big business idea from the owner of that bike shop. Typically, a new customer would have to wait two weeks after purchase for the bike to be assembled and ready to take home. To beat the competition, Bucky convinced the owner to break all kinds of labor laws so that Bucky could have all the bikes preassembled and ready to be taken home the day of purchase. He used his ADHD energy and hyperfocus to stay up all night on the shop floor, bringing out dozens of new bikes for assembly each day. Next, he made up a sign to put outside the shop, advertising same-day delivery. From that point on, business had never been better.

But the budding entrepreneur wasn't done yet. He did the math and realized that the sales markup for bike accessories like helmets and locks was much higher at 200 percent for a lock versus 15 percent for the bike. So he went to his local library and pulled police reports about local bikes being stolen, along with articles about head injuries from bike accidents, laminated them and posted them next to an in-store display of locks and helmets, selling these items to every customer who walked into the shop. He convinced the owner to pay him 10 percent commission on all accessories sold.

"I started making up to four hundred dollars a week extra and I loved it! That was my launch," Bucky recalls.

But Bucky was fortunate to have mentors early on in his career. The manager of that bike shop introduced him to one of his in-laws at a wedding, who happened to be a senior executive in the trade show industry. He hired Bucky to work in sales after he graduated from college and became "like a second father," teaching him every aspect of the trade show business. For seven years, he became the company's top sales rep, becoming the company's biggest revenue earner.

Creating a Context

Although Bucky was an employee of the business, he was effectively running a company as a 100 percent commissioned sales rep. He carved out a spot for himself that fit his ADHD strengths, breaking down elements of his job into positive revenue-generating and negative revenue-generating activities. Meeting clients live or talking to them on the phone made money, but coming up with price quotes, researching or calling vendors did not, and yet Bucky was spending about 80 percent of his time on negative dollar-generating activities. Showing his boss the numbers convinced him that Bucky should hire a project manager and assistants, so that Bucky could concentrate on his first love, sales, which then quickly multiplied.

When the company eventually sold, Bucky left to accept a minority partnership in a firm that manufactured metal trussing and sold exhibit installations in five locations across the country. This time, he had to build the business from scratch, learning everything from banking and payroll to how to drive a forklift to building crates and designing on the computer design program AutoCAD—even though Bucky had barely learned to turn on a computer before then. "It was the MBA I never got," he recalls. Because he'd just married and moved to Orlando, it was one of the toughest years of his life, but Bucky's high energy and ability to multitask helped him get things up and running until that company liquidated, prompting him to move back to Chicago and start his own trade show business. Today, Bucky owns an exhibit/event company that has been recognized three times by *Inc.* magazine as one of the five thousand fastest-growing companies in America, and sits on multiple community, charitable and corporate boards. His ADHD strengths have served him well on various business, social and personal fronts.

Natural-Born Risk-Taker

Bucky has also entered the real estate game, because the trade show business practically runs itself now, and he needs new challenges. After the real estate market crashed, he decided to buy up foreclosed townhomes at rock-bottom prices and rent them out to families who'd had perfect credit until it was destroyed by the mortgage crisis.

As a husband and father of twelve-year-old triplet girls and an eleven-year-old son, and owner of a couple of Swiss mountain dogs, Bucky was warned by friends and associates that he was gambling with his family's future. But Bucky didn't see it that way. It was one of many calculated risks he's taken without a moment's hesitation.

"I didn't even recognize it as one of my ADHD strengths until midcareer, but my ability to make rapid-fire decisions with limited information and make them in a confident enough manner in front of others, so that they can run with it, is what makes me a successful business owner and leader today," says Bucky, who believes that his successes will outweigh his failures because he got to market first.

He may be on to something. At latest count, Bucky owns ninety-eight fully leased homes, along with a growing commercial-property, land and improved-lots portfolio. He's so busy, in fact, that during the twenty minutes he was speaking with me on the phone he was dealing with over fifty-five incoming emails related to his exhibit business, a complex commercial property transaction involving the sales of two buildings that were closing that day, and a cancer charity marathon that he'd volunteered to organize. "This is my happy place," he says. "If I was sitting at a desk all the time, I wouldn't be nearly as stimulated as I am now."

A Place Where You Belong

Dozens of other successful business owners interviewed for this book were instinctively drawn to the entrepreneurial path. Others find themselves hitting a career wall, and entrepreneurship becomes a way through.

DeShawn Wert, who worked as an educator, used to achieve success in her job by "working harder and staying longer." But that no longer worked when she became an administrator, where politics, process and time management became more important than results. Her tendency to hyperfocus caused her to focus on a single project and miss meetings, and sitting in endless conferences that achieved nothing was torture.

"I couldn't be who I genuinely was," recalls DeShawn, who was first diagnosed at forty-eight. "I had gotten into education to help people, but this was much more about winning and do as I say. It was not serving a bigger purpose."

DeShawn, was especially frustrated by the "busywork," and the inane decision making of the group. Her solution was to start her own coaching and consultancy company, and take on a part-time job administering a private preschool, a position that gave her the flexibility to develop her business on her own terms.

"I still get that kid connection, which I love, but I get plenty of bandwidth to work on other things I am passionate about."

Campus CEO

Many ADHDers, like Brian Scudamore, the bingo brain CEO from Chapter Seven, find out their purpose as business leaders before they even finish college. When he was in college in Vancouver, Canada, and trying to figure out a way to make extra money to pay for his room, board and tuition, he spotted an old pickup truck for sale in the parking lot of a McDonald's. It had plywood sides with the words MARK'S HAULING on the side, and it gave Brian the idea to start up a hauling business, so he scraped together $700 from the little savings he had to buy the vehicle. It quickly became a thriving business, so Brian dropped out of college and, twenty-five years later, it's a $150 million empire with two hundred locations in the United States, Australia and Canada. Brian has also gone on to found two more businesses: a house-painting brand called WOW 1 DAY Painting and, most recently, a moving brand called You Move Me. And many more ideas are percolating in that bingo brain of his.

"As I learned of other entrepreneurs with the same need for a change of pace and desire to jump from thing to thing, I started to realize that what people label ADD or ADHD might be a badge of honor in the entrepreneurial world," Brian observes. "It's a gift, not a weakness. I need to leverage the parts that help make me who I am and take advantage of this opportunity."

Entrepreneurial Tool Kit

Of course, leveraging your entrepreneurial strengths requires a set of tools. A propensity for hyperfocus is all well and good if it's related to your core business, but an all-consuming passion for a subject can also get you sidetracked from the jobs that need to get done. Multitasking can also result in a lack of follow-through, and bingo brain can distract from the development of a few solid ideas. What separates the ADHD entrepreneurial success stories is an ability to enhance those strengths and minimize their potential flip sides. They have tool kits that get them to the next level.

Brian recently wrote an article for the Canadian magazine *Profit Guide*, "Given to Distraction," which offers tips for others he describes as having EADD: Entrepreneurial Attention Deficit Disorder.

"I think all entrepreneurs have some variant of ADD in their DNA," he writes. "And, if you're like me, it sometimes makes you crazy! But EADD is also a good thing: it's part and parcel of our creativity and out-of-the-box thinking. But too often it gets in the way of running our business."

It's not a lack of ideas that's the problem, Brian goes on to say. It's the fact that we have so many, and no filter. We allow ourselves to get excited by an idea in the moment that may not be as important in the bigger picture. So he recommends having a "painted picture" of what the company you want to build will look, feel and act like at some point in the future. Then, whenever you come up with a new idea, ask yourself, "Will this bring me closer to my vision?"

"If the answer is no, toss the idea. (Experience has taught me that if you trash what could have been a good idea, it will eventually come back at you)," Brian writes.

It's great advice, and Brian gets systematic in the way he applies this principle to his daily working life. For the small, daily distractions, he has developed a tool he calls the "Top 3." Every Monday morning, he draws up a list of things that he needs to focus on that week, in order of importance. All three of these items must somehow get him closer to his big picture vision. He then draws up a Top 3 list for what he needs to do daily to ensure he achieves his weekly Top 3—a simple system that works.

Brian applies this rule to the distractions caused not only by his bingo brain, but by the many people who demand his attention throughout the day.

"If I don't think I have the time and energy to satisfy their needs without compromising the completion of my Top 3, then my goals win out," he writes.

Whatever Works

In addition to the Top 3, Brian uses multiple methods to help him stay focused. Changes of scenery are essential to helping him stay inspired and on task, so he allows himself to move regularly throughout the day. 1-800-GOT-JUNK doesn't have offices. Instead, people work in pods, or work areas of desks. Typically, Brian roams his headquarters with his iPad, switching from the lunchroom to various pods, seating himself near someone he needs to consult for help with solving a problem. He works in spurts, roaming the office halls until the next brain wave hits. Periodically he'll move to a favorite coffee shop near his office building, where a few strong espressos clear his head and the comings and goings of other customers create just enough chaos to keep him clearheaded and calm.

He schedules times throughout the day and week to put himself in places that inspire him, like the beach or, better yet, the woods near his house, where he will sit for hours on a bench with his iPad in a state of hyperfocus.

"I work best when I am in a new environment," explains Brian, who takes the same approach to his most important business meetings. This is true for many restless ADHDers, who benefit from the stimulation of a change of scene.

Brian recently did a "ski day" with his company president and right-hand man, conducting productive meetings on the hour-and-a-half drive to the mountain resort of Whistler, and having some of his most productive talks on the chairlift.

"The moving scenery helps keep me focused and engaged," says Brian.

But despite the freedom he gives himself to roam, this entrepreneur self-imposes plenty of structure through his calendar, which drives his day.

"My assistant knows that if something is not on my calendar, it does not get done."

He doesn't like a cluttered office, and he has his assistant go through and delete any nonessential email. The external order helps give him internal structure, free from extraneous information.

"I don't want to keep it all in my brain because there is already too much in there," says Brian, who's currently percolating ten different brand ideas and developing franchise operations along with balancing his time between a family of three kids and three growing companies.

"I can still do more. It's fun. It's a buzz," says Brian, summing up the sentiment that drives ADHD entrepreneurs the world over.

THE TOOL KIT

- Find something you love! Only then will you be able to maintain focus.

- Give yourself permission to fail a few times before you succeed.

- If you realize you are getting bored with a project, rethink it; it may not be for you.

- Embrace multitasking!

- Recognize you are a "big picture" thinker and will need an assistant or partner with detail orientation.

- Do a periodic brain dump. Writing the ideas down will lessen the distractions of your bingo brain.

- Leverage technology—like Google Calendar and Outlook—to impose structure and keep you on track.

- Prioritize and filter ideas. Don't worry about missing a great idea. If it truly is good, it will eventually percolate back to the top of the pile.

- Hire people whose strengths balance out your weaknesses—people with good follow-through skills and organizational ability.

- Know your own strengths and delegate your weaknesses.

CHAPTER ELEVEN

In the Zone

The ADHD Athlete

When former NFL quarterback Dave Krieg was in the huddle, he had seconds to call a play while also answering questions from running backs and receivers, thinking about the yards needed for a first down, the score of the game, the time on the clock, which player needed some extra motivation or an "atta boy," and which play could be run next based on the success of the last one. And all this was done while thousands of fans were screaming at the top of their lungs, which often made it hard to think, much less hear. So for those of you who think being an NFL quarterback is only about arm strength and accuracy, think again.

"You've got to have poise under pressure," Dave told me. "Being able to step into a huddle, be in the moment and assure your teammates that you can get all this done—you've got to thrive in these situations."

While he has never been formally diagnosed, it's clear from my conversations with Dave—one of the most prolific passers in NFL history, who played for the Seattle Seahawks, the Kansas City Chiefs, the Detroit Lions, the Arizona Cardinals, the Chicago Bears and the Tennessee Oilers—that he scores high on the ADHD continuum. He exhibits many of the hallmarks of the trait, and was a leader in a sport where success depends just as much as on mental agility as it does on physical ability. In my opinion, the strengths of ADHD help to give him that edge.

He's not alone. Michael Phelps, Terry Bradshaw, Pete Rose, Bruce Jenner, Justin Gatlin, Michael Jordan, Andrés Torres, Greg Louganis, Chris Kaman, Cammi Granato . . . the list goes on.

With so many medal-winning, record-breaking sprinters, swimmers, pro-ballers and Olympians diagnosed with the condition, there ought to be an ADHD Sports Hall of Fame. There is something about the trait that lends itself to athletic greatness. Equally, there is something about athleticism that helps to ameliorate the restlessness and distractions commonly associated with ADHD, allowing those who indulge their physical nature with exercise and sports to focus and perform better in many other areas of life.

It's a win-win, and something worth exploring as we develop, educate and treat the next generation of champions. It's also worth noting that many of the names on our list either never took stimulants or made the decision to go off their meds before making sports history.

Major League Connection

If the recent statistics put out by Major League Baseball (MLB) are to be believed, the incidence of ADHD among their ranks is twice as high as in the general adult population, at about 9 percent versus 4.4 percent in the population of adults ages fourteen through forty-four, according to a study commissioned by the National Institute of Mental Health in 2006. (In contrast with those under the age of seventeen, the adult population rate is about half has high.) Many sports psychologists extrapolating from this contend the percentage could be as high as 20 percent among the general pro-athlete population.

I can't vouch for these numbers entirely, because there's no telling if they reflect a higher incidence to aid and abet stimulant use, which has exploded in pro sports in recent years. However, they do make perfect, logical sense. Athletes with ADHD tend to perform better in sports that require hyperfocus—intense bursts of attention. They can be in the moment, with a heightened awareness of their immediate environment. They excel in chaotic conditions and thrive under pressure. They are risk-takers who can come up with creative, out-of-the box solutions, and they don't overthink, enabling them to make a play without hesitating over possible consequences. Their impulsivity, if controlled, can also lead to quicker reaction times, saving precious milliseconds that can mean the difference between losing or winning a game.

Of course, top athletes need to be physically and genetically blessed and possess the talent and discipline to train hard. But in the right sport, these ADHD traits are the ingredients that separate the good from the great. As Rob Manfred, executive vice president for labor relations and human resources at MLB, puts it:

"Our population doesn't look like the nation," he says. "We are younger. We are higher income, and there's no question attention is a key part of what these athletes do. So the idea that we would have a higher incidence rate [of ADHD] than the general rate is really not that surprising."

The Trait of Champions

Consider the trajectories of some of sports' brightest stars, and the prevalence of ADHD makes even more sense. Michael Phelps, who won a record-breaking twenty-two Olympic medals, was told as a child by a wrongheaded teacher that he'd never be able to focus on anything. He was bouncing off the walls, and the pool became a place where he could burn off all that extra energy. But it was also something that engaged him so much that he never missed a practice and would sit for hours waiting to compete. It gave him peace and a sense of success.

The athlete, known now as the world's greatest Olympian, does it all without meds. Put on Ritalin at nine, he hated it, and convinced his mother to let him go off the medication at the age of eleven. He knew more than his doctor and all his teachers realized, because the structure and discipline of his swim training carried over into his schoolwork. In fact, had he not come off the drugs, he may never have realized his true potential.

Justin Gatlin made a similar decision. The Olympian runner, gold medal winner and one of the world's fastest humans says racing helped him focus, and he came off his ADHD meds in 2001 after testing positive for a banned substance by track-and-field officials. Far from holding him back, being off ADHD drugs propelled him to the top of his sport.

Even before she knew she had ADHD, Cammi Granato scored more goals than any other player in the history of U.S. women's hockey. She was nicknamed "Little Tornado" by her parents, and all that energy helped lead her team to a gold medal at the 1998 Winter Olympics in Nagano and a silver at the 2002 Games in Salt Lake City.

"The sport doesn't require a lot of thinking," she told ADDitudemag .com in an interview. "You just react. You're in the moment. I was a natural at that."

Basketball was the one thing Dallas Maverick Chris Kaman was able to focus on in school, but meds were holding him back and keeping his weight down. At seven feet tall he was only two hundred pounds, so he'd get thrown around the court. But he stopped taking medication after winning a college sports scholarship. Not only did he get competitive enough to make the first round of the 2003 NBA draft for the Los Angeles Clippers, his grades also improved!

A Friendlier Place

It makes perfect sense that many with ADHD turn to athletics. As they struggle in school, sports become an escape route. These young men and women are willing to put in hours of training because it comes as a relief from the pain of the alternative: sitting at a desk and studying. It's something they're good at, and it's fun, which in turn helps build a level of confidence they don't find in academics. The field, the pool or the track become a friendlier place—their whole world. They become successful in sports because, for many, it's their only option.

"If it wasn't for football I'd probably be working a swing shift at a paper mill in Rothschild, Wisconsin," says Dave Krieg the quarterback, who struggled in school. "It gave me self-esteem and focus. It was kind of like my Ritalin."

Dave began playing football around the age of five, after watching his local team, the Green Bay Packers, on television back in the sixties, when his beloved Wisconsin team was winning championships. He'd always been fidgety and needed an outlet, playing sports like basketball and baseball. But football was the game that captured his imagination.

"I could visualize how the whole game should be played, and I took what I saw on the television into my backyard, playing one-on-one."

Dave moved on to tackle football, playing pickup games throughout middle school and practicing whenever he could. He had a good arm, although physically he wasn't the biggest kid—at six feet tall and weighing just 185 pounds he is unusually small for a quarterback, which may be why he never made all-conference in high school. But his secret weapon was his mind, which was much more advanced than his peers' when it came to strategizing and making plays. He could see where he needed to go, and how he had to get there. Being good, if not the best, built up his self-esteem despite his inability to focus or catch up in school, and he knew if he kept at it, practicing for hours a day, he could get better.

"God blesses you with a certain talent if you work at it," says Dave.

His high school career helped him make friends and "show the other guys what I could do." Hard work and practice got him into

Milton, a small private college in Milton, Wisconsin, that no longer exists. Dave started as a seventh-string quarterback on the school team, which meant he spent a lot of time on the bench. But his chance to show what he could do came in the fourth game of his freshman season, when he completed four passes, three of which were for touchdowns. He was such a strong and consistent performer that his coach had him start for the rest of his college career.

Next, he made the Seattle Seahawks as an undrafted free agent, starting out his NFL career as the ultimate underdog.

"I came from a small farming town and a college that no longer exists, I didn't have a scholarship, I didn't get drafted and had never even flown on a plane before, so for a quarterback I was a bit of an oddball," says Dave, who was competing alongside stars from top-tier Division I football schools who'd already been groomed for the big leagues and courted by the top NFL teams.

Poise Under Pressure

That first season was overwhelming for the farm boy. His first game was in front of seventy thousand people, and having to perform in front of all those people threw him into a panic. He started hyperventilating, and when he walked out onto the field, "I couldn't get past the end zone without putting my hands on my knees." But once the game started, his focus was laser-sharp.

"You feel like a gladiator with everyone looking at you," he says.

That pressure to prove himself and perform intensified early on in his NFL career when Dave was named starting quarterback. In 1983 his team made the AFC playoffs and won two postseason games before losing in the AFC championship game.

Dave was the perfect complement on a team of strong players, and he performed well throughout that season, but the other team's offense was stronger. It was a devastating blow.

"I didn't know I was good. I had all these big players telling me I was good, but I felt I had to keep proving myself."

Relentless Resilience

Because Dave was one of those players who never gave up, setbacks just made him work harder—another example of ADHD's resilience or, as Dave prefers to call it, "persistence." Knock him down and he gets back up, literally. In 1990, during a game against Kansas City, a team the Seahawks had never managed to beat, Dave was sacked by Chiefs linebacker Derrick Thomas—all six-three, 255 pounds of him—a record seven and a half times. And Dave's pummeling wasn't over. He got sacked two more times by other players during that game. But what's even more extraordinary was the way Dave was able to disrupt that eighth attempted sack by Derrick. He somehow whipped around and got free of him, or, as he now jokes, "I wore him out by letting him tackle me so many times."

That thwarted sack could have ended the game in Kansas City's favor, but when Dave escaped Derrick's grip he threw the ball to a teammate who leaped for a reception at the twenty-five-yard line, setting up a field goal.

"I thought I had him," Derrick told the sports media after the game, referring to Dave. "He just stumbled back and caught his balance and threw the pass. That last sack I didn't get is the one I'm going to remember."

Each time he was tackled, Dave got back into the huddle, and, with a minute left and no time outs, got his teammates focused and believing in the next set of complex plays, which they executed perfectly, driving the ball seventy-five yards.

It was multitasking for the big leagues, an ADHD strength that found its perfect context in Dave's role as quarterback. So was his nonlinear thinking. Dave had a way of seeing the situation on the field from multiple angles and coming up with plays that no one else would have thought of. The more chaotic and unpredictable, the better.

"I am a scrambling quarterback who, when I get out of pocket, can make things happen. I can see it better than if it was all one perfect geometric design," says Dave.

He likens his way of viewing the world to "one of those artists at charity events who throw paint at the canvas with music playing, dancing around as he's creating something that looks like nothing to other people until he's finished, then he turns the canvas and it's a portrait of Elvis or Mozart or somebody."

Being a quarterback leveraged Dave's strengths so perfectly that he did everything he could to stay in the game. When he lost his position as starting quarterback for the Seahawks, he took a pay cut to join another team, and another, and another . . . just so that he could keep playing the game he loved. It's why he holds the NFL record for most seasons in a career having played every play at quarterback in a year.

Drug of Choice

Deep down, on some level, Dave knew that being a quarterback was his ideal context—his way of using his ADHD energy and strengths to become successful and reach his maximum potential. It's why he played in 213 games over nineteen seasons, as well as in twelve post-season games. Despite the physical toll the sport was taking on his body, he never wanted it to end.

"There was nothing else I knew or wanted to do," he told me.

Since his retirement, after the 1998 season for the Tennessee Oilers, Dave admits to feeling a little lost. Those first few years he enjoyed the interests he developed in his off-seasons, like fishing, waterskiing, snow skiing and deer hunting. After almost two decades of intense physical workouts and pressure, he needed a break. But it wasn't long before he started missing the discipline, structure and camaraderie of the game. Above all, he misses the heightened drama of those moments when he was calling risky and complex plays during the last thirty seconds of a game. Those moments, and all the anticipation and training that went into being ready for those moments, kept his ADHD brain stimulated and focused. It gave him purpose and an outlet for all that gladiator energy.

Today, Dave is finding new contexts for his ADHD strengths.

Since his retirement in 1998, he has become a motivational speaker teaching leadership skills, as well as a real estate investor in Phoenix, where he now resides. He also became part owner of the indoor professional football league's Green Bay Blizzard team. He hopes to do more, using that poise under pressure and ability to multitask to develop more businesses, and channeling that passion and energy into a renewed sense of purpose.

"I know if I put my mind to it I can do a lot more," says Dave.

A Transfer of Skills

It's no coincidence that many of these athletes go on to become entrepreneurs and motivational speakers flown around the world to coach leaders at Fortune 500 companies. Many of the same qualities that make sports champions translate perfectly to the business world.

Tatiana, whom you first met in Chapter One, was a champion college volleyball player who competed around the world on Junior Olympic feeder teams. But she decided to apply her athletic discipline to academics and, later, the business world. The twenty-three-year-old, who was diagnosed with ADHD at four—an unusually young age—now works for a start-up incubator in Chicago after graduating magna cum laude in economics, finance and business law. And she attributes all of her successes in life to her athleticism, which gave her the structure and focus to channel her ADHD strengths to their maximum potential.

Tatiana began playing volleyball at ten. Before then, the second-generation Ukrainian-American was studying ballet, but there wasn't enough action to keep her ADHD brain stimulated and engaged. Volleyball, on the other hand, was an "immediate click."

She was so passionate about the sport she found she could zone out for hours, losing track of how much time she was practicing on the court. Typically, she would play for three hours a day and do lifting for an hour. That four hours, plus an hour each way between home and the gym, took up a huge chunk of her life throughout her teen years, "but it was not a sacrifice for me. I would go to any lengths to play volleyball."

It was a great way for her to channel all that excess energy. But what Tatiana enjoyed most was the immediate feedback of the fast-paced sport.

"I have a short attention span, so if I don't understand the value of something I won't put a hundred and ten percent of my effort into it," explains Tatiana. "But volleyball is so results-oriented, it gave me the immediate feedback I needed."

Volleyball taught her how to constructively harness all that ADHD restlessness, work with a team and commit to a goal. At the highly competitive level she was playing, the game also taught her to learn from her mistakes, as she rated herself daily and set benchmarks in order to surpass them.

"I kept pushing myself farther and harder to keep my competitive edge; it was always all or nothing. It's natural for someone like me to be an extremist," says Tatiana, referring to her ability to hyperfocus on the game she loved.

Her passion and hyperfocus on the sport made it easy for her to commit hours to practice. Her ability to be calm under pressure helped her to mentally slow down the chaos around her, enabling her to observe her external environment and make smart decisions right in the moment, under conditions that could fluster others.

"Being in tune with the environment is a big part of athletics and team sports," says Tatiana.

Thriving in Chaos

The volleyball court also became the perfect forum for Tatiana's impulsivity and risk-taking.

"Rash action is stimulating for my ADHD brain. Things are moving so fast in sports, and events are so unpredictable, that you have to react to things as they are occurring," she explains. Whether it was the personalities and relationships between the different players on her team, the direction of the ball or analyzing in microseconds the best position from which to slam home a point, "I am so tuned into everything that is going on in the moment, when things are flashing before your eyes. In fact, I kind of like it when the pressure is on." Tatiana exemplifies calm in chaos.

While she hated losing, she enjoyed the noticeable improvements and challenged herself to get better, demonstrating the ADHD strength of resilience.

But in college Tatiana became disenchanted with the level of playing, which wasn't challenging enough, and decided to focus on her studies. This happens often with ADHDers. They will find an interest, play it out as far as it can possibly go and then move on. It's not that we give up on it entirely—but it no longer is as all-consuming. Something else has come along to stimulate us and ignite our hyperfocus.

For Tatiana, that something else was academics, with the end goal of becoming an entrepreneur. Years of playing volleyball gave her a host of life skills that she could apply to being a good student. The game gave her an external structure and discipline, forcing her to show up on time, remember things and follow through because her other teammates were depending on her. It didn't hurt that being great at something also gave her a huge boost of confidence. She knew that if she could get better and better at volleyball, she could grow and maximize her potential in any endeavor.

"Getting that immediate feedback from volleyball, and being so result-oriented, motivated me to see myself improve, and that is exactly how I operate in my life today," she says.

She taught herself organizational skills, figured out how to prioritize and generally learned how to learn—by repeating back what she thought a teacher was saying, to make sure her understanding was correct, in much the same way she would take instructions from a coach.

"Athletics gave me the structure to continue to be successful, appreciate the value of teamwork and learn from failure. It's prepared me for a greater purpose," says Tatiana.

These days, at the small-business incubator in Chicago, she unleashes her ADHD bingo brain on innovative ideas for multiple business start-ups. As in the fast-moving plays on the volleyball court, she thrives in a business where different challenges come up every day. She can't switch off her mind, which is constantly coming up with innovative ideas, just as it came up with creative plays on the volleyball court.

"I feel like my ability to generate ideas and push the envelope—that innovative spark—is appreciated by my boss," says Tatiana, who has found a challenge that stimulates her ADHD brain as much as sports. "I love ideas that are new and unheard-of, and being at the forefront of a business with a level of unpredictability. But getting to this level would not have happened without sports," she says, adding that she still gets up early most weekends to play a few intense rounds of volleyball on the beaches of Lake Michigan. It keeps her sharp, both mentally and physically.

Getting Barreled

Former pro surfer Erik Heimstaedt discovered just how capable he was at focusing and remembering—two things that eluded him in school—when he took to the waves. A native of Newport Beach, California, he grew up around surfing and was encouraged by his father, who was also a surfer, to take it to another level and start competing when he hit middle school.

"With all of these problems I had in the classroom, I was the complete opposite when it came to surfing," Erik told us. "I could tell you exactly what went wrong or what I was thinking or feeling in the exact moment of a wave that I had caught months ago, whereas I couldn't have told you what I read fifteen minutes ago."

What he loved most about the sport was the fact that, for the hours he was on the water, nothing else existed. Getting inside the "barrel"—that hollow inside a curling wave when hundreds of pounds of seawater can crush down on top of a surfer in any given second—was his sweet spot. Time would slow down, and it was like "stepping away from reality." That sense of risk, and the clarity it gave him to make decisions that were exactly right in the moment, felt soothing, like a balm that took away all the frustrations of his struggles in school.

"You are in there, watching everything going on, and then you come out of that barrel feeling an adrenaline rush, with all this excitement and joy afterwards," Erik explains. "When I go surfing I know that for the most part I am going to have a good day."

Erik was obsessed with getting better at the sport he loved, and had his father film him from the beach so that he could watch himself later and see how what he was feeling out on the water actually looked like. He would then upload the footage to his computer and study every wave for hours, going click by click. Although he couldn't study his academic work for more than fifteen minutes at a time, Erik's ability to study and memorize each wave is a testament to the fact that ADHDers can focus and learn, as long as it is a subject they love.

"I thought that it was normal practice to just pick myself apart for hours, even going into the night, neglecting schoolwork, just to figure out how to change my body position during a particular maneuver," says Erik.

His father noticed this intense focus and told him that if he could apply it to school he would become extremely successful. But nothing quite captured him the way a wave could, so Erik continued to struggle with his academics. Then, when he graduated from high school, his parents sat him down and asked him if he was going to continue as a pro surfer or focus on building a career on dry land. Realizing that the risk of injury was too high and could cut short his vocation on the waves, Erik decided to turn his attention to a college degree in business—the one topic that captured his interest almost as much, if not quite as much, as surfing.

At Pepperdine University, where the twenty-two-year-old has just graduated with a degree in business administration, Erik discovered that he could, in fact, focus on something else besides his sport. (Again, this was a phase shift similar to what we often see.) During a summer course on policy, which was considered the toughest in one of the most challenging majors at the school, he finished at the top of his class. He did it by tuning out everything else in his life, including surfing, spending every day in the library until 3:00 a.m. analyzing a company—much the way he could dissect in detail the break of a wave.

"I know I can do it, it's just a matter of me honing in and using that focus," says Erik.

Part of his ability to focus and commit his attention to that class was fear. The class had been built up as the hardest, and Erik felt intimidated. Being nervous stimulated his brain and launched him into hyperfocus mode, just as a monster wave could.

Today, he wants to apply some of the ADHD strengths he has leveraged in surfing into a career in stockbroking, or possibly as an entrepreneur. He believes that all that time he spent studying the waves, enabling him to quickly adapt to changing conditions, makes him especially good at spotting new trends.

"I want to be able to apply that kind of thought process to the market," says Erik, who still surfs regularly.

A Daily Dose of Exercise

Just as sports can lead natural-born athletes on to other endeavors, athletics can help those with ADHD who may not be as physically blessed to find more focus. Unlike diet and nutrition, which we cannot say conclusively has much direct impact on the ADHD brain, the benefits of regular physical exercise can be huge.

A recent small study published in the *Journal of Pediatrics* compared two groups of twenty children with ADHD ages eight through ten who either did twenty minutes on a treadmill, or sat and read. They were then asked to complete a short reading comprehension and math test, as well as a computer game that assessed their ability to ignore distractions and focus on a goal. The children who exercised performed better.

"This provides some very early evidence that exercise might be a tool in our non-pharmaceutical treatment of ADHD," study leader Matthew Pontifex, an assistant professor of kinesiology at Michigan State University, said in a university news release. "Maybe our first course of action that we would recommend to developmental psychologists would be to increase children's physical activity."

Exercise works in both children and adults by activating the executive functions of the brain and causing a burst of neurotransmitters like dopamine and norepinephrine to be released in the brain, which affects focus and attention. It improves working memory, impulse control, problem solving, planning and organizational skills while boosting mood and confidence. It also boosts levels of a protein called BDNF, or brain-derived neurotrophic factor, which is involved in learning and memory—which tends to be deficient in those with ADHD. In effect, it acts as a stimulant without the side effects of medication.

Certain types of exercise, which require participants to pay close attention to body movements, can be particularly helpful in sharpening focus, according to Harvard clinical psychiatry professor Dr. John Ratey. He notes that studies have also found that tae kwon do, ballet, and gymnastics, which require close attention to body movements, focus the attention system. "A very good thing for kids and adolescents with ADHD," he says.

For both adults and children, dancing is indeed something equally physical that lends itself to the ADHD brain. Karina Smirnoff of *Dancing with the Stars* fame is a case in point. She got into dance because her parents realized that she desperately needed an outlet for her high energy.

"My parents tried anything and everything just to address my inattention and provide an outlet for my hyperactivity," she says. "They enrolled me in activities that held my interest like figure skating, ballet, gymnastics and playing the piano."

Dancing in particular has helped her to channel that energy into something that has given her an incredible career, with sixteen seasons of the hit show under her belt. As a five-time U.S. National Champion, World Trophy Champion and Asian Open Champion, she's without a doubt one of the top dancers in the world, and that extra ADHD energy is a big reason why.

Even after practicing fourteen to sixteen hours a day, she could keep going. The restless Ukrainian beauty never gets tired.

"Dancing is one of the few things I can really focus on," Smirnoff says. "It's never boring, and that's very good for someone with ADHD."

The good news is the kind of exercise that's needed to make a difference doesn't require any special skills, artistic grace or athletic prowess. The trick is simply to find something you enjoy doing enough to be consistent, so that your ADHD brain doesn't get bored and move on. And make sure you get your heart pumping with some cardiovascular activity.

Until recently, Bucky Buckman, the trade show and real estate entrepreneur you first met in Chapter Nine, had always done weight training. He was never a fan of more rigorous, steady workouts that raised his heart rate until he came across some research suggesting exercise that increases blood flow can help him activate neurotransmitters and improve cognitive function.

"Think of it like your lawn. You have thousands of ungerminated grass seeds that can be sitting there stagnant for years, just waiting to be activated, and the only way to activate these grass seeds in your brain is to exercise," explains Bucky.

Taking this new information to heart, he signed up for a charity marathon, and loved the adrenaline rush he experienced, followed by the relative calm and focus it gave him throughout the rest of the day. Now he makes a point of getting up early to run and get his heart rate up to at least 70 percent of his max for twenty minutes each morning. He still doesn't love running, but he's so thrilled with the way it makes him feel afterward that it has sparked another passion.

"It helps get my blood flowing, so I am prepped and ready to go into battle," he says. "After my run, I can take on the most problematic issues of the day."

So exercise is one of the most fundamental tools in the ADHDer's tool kit.

THE TOOL KIT

- Try—or let your child try—many sports until you find the one that captivates. The ADHD brain often needs to sample a few things first.

- We ADHDers need to be passionate enough about something to put in the hours necessary to become champions. So find something, or several things, you love to do.

- Being good at a sport will help build confidence that can translate to other areas of life that are more of a struggle.

- Remember, it's not just physical. Great athletes can leverage mental agility. Know that you can adapt this strength to any other circumstances.

- Certain types of physical activity may be better at sharpening focus than others—such as dancing and martial arts, which require you to pay close attention to body movement.

- Team sports can help hone interpersonal skills in dealing with others. Something the ADHDer may otherwise find difficult.

- Committing to a competitive sport requires discipline and structure. From sports we are more likely to come up with organization tools that help us to show up on time for our teammates and coaches.

- While winning builds confidence, losing enables us to leverage one of our key ADHD strengths: resilience.

- Even if you are not an athlete, daily bursts of physical activity will help you sharpen your focus.

- Just make sure that activity is something you enjoy doing enough to do it on a regular basis. Consistency is key.

CHAPTER TWELVE

Relationships

Life of the Party

If there is one thing Ty Pennington can't live without, it's his long-time girlfriend and manager, Drea Bock. As someone who is grounded, practical and focused on the details, she complements him and keeps him on track.

"When you have ADHD, you've got to find someone with the right amount of patience and a lot of organizational skills who is also secure, with their own purpose and social life," says Ty, who feels fortunate that he has found the whole package in his significant other. "She's someone who is excellent at handling the chaos of other people's lives."

Ty's own experience is something I've found to be true of most ADHDers—opposites attract. In many ways, though it sounds extreme, someone with OCD would be the perfect mate, because their strengths—remembering details, following through, executing and perfecting an idea—fill in our gaps and complete us. Or, as Ty puts it:

"We bring the fun, but we need the function."

That just about sums it up. Those of us with ADHD can be the life of the party, so curious and excited to meet a variety of other people that you'll often find us in the middle of the room, surrounded by a laughing crowd that's enjoying our quirky observations and humor. We tend to be a gregarious bunch, with a wide and eclectic collection of friends. While there's no research on this topic, and the underlying reasons remain unclear, many of us seem to have charisma in abundance, with a sense of humor, adventure and fun that tends to draw others into our orbit. We love being out in the world, bouncing from conversation to conversation, and are up for anything. But we always need that anchor, that person who gently reins us in and keeps our ADHD from veering into dysfunctional territory.

Opposites Attract

That doesn't necessarily mean that finding your opposite is a must. Of course, it is possible to form lasting, healthy relationships with all kinds of personality types. But, in our closest relationships, ADHDers in particular require balance. It's the one thing I have noticed both in myself and the hundreds of ADHD success stories we've interviewed. There is always someone: a spouse, a business partner, friend or family member, who is the ying to our yang; who completes us, romantically or otherwise. Leveraged and understood, a healthy relationship is key to maximizing our full potential, in our careers, in our businesses and our lives in general.

But it can take time to find that person, especially when it's a romantic partner. Just as we need to try out a few careers and lifestyles to see what fits, we may need a few tries before we figure out the kinds of partnerships and friendships we need in life to keep us on track. The good news is that our low boredom threshold will act as a natural filter, to help us find the right person. Once we find our mates, there are multiple steps to make sure that the partnership is healthy, and that both sides are accepting and supportive.

Getting to Know You

One of the issues that comes up when we get together with our opposite personality type is that at times it can seem like we come from different planets. It's alluring and confounding at the same time.

"Everyone I speak to is in a relationship with someone quite op-posite to them," notes Shanna Pearson, the ADHD coach whom you first met in Chapter Two. "Those with ADHD tend to have totally organized partners who are more linear; it drives a lot of them crazy, but at the same time it is what they are attracted to."

As it happens, ADHDer Shanna is married to someone she de-scribes as "calm and organized." Jeremy, who also has ADHD but is much lower on the continuum, is Shanna's business partner, life part-ner and helpmate at home, where they have young children. But it's a shared responsibility, with give-and-take based on truly trying to understand what it is like for the other person. If things aren't work-ing, consider a therapist or a coach. This mutual appreciation can come through a neutral setting, and by talking things out with a third party, which is something Shanna and Jeremy encourage their clients to do.

"When you are seeing an ADHD coach, it's helpful to involve the non-ADHD spouse so they can understand what the ADHDer is ex-periencing, what kind of world they live in, and so that the ADHDer can hear how frustrating it is for the spouse at times," explains Shanna. "Understanding has to come from both sides."

What makes the ADHD relationship even more challenging is we ADHDers tend to be a rebellious bunch. We don't like being told what to do, question everything, and can get irritable and argumentative when we perceive someone as an authority figure. So if a partner starts telling us what to do, our knee-jerk reaction might be to turn around and do the opposite. It's not intentional. It's just one of the many ways we are wired differently from the people we love.

Work at It

So it's not all champagne, rose petals and joyful spontaneity, even when we've found "the one." Relationships take work, regardless of our individual traits, but they can be especially challenging for ADHDers. Our partners often misinterpret our forgetfulness and tendency to get distracted as lack of interest. People in our lives get frustrated when we habitually turn up late, and resentful when they have to pick up the slack for day-to-day chores and child care. The divorce rate is nearly twice as high for people with ADHD than for those without, according to Melissa Orlov, author of *The ADHD Effect on Marriage*, whose own marriage to an ADHDer nearly ended until she delved into the topic to understand it better.

That said, plenty has been written about the problems, especially from the perspective of the more linear thinkers in a relationship, and not enough has written about the "fun." ADHD relationships *can* work extremely well—they can even be tools for successful lives in and of themselves. Just as someone like Ty's partner can help keep their spouse calm, focused and functioning, ADHDers remind their partners how to be in the moment, take time out for their passions and go with the flow. Their resilience, and ability to laugh at their own quirks, can help their partners learn how to let things go. Hey, sometimes it can be healthy to just throw your hands up in the air and laugh. And sometimes an ADHDer's curiosity and enthusiasm for a new topic or interest can be infectious. Everyone could use a natural-born explorer in their lives.

After seven years of marriage, Guadalupe, the Spanish photographer you met in Chapter Seven, discovered how well she and her husband, Stefano, complement each other. It was a struggle at first, but things fell into place when she was finally diagnosed in 2013, at thirty, and both husband and wife began to better understand the differences that had been creating conflict.

"My husband is my opposite. He freaks out if we change plans, and I freak out if we plan a week ahead. But we are extremely in love, and finally we are living the way we always wanted to," Guadalupe says.

For those first years of marriage, there were many arguments. Neither of them understood why the relationship was so hard, and each thought the other was being unreasonable. The fights about her constant lateness, her inability to remember things and the fact that her mind could easily wander off right when he was midsentence were frequent, and when their first child was born, it got worse. Guadalupe was always tired, never able to sleep through the night, and that made it even more difficult to focus on the day-to-day tasks of her life.

The fact that she was dissatisfied with her job in communications—where she did not feel she was reaching her full potential—did not help. She started channeling what was left of her energy and attention into her hobby, photography, which was blossoming into a profession, and worked on taking and editing photos on the side, often during those sleepless small hours of the morning, leaving little quality time left for her and her husband.

"This has been a path that we have had to walk," says Guadalupe.

Her diagnosis lifted that insecurity Stefano felt about her behavior. Until then, he thought her lack of focus and forgetfulness about things that were important to him meant that she did not love him, but then he realized that was just the way her brain was wired and it wasn't because she didn't care. But this new understanding created new problems in their relationship. He went beyond acceptance and tried to do everything for her. It made Guadalupe feel like she was something broken that needed to be fixed, and felt it changed the dynamics of her relationship. Instead of feeling like the woman he loved and admired, she started feeling like his burden, noticing he was getting burned out, and that created a different kind of tension.

"I thought he wasn't having fun with me anymore," recalls Guadalupe.

Time and therapy helped, and the couple have come to terms with the contrasting ways their brains are wired.

"Now I feel the freedom to ask him to help me," says Guadalupe, who calls him when she gets stumped over scheduling issues to ask him to help her come up with a realistic timetable. He also takes care of "things I am not good at," like the family finances.

Stefano, in turn, benefits from her example. He used to be "rigid" with his job, never doing anything that he didn't consider to be practical. The responsibilities of being a husband and father took over, and he gave up one of his passions, music, until he saw how fulfilled his wife was when she followed her dream of becoming a photographer. Now he blogs about his favorite music genres—punk and hard rock— which gets him free tickets to concerts and opportunities to interview his idols.

"Looking at me, he realizes he can live for the moment, and nothing is as urgent as life and death," says Guadalupe.

In fact, her calmness amid chaos has helped him through some major crises. Although both are earning money, in Spain's economy their clients and employers don't always have the liquidity to pay them on time.

"The other week we literally ran out of money, and I had to turn down a job because I couldn't even pay for parking," Guadalupe says with a laugh. "But when things go extremely wrong, I am fine. I love the excitement."

Stefano still panics under those circumstances but looks to her as his rock and trusts that they'll both survive.

"And meanwhile I trust him to organize a family weekend that won't cause me to sink into the nothingness of routine!" says Guadalupe.

At their best, and with awareness and understanding, they balance each other out.

Mixed Signals

But lack of awareness can wreak havoc when couples enter into a relationship. When one spouse has ADHD and the trait has either not been diagnosed or is not properly understood, it can lead to unhealthy patterns as the more linear thinker in the partnership reacts to some of the typical things his or her partner struggles with, including:

- **Difficulty paying attention.** "Where did you go just now?" is a typical annoyed remark heard by ADHDers, whose minds often wander in the middle of a conversation. We also have a tendency to interrupt by blurting out whatever we are thinking in the moment. This can make partners feel as if what they have to say isn't important.

- **Forgetting to follow through.** Let's admit it. We're not good at remembering birthdays or anniversaries. We may have every good intention of picking up the milk on the way home, but get distracted by a great song on the radio. Not being able to finish what is expected of us can again be misinterpreted as a lack of commitment or caring.

- **Our minds are all over the place.** As a result, we may forget to pay the bills, or get distracted and walk away from a task, leaving an open can of turpentine for a furniture refinishing project, which gets knocked over by the dog and tracked through the house, infuriating our better halves.

Partners of people with ADHD need to know what they are signing up for. Even when there is awareness about ADHD, and our partner is attracted to our energy and zest for life, we can be a lot of work. Let's face it, while we are off being visionaries, hyperfocused on that creative pursuit of the day, we are not necessarily paying the bills, watering the flowers or taking care of the kids, and often that burden falls on the shoulders of the person in the relationship who is good at executive functions. No matter how much love, compassion and understanding the non-ADHD person has, it can be exhausting, especially if they are not prepared for it.

The Wrong Fix

And "fixing" the problems can often make things worse—because the person doing the fixing may not understand that what seems like the most logical approach simply does not sync with the way the ADHD brain is wired.

Take list-making, for example. Lists are always helpful tools for

ADHDers, whether the ADHDers are writing up an inventory to get ideas on paper, establishing a set of goals or simply reminding themselves of things that need to get done. Lists can also be useful ways for partners to remind ADHDers about things that need to get done. They can be effective ways to share responsibilities. But the key to successful list-making for ADHDers lies in the presentation. Often a non-ADHD spouse will assume that all they need to do is write up a schedule and give their partner a list of five things to do for that day—take out the trash, pick up milk, drop off the kids at school, etc. They may also repeat that list five times, thinking, *He's so smart, he'll be able to hear me; he'll know what to do.* But often our brain shuts off after the first two things on the list. We genuinely forget, and get distracted by something else. By the time we are halfway done with the laundry, we have totally forgotten what the other things on the list were. This then turns into a fight, because the spouse feels that what was important to her was not important to her partner.

"How many times do I have to tell you?" he or she might say, while the ADHD partner shuts down and sulks (although usually not for long).

"They start thinking of their mother, their teacher and all those people in their lives telling them they are not enough," explains Aaron Smith, the ADHDer and motivational coach you met in Chapter Six. This causes the ADHDer to start beating themselves up, which is counterproductive, "because you can't be motivated when you are feeling bad about yourself." Instead, those old feelings of anxiety and self-doubt creep in, and the ADHDer avoids the tasks altogether. It's not that they don't care about their partner's wants or needs, or that they have no desire to do it successfully. Quite the opposite. They are afraid to fail yet again.

Symptom-Response-Response

It's part of a vicious cycle that Melissa Orlov calls "symptom-response-response." The so-called symptoms of our trait aren't necessarily the problem so much as how the non-ADHDer reacts to it. So if you as an ADHDer don't appear to be listening as your partner is speaking because you are lost in thought inside your bingo brain, you partner may feel dismissed or ignored. Understandably, the non-ADHDer reacts in anger, which causes you to withdraw even further into whatever it is that is more stimulating and fun to think about than the present reality.

Aaron suggests a different approach. The burden shouldn't fall on the non-ADHD partner to come up with all the solutions. Instead, a couple should work on them together, taking into account the different ways our ADHD brains function. So instead of giving that list in the morning, for example, a couple could create a Google household calendar to send the ADHDer Google alerts throughout the day as task reminders. Or simply send bulleted texts spaced throughout the day, with no more than one or two items at a time. They are neutral reminders, done through technology, that lessen the stress of a spouse who might otherwise feel the need to constantly remind an ADHD partner of all the things he or she is supposed to do.

"That way, you take the non-ADHD partner out of the role of enforcer or helping professional," says Aaron. "It avoids triggers for self-esteem issues, or anything that makes the ADHD partner feel like they need to do better."

Mood-Killer

This also takes the non-ADHDer out of that parental role, or what Orlov calls the "parent-child dynamic." If the ADHD partner isn't using the tools to leverage the trait and become more reliable, she says, the one without ADHD will start taking on more and more responsibilities—much the way Guadalupe's husband did. The partner without ADHD becomes overwhelmed and exhausted, viewing their spouse as the child in the relationship, and the one with ADHD starts to see their partner as more of a caretaker or authority figure. Not only can this turn the non-ADHDer into a parent, it's a definite mood-killer! This is true for both the ADHDer and the non-ADHD partner, and why many spouses I spoke with say that, while they are supportive and compassionate, they try to take a step back and not get too involved.

"A lot of times the non-ADHD spouse becomes the full-time organizer," says Shanna Pearson. "It's hard for them to be attracted to someone they have to remind to bring their lunch to work every day."

So don't think your ADHD gives you a free pass to let your partner shoulder all the mundane tasks of life. This is key. We have to take responsibility too; we have to at least try. It's not a case of, "Accept me as I am, like it or not." The ADHD partner has to take responsibility, otherwise it will impact the marriage.

Conversely, the non-ADHD spouse needs to learn to relax. Heidi, the other half of Chicago entrepreneur Bucky Buckman, for example, approaches the typical ADHD situations with a healthy sense of humor. Whenever they are talking and she sees him going into bingo brain mode, she shouts, "Squirrel!"—referring to the dog character in the movie *Up*. The fact that the dog keeps getting distracted and chasing these rodents, even in the middle of the most urgent dialogue, is so bang-on that it gets the whole family laughing, and reminds Bucky in the nicest possible way to bring his focus back to them.

Gentle Guidance

There's plenty of solid advice out there for couples in ADHD relationships if you know where to look. On the website Psych Central, Margarita Tartakovsky, based on an interview with Melissa Orlov, came up with a number of helpful suggestions for ADHD and non-ADHD partners to work with each other while keeping the spark alive, and I have paraphrased, clarified and elaborated upon a few of these in this list:

• **Be patient.** As you're starting to work on your relationship, an ADHD spouse may react defensively, assuming they'll be blamed for everything. Persist anyway. Once they realize the non-ADHD partner is also willing to change and adapt, managing their own anger or tendency to nag, the defensiveness will subside.

- **Make time to connect.** This is key. Relationships need to be sustained by attending to each other's needs beyond the day-to-day logistics of life, whether that's scheduling time for a dinner date or, yes, even sex. We ADHDers can get so carried away with researching something on the computer, for example, that by the time we think to go to bed, it's 3:00 a.m. and our partner is already asleep. Another mood-killer!

- **Empathize.** "Put yourself in their shoes. If you don't have ADHD, try to appreciate just how difficult it is to live every day with a slew of intrusive symptoms. If you do have ADHD, try to understand how much your disorder has changed your partner's life," writes Tartakovsky. I couldn't have put that one better myself!

- **Remember why you love this person.** This may seem obvious, but when you are so focused on scheduling, planning and bringing order to the chaos of your lives together, you might forget what attracted you in the first place. Guadalupe's husband needed to learn to stop taking care of her and simply sit back and appreciate her passion, curiosity, free spirit and stunning beauty.

- **Don't try harder, try smarter.** Trying too hard can lead to huge disappointment, despair and resentment. But what might seem like the logical answer simply may not be an "ADHD-friendly" strategy based on a clear understanding of how the ADHD brain does and does not work.

- **Avoid the blame game.** Without insight into how the ADHD brain differs from a non-ADHD brain, there is a tendency to blame the ADHD partner. But just as neither one of the couple is to blame, both are responsible for coming up with realistic ways to share tasks and improve how a relationship functions.

- **Don't set the ADHD spouse up for failure.** It's not helpful to insist on teaching an ADHDer how to do something that is simply not one of their strengths. Share tasks, by all means. Have expectations, but make sure they are realistic. If you are going to cook a meal together, for example, let the ADHDer get creative with the ingredients while the non-ADHD partner remembers to screw the top back on the chili powder container and put away the knives. It's fine to let your restless spouse clean up, but don't expect her to follow through with drying and putting the dishes away. By then she will have been distracted and moved on to something else. As Orlov suggests, repeat this mantra: "I am never my spouse's keeper. We will respectfully negotiate how we can each contribute."

Too Much of a Good Thing

Yes, it's a long list. Making an ADHD/non-ADHD relationship work takes serious commitment. But it's probably better than the alternative.

Shanna's earlier relationships tended to be with other ADHDers. Still completely unaware that she had ADHD, she was attracted to their spontaneity and sense of adventure. It was part of her ADHD brain's need for stimulation and drama. But the relationships never lasted for long.

"Some of the most fun boyfriends I've had possessed the trait, but there was no way I could have married them," she says. "There was too much fire; it would have been explosive."

Again, you don't necessarily have to seek out your opposite for an intimate relationship. But be aware of the potential for burnout when you choose a mate among your own tribe. Anecdotally, Aaron Smith has observed that many of ADHDers' first marriages were with other ADHDers, often because neither party had a diagnosis or possessed the slightest self-awareness.

"That can be its own kind of storm," he says.

The same spark, excitement and impulsivity is what draws ADHDers together. They share a huge variety of interests and fuel each other's energy. But these intense connections, so appealing in the beginning of a romance, often fizzle out quickly. Both partners, if they haven't found ways to control the flip side of ADHD, and instead let it control their lives, end up living a life together that is so chaotic it is unsustainable.

"When you are each bouncing between different jobs and trying to do five different things at once, it can create a very stressful situation," notes Aaron.

Enjoy Your Tribe

Okay, so maybe dating another ADHDer isn't always the best idea. Our intimate, day-to-day relationships need a different kind of dynamic in order to last for the long term. But, outside of romance, we shouldn't seek out one personality type to the exclusion of another. As ADHDers, we need variety, and there is nothing more freeing and exhilarating than getting together with fellow members of our nonlinear tribe and letting topics bounce all over the place. We are natural adventurers, so we need to give ourselves the space to let our ADHD freak flags fly and be instantly understood. And when we do find each other, it's a relief.

Guadalupe experienced this recently when she met two other ADHDers at a party. She felt as if she'd known the men forever, and the conversation she had with them was completely open and in the moment.

"I recognized them like brothers," she told me. "We were like volcanoes, changing topics all the time and excited about everything."

Personally, I have noticed that most of my male friendships are with fellow ADHDers. It's not a conscious thing—it's a gravitational pull. Our common interests and energy bring us together, and we get such a kick out of being in each other's company. Many of my best friends I've made through whatever pursuit I am into and exhaustively exploring in that moment, whether it's playing poker, kayaking, sailing, cross-country cycling, investing, diamonds, real estate . . . And we pick up each other's interests. Durrell Hudson, the diamond importer whom you first met in Chapter Three, got me so much into diamonds I even completed my GIA (Gemological Institute of America) certification, for example.

I meet with some of these guys occasionally for a weekend trip. We'll happily sit there talking over one another for three days straight. It's our chance to go a little crazy. We open the gate and let our ADHD selves go run in the pasture. As we've gotten older and a little more settled, we're not as out there as we used to be, but I still need to be able to get together with them once in a while. Then, after one long weekend, I'm good for a while. I've had enough!

Accidental Friendships

These ADHD connections often happen by accident. We don't necessarily seek each other out, but somehow we always seem to fall into each other's orbit.

Bucky found himself surrounded by ADHD fellow travelers when he joined Vistage, a board of directors peer group.

"Literally fifty percent of my sixteen members absolutely have the 'condition,'" he told me.

Cynthia Kaye Alexander has noticed the same tendency in herself to fall into ADHD friendships. The former fashion model turned "crisis counselor" and life coach for a circle of prominent families, entertainers and CEOs, Cynthia was diagnosed later in life, when her adult son was identified as having the trait. It so happens that many of her dearest friends are also ADHDers, who find relief in the free flow and exuberance of each other's dinner party conversations.

"Anyone listening to us wouldn't have a clue what we were talking about," says Cynthia. "We'll start a topic, digress and then pick it up again two hours later, but we have no problem following the thread. We always understand each other." I can relate.

Daniel Sandler, a twenty-six-year-old entrepreneur from Manchester, England, feels the same way. Studying law, he didn't meet anyone who shared his trait, and often found himself misunderstood. But on a visit back home he reconnected with a platonic female friend who had since been diagnosed as well. Talking with her was a relief.

"Within five minutes we were talking about fifteen different topics. No one else would have a clue, but it was so much fun!"

Again, these nonromantic relationships are key, whether social, at work or within the family dynamic. We ADHDers thrive in company, and need a healthy balance of personality types to interact with to bring out our best.

Perfect Partners

In Daniel's case, the perfect complement is his father, and boss. When Daniel finished his law degree, he was lucky enough to land at his father's firm, which extends the supportive environment of the home in which he was raised. Daniel's dad knows that the drudgery of legal contracts and the routine of sitting at a desk put him to sleep, literally. (He was once jolted awake at his desk when his elbow slipped off the desk and his head crashed on the desktop.) So he assigns Daniel more responsibilities he knows will play to his son's strengths, such as engaging with clients and strategizing over business-related decisions for the firm. Daniel's father treats him as a confidant, sharing with him the inner workings of the office to get his son's insights and vision.

Daniel, in turn, has picked up some of his father's slightly OCD organizational tricks, such as a decluttered desk. His father's more methodological approach to decision making has also inspired Daniel to take more calculated risks in his new business venture, into which Daniel has invested the majority of his savings. (More on that later.)

"My father really balances me. It's a ying/yang thing, without question."

Brian Scudamore, the CEO of 1-800-GOT-JUNK? whom you first met in Chapter Seven, has also found the perfect partner in his company president.

"We are like two people in a box—stronger together than when we are separate," Brian told me.

Brian's bingo brain—his constant stream of ideas—is often hard for others to follow. Although he is able to see something in a complete picture, "I can't necessarily articulate that well to others." So he relies on his president to "dive deeper and extract the details" and then push those ideas forward.

"He is much more rigorous than me; always work, work, work, and he likes rallying the team and seeing the results happen," says Brian.

"I am about where we are going, and he is about how we are going to get there."

Bucky Buckman also leverages his relationships in business, and he is very deliberate about it. For each hire he uses a culture index—a questionnaire that takes into account all the personality traits and how they manifest in terms of speed of work, attention to detail, leadership style and so on.

"My attention to detail is absolute zero but my work pace is off the charts," says Bucky. "I am also very autonomous."

So he often hires people to be his project managers who are his opposite: detail-driven and less autonomous, therefore better able to take direction from him.

"The only time I have functioned well has been when I have had someone extremely detail-oriented sitting by my side," Bucky explains.

Charisma

Fortunately, Bucky, Brian and Cynthia have a quality that makes others want to execute their ideas and follow their lead: charisma. As noted ADHD expert and author Dr. Edward Hallowell observes, charisma could be regarded as one of the trait's gifts. Although there's no scientific way of measuring whether those with the diagnosis possess more charm than those without, anecdotal evidence abounds. In addition to having ADHD, charisma was the one thing the dozens of men and women who were interviewed for this book had in common. They had a kind of affability, a quirky sense of humor that was also self-deprecating and an openness and sincerity. Getting them to share stories and ideas was easy, because they were curious and excited to speak with someone new and make a connection.

Our lack of a filter can, at times, become a social and career liability as we blurt out our thoughts as they come, but it's an unaffected and open way of interacting with the world that's infectious. It's also the stuff that makes great leaders.

Christopher Lauer, whom you first met in Chapter Seven, is a great example of this. As the German head of a political movement comprised of young radicals throughout Europe, this young firebrand has a charisma and attitude that attracts thousands of voters. While still a somewhat fringe organization, under Christopher's leadership his party managed to win 8.9 percent of the seats in the Berlin city-state legislature in 2011.

Christopher has since become something of a local celebrity on the streets of Berlin, where he is best known for his quick-witted, fiery speeches calling for an overhaul of patent laws, greater freedom of information, civil rights and more direct participation in government. The young politician, who was diagnosed with ADHD three years ago at twenty-seven, mesmerizes audiences with his powerfully articulated ideas about the power of Google and copyright law reform.

"Speeches and debates, that's where I do well," Christopher told me. "I may be one of the best speakers in the Parliament."

In fact, one of his public talks got 250,000 clicks on YouTube, which is a remarkable number for a local German politician, he notes.

And yet that "shoot first, ask later" style that does so well on the podium, where he lets his impulsivity and bingo brain fly, doesn't help him as much in his interpersonal relationships. He can attract the crowds, but his lack of a filter hurts his more intimate relationships.

"In person, I annoy people," he admits. "Even for a German, I am too direct."

Serial Daters

No one is more annoyed, perhaps, than Christopher's ex-girlfriends. Once the initial bloom is off the new romance, we ADHDers are susceptible to getting restless and moving on. It's a cycle we tend to repeat again and again, and the German political star is no exception.

"I do tend to get bored in relationships," he says, having ended his last relationship not long before we spoke. "I hope that will change as I get older."

It does. Christopher's low boredom threshold in relationships is similar to what I experienced at his age. My marriage lasted more than twenty years, though ADHD was at least partly responsible for it ending, and before I was married my relationships with girlfriends never lasted more than two or three months. I would be initially thrilled. When it was fun, exciting and new, I was all in. But then I would get bored quickly.

That's how I am with almost every aspect of my life. I love to start something new, put it in motion and then I am done. Fortunately, this tendency has helped me be successful in my career. I'd built up multiple successful practices along with other ventures. But it wasn't working in my relationships. Then I wrote my first book, and when I got to the chapter on ADHD, it was transformative. It forced me to delve more deeply into my own history—especially when I did the research on the continuum questionnaire and drilled down further into this topic, organized my thoughts and answered my own quizzes.

You may well be wondering how a psychiatrist could not have diagnosed himself much earlier. After all, I had worked with countless ADHD patients, and I was well versed in all the signs. But self-awareness can be hard to come by, especially when your ADHD brain is preoccupied by a multitude of different things at once! It was an incredible aha moment that gave me huge insight into who I am and what I tend to do. Suddenly my past decisions made sense. And you need that self-awareness when entering into a serious relationship. Knowing your various patterns is key.

So when I met my girlfriend, Wendy, I was ready. She is my first relationship post-diagnosis, and in many ways meeting her has been a kind of catalyst for change. I was up-front with her about who I was, and what I had, and gave her a thorough heads-up on what to expect. I told her, "Now, I am probably going to do A, B and C, but it's not about you or my lack of respect for you. It is my personality type." That didn't mean a free pass for me. As we age, some of these symptoms—like thrill-seeking in short-term relationships—tend to moderate. And knowing when it is my trait speaking doesn't make me any less responsible for my actions. I do have control over this and can make logical decisions.

Of course, we went through the usual cycle. The initial intense excitement of those first months together leveled off and, for a brief moment, I struggled with my ADHD impulses to move on. But this time I understood why it was happening, and appreciated the value of what I have in this relationship and the rewards of working past that restlessness.

To her great credit, Wendy has been incredibly understanding and patient. My personality can be overwhelming, yet she knows my ups and downs, and can deal with my sporadic nature. She gets it, accepts it and even enjoys it, most of the time.

I've found a good match in Wendy. While I wouldn't say she is OCD, she is in many ways my opposite. Wendy is well organized and focused, or what she describes as "regimented," while I bounce around all over the place. She's an amazing listener, and I happen to be quite the talker. Socially, she's a little shy and withdrawn, whereas I like to be the center of attention.

"I enjoy the fact that you like to shine," she once told me. "You can go in and grab the attention in a room—that takes a lot of the pressure off me."

That said, with one meaningful glance she can rein me in when I go too far. I can be entertaining at a dinner party, but there are times when I get a little too loud and outrageous and talk over everyone. A word or a look always brings me back, and now I have the insight to know that she is right. Even better, she sees the humor in these situations, and we can laugh about it together.

For her part, Wendy is attracted to my energy and zest for life. She likes the fact that I get interested in something, hyperfocus and then learn everything about it, inside and out. She finds my enthusiasm contagious, and picks up new skill sets just by watching me go after something.

"You expand my world and take me to a place I didn't necessarily know I could go and exist," she told me.

A great partnership can also be a tool that helps us leverage our ADHD strengths. As ADHDers, we need someone in our lives who can check us, talk things through and generally help us along. Wendy is my anchor. Without her I would just be bouncing around on the white water like a loose raft, hitting every rock. My life is so much better with her in it.

If you haven't already, I hope you find that in your own relationship. Because we ADHDers could all use a little extra love, compassion and gentle reminding.

THE TOOL KIT

Tips from ADHD partners, for ADHD partners:

> To get him to leave the house, don't ever say, "Hurry up!" That will only make him more scattered. Instead, sit in the car and wait patiently. I always know he is going to come to the car three times, forget something and come back again. It's a ritual now. It's never going to be a single exit, so you might as well relax and read a magazine until he's finally ready to roll.
> —WENDY LASTRAPES

> Learn how to keep up. Shane does everything at a fast pace, from eating and walking to getting things done. No time is wasted with him, and coupled with his need for being productive at all hours of the day, it means I have to keep up with him or be left in the dust . . . Be ready to always feel exhausted!
> —TERI MIYAHIRA

Get your timing right. When we were about to be married he was in the middle of his busy season and he was so hyperfocused on work that any wedding talk was useless. After four and a half years I am finally figuring out when to bring up certain conversations.　　—LINDSAY BLANCHARD

If you really want something, get eye contact and then you know they are focusing on you and not a bunch of other things at the same time.　　—HEIDI BUCKMAN

ADHD can be challenging. But acceptance is the starting point, so don't force them to change. My role is to help my wife change only what she wants to change, not to fix her.
　　—STEFANO CAZZANELLI

Involve the non-ADHD spouse in any coaching sessions so they can understand what the ADHDer is experiencing. What's the world they live in? What is it like? A lot of times you may think they are doing it on purpose but they are not. The ADHDer also needs to hear how frustrating it can be for the spouse.　　—JEREMY PEARSON

The biggest benefit of being with an ADHDer is that you never get bored. When we're on vacation, I let him do all the planning and go along for the ride because I know that he needs to have a jam-packed schedule.　　—TERI MIYAHIRA

Work with what you have. His memory is selective, and he always forgets the little things, like picking up eggs on the way home. But if I give him a phone number or address, that's the kind of thing he stores. I am the one who gets things done around the house. But he is the one I can come to if I have a work problem. He's all over the place, and I bring him back down to earth. So it all balances out. —LINDSAY BLANCHARD

You're in this together so just go with it. If they know that they have that rock and anchor at home, it takes a little bit of weight off and they can be the risk-taker, and act like they have it together at work. Let them know that you trust them and have their back through thick and thin. They can be on top of the world one time and in their parents' basement the next, but as long as they have the support of their partner, they can do anything.   —Heidi Buckman

Seeing him always being productive helps to push me to be productive as well. But since I am a "normal person" and need rest, I can't keep going the way he does. How I wish I had his energy!   —Teri Miyahira

Let the coach become the nag or the nudge, not the wife or the husband.   —Jeremy Pearson

Appreciate the gifts of passion and adventure that they bring to your life.   —Stefano Cazzanelli

Communicate your expectations, because if you go with the flow sometimes your needs are not going to be met. Sometimes I have to step up and say, "I need for you to hear this." And the best approach is to ask for advice, because he always has an opinion!   —Wendy Lastrapes

He's the adventure in my life and I love it. Of course, I can't stand it when we can't find his keys and end up looking for an hour and they were on top of the shoe rack the whole time. But that's just Ben.   —Lindsay Blanchard

Life with an ADHD spouse can be a roller coaster, so enjoy Mr. Toad's Wild Ride!   —Heidi Buckman

CHAPTER THIRTEEN

Find Your Fit

One look at Anita Erickson's résumé would make any prospective employer dizzy. At forty-eight, the Austin, Texas-based entrepreneur, whom you first met in Chapter Seven, has held forty-five jobs across a breadth of different fields. It wasn't until later in life that Anita finally found her fit, as a self-employed interior designer and founder of a website for online home furnishing sales.

"For the longest time I had no idea what I wanted to do," says Anita, who has worked at everything from waiting tables to being a radio DJ. She held jobs as an account manager for several ad agencies and as a marketing executive for Dell before working for several start-ups, including running operations for a car magazine.

Anita couldn't pick a path, simply because she was interested in too many different subjects.

"I was intrigued by a lot of things," says Anita, who loved literature, particularly Shakespeare, "but not early American history," she adds. She studied geometry, anthropology and etymology, dropping one new interest for the next throughout college, where she managed to get a BA in communications but "was probably more into socializing than going to classes."

There was no particular reason for choosing that major, other than the fact that it was easy and "there were a lot of football players in my class," admits Anita. "But I had no idea what I was going to do with my degree."

Anita's story is typical of so many with ADHD who struggle to find the right career path. We don't do well in a lot of work environments, because often the constraints of a typical workday, from the nine-to-five hours to sitting still at a desk or a cubicle, are a misuse of our strengths and run counter to everything that stimulates the ADHD brain. Until an ADHDer can zero in on something that's the perfect fit, there's a lot of changing course—some might even say flailing. Many of the success stories we interviewed didn't hit their stride until they reached their thirties, forties, even fifties.

"Deciding what I wanted to do became like an algebra problem," explains Bobby Chinn, the chef whom you met in Chapter Four. "I had to get rid of all the other variables that didn't make sense in the equations and whittle it down."

Everyone talks about the importance of finding your passion in choosing a career. Every advice book that's ever been written says it's all about doing what you love. No kidding. But for the ADHD brain, there really is no other option. Unless you are completely engaged in what you're doing, unless it's exciting, self-starting, unrestricted and unstructured, you might as well still be sitting in the back of your sixth-grade math class, staring out the window. Whatever it is, whether it's trading stocks, arguing legal cases or meeting a reporter's deadline, it has to stimulate you and trigger that increased dopamine tone in the brain.

I cannot stress this point enough. In this book we've worked hard to explode the myths and change the negative misperceptions of ADHD. But it remains a fact that there are many bleak statistics associated with the diagnosis, including a high school dropout rate of 32.3 percent, a 40 percent incidence of ADHD among long-term prison inmates and a 25 percent prevalence of ADHD among lifetime drug and alcohol abusers.

But I am convinced that a large part of these statistics is a result of the fact that the education system, along with the rest of society, has not made room for this different style of learning and operating in the world. Those with ADHD start out in life constantly being told to change, to fit, to conform . . . When they cannot conform because that is simply not the way their ADHD brains were made, they turn on themselves, flipping their strengths into weaknesses and burying those superpowers under layers of low self-esteem, anger and frustration.

It doesn't have to be that way. The fact is, someone with ADHD can perform well in every profession imaginable, especially in a global economy driven by technology, innovation and change. And these days, there's no reason why any job should require being chained to a desk, although it requires a progressive and understanding employer who is more focused on results than hours spent at the office.

ADHD career coach DeShawn Wert, whom you met in Chapter Ten, notes that the difference between someone who is successful with the trait versus someone who is struggling is about context.

"There is a difference between fitting in and belonging," she notes. "When you are fitting in, you are contorting yourself, but you don't have to do anything to belong. You're not hiding your ADHD superpowers, you are leveraging them and being productive in a driven world."

For those who try to force themselves into a career or rigid work environment that doesn't feel natural to an ADHDer, or fails to ignite their passion, DeShawn recommends a process of trial and error. Allow yourself to fail as you figure out a context that will work. When you know something is not natural to you, don't give in to the external pressure to conform to the world's expectations. You have to give yourself permission to try things and fail until you either come across a business idea, or connect with a boss or partner who gives you the freedom to work your own hours, in your own space.

"ADHD people have something to offer, but that gets stunted or muted in a regular workplace," says DeShawn. "If only people could learn to leverage what they are good at, ADHD would become a nonissue."

I couldn't agree more. ADHDers also need to find the right niche within their chosen fields. Perry Sanders the attorney, from Chapter One, is best at what he does as a trial attorney, thinking on his feet in front of a courtroom, as opposed to meticulously poring over corporate contracts. For most with the ADHD trait, a nine-to-five job probably won't maximize your gifts, nor will jobs that require great organizational skills, like executive assistant or accountant, or careers that are routine and predictable, like being a banker, a government worker or something that requires clocking in and shuffling paperwork. These are not vocations that would leverage the many ADHD strengths you possess. But if you find the work fascinating, then anything is fair game. Through my work, friends and acquaintances, I've met ADHDers in virtually any profession or industry you can name. There's a wide-open field of career paths that can work. The trick is figuring out which one is right for you.

Process of Deduction

And if it takes time, as it did in Anita's case, that's okay, as long as you are learning, growing and getting closer to finding your fit. It's never too late. Often it takes trial and error for people with ADHD to figure out what they're good at and what, more importantly, ignites their passion. Many with ADHD are late bloomers, but they keep trying. It's their resilience and optimism that gets them where they need to go.

Anita's exploring nature led her to sample professions, and each job she tried taught her something. Through radio, she developed her communication skills, and her advertising agency experience helped her to leverage her creativity and apply it to a business context by working to please clients. The job at Dell forced her to work within a corporate structure and introduced her to her business mentors—three Dellionaires who started a small ad agency. Because it was a small company, Anita got involved in running every aspect of the business and found herself drawn to smaller accounts.

"I could be more involved in business planning, and had my hands in everything," she told me.

The ad agency gig led to the job at the car magazine start-up, where Anita, the first employee, virtually ran the show. Her boss taught her every aspect of the business and, "I soaked up all this new information like a sponge," she says.

Anita relished the chance to be strategic, seeing how all the pieces of a small business fit together. She could step back, see the big picture of what the business needed and move from one task to the next. Her nonlinear thinking enabled her to see connections that could take the business to the next level. Anita also learned a new skill she enjoyed—financial planning. "I became the queen of the spreadsheet," she says. It was a surprising discovery for Anita, because you wouldn't think an ADHD brain would go there.

After another job at a start-up, which ended with the recession, Anita finally realized what she was meant to be: an entrepreneur. But, in order to make it work on her own, the business needed to revolve around the one pursuit she'd consistently enjoyed since she was a teen: interior design. Together with her husband, a software engineer, she created Red Door, a "Craigslist for furniture," selling unique pieces she'd found and restored from flea markets.

Starting her own business was a risk, but combining the skills she'd picked up over the years exploring different careers with her original passion has paid off. The network she's built up with other interior designer clients and friends even inspired her to start another business—a beautifully designed, membership-based conference center for sole proprietors who need a structured place to bring clients for meetings. It's become a faster way to generate revenue, and an ingenious way to strategically leverage her relationships with other designers in Austin, on whom her website business depends for sales and client referrals.

"Now I am happier than I have ever been," says Anita. "The thought of going back to work for someone else is painful."

Know Yourself

Again, self-awareness is key. Knowing your own ADHD strengths can help you save time and channel your energies in the right direction.

From his first day in school, Brennan Benglis knew he was different. Brennan, the private investigator introduced in Chapter Nine, used to beg his mother to let him stay home, and although he was a friendly, likable kid with great social skills, he bristled at the idea of sitting at a desk and being lectured to.

"I just never liked authority," Brennan recalls. "It affects everything I do."

While his friends went off to college, Brennan struggled, wondering what he was going to make of his life. For a moment, he thought about becoming a sports coach. He loves working with kids, and he's athletic, so it seemed like the perfect job, but the money wasn't what he felt he needed, and getting the appropriate degree just wasn't in the cards. After two years of college, he realized, "It wasn't for me."

Brennan, who is twenty-eight, spent a couple more years drifting, playing poker and dealing cards in a casino, but it was time to get a "real job." His older sisters owned a private investigator business and suggested he give it a try. The possibility of earning a good living in a job where he could make his own hours, and was answerable to no one, was too good to pass up, so Brennan put in just enough hours in PI school to get his license, and there's been no stopping him since.

"This is right up my alley. There's no one to listen to. I can just take a case and go from there."

Brennan is particularly good at this line of work. He uses his bingo brain to crack cases, his people skills to extract information from people and his calm-under-pressure demeanor to handle on-the-job dangers and stresses. He uses his instincts and ability to react to the moment to blend in undetected and observe details that others might overlook.

Brennan especially loves that the work is unpredictable, and he never knows what city or establishment he's going to be working in from one week to the next. The only drawback is that, when he is on a stakeout, he has to spend hours in his car, alone. But his iPhone and social media keep him engaged and multitasking while he's watching his subject, and the long hours have taught him patience and made him a better poker player.

"This fits me for sure," he says.

Taking Stock

Of course, there are some shortcuts to finding the right vocation for your ADHD brain. You don't have to spend half your life running up blind alleys. Andrew Ryan, whom you first met in Chapter Five, figured this out after some careful soul-searching in his midtwenties, around the time he was diagnosed with ADHD.

"Certain aspects of my life were not going well and I needed to find answers," he told me.

His diagnosis inspired him to find tools and techniques to improve his quality of life, which had been hampered by his lack of career fulfillment. He wasn't performing to his maximum potential at work, couldn't focus and struggled with anxiety and depression, which led to some substance abuse problems.

"I felt almost no motivation, and although you could say I'd accomplished quite a bit, I was not content," he recalls. "Waking up each morning and not looking forward to your day is no way to live."

Despite his past struggles in school, Andrew was skilled at math and problem-solving, so he eventually forced himself to get a university engineering-physics degree.

After graduation, he moved in and out of jobs. There were so many he can't remember all the companies he worked for.

"It is very frustrating to be in positions that you have no desire to be in, that are just not fulfilling," Andrew observes. "The saddest part is that your talents are being squandered."

It was especially demoralizing to hear how excited so many of his peers were about their jobs. The more he heard how focused and de-voted they were to what they were doing, the more it brought home to him that he was wasting time and he began to fear he would never live up to his true potential. He woke up to each working day in dread, but not because he couldn't perform. He just couldn't face the boredom and futility. The jobs he drifted through were detail-driven, with little independence and almost no human interaction. He felt completely disengaged, had bad relationships with coworkers and management and found few opportunities to use his natural strengths.

"Looking back, I realize how miserable I was in past positions; I had a predominantly negative experience day in and day out," Andrew recalls. "It was truly getting in the way of my happiness."

So when Andrew was diagnosed with ADHD, he embarked on a period of self-reflection. He understood little about the trait, assuming it was relegated to the boisterous "problem" children who were "bouncing off the walls." But research brought greater self-awareness, and his interests and habits finally made sense. He saw his past life and career choices in a whole new context, and realized that he needed to find a pursuit that was a better fit for his ADHD brain, with daily routines that would enhance his lifestyle without suppressing his restless energy, risk-taking nature and nonlinear thinking.

Of course, the solution wasn't immediately obvious. Understanding which career path was best for him was a process. He started taking long walks, thinking deeply about what he was good at, activities he enjoyed and what his weaknesses were.

"It took me some time to really find the key to getting to where I wanted to be, to determine what kind of careers for ADHD could work for me and then diving in more to learn more," explains Andrew.

His process of self-analysis involved looking deeply into his past. He thought about what he was good at in school, as well as the things he chose to do during his personal time. Andrew was systematic about it, making detailed tables with "good versus bad" experiences. He wrote down the things he enjoyed about past jobs and, through the mechanics of writing these things down on paper, he was able to create a road map of where he wanted to go in his career. But his choices were not career-specific. It wasn't about an industry or a product. Andrew was more interested in the day-to-day challenges of a job, the variety of work and the level of autonomy. He knew he couldn't take one more day in a cubicle with someone looking over his shoulder.

Once he narrowed down the field of choices, Andrew sought out individuals in various industries, asking them questions about their careers. Instead of just randomly pumping his résumé and taking the first job that came along, he came up with a wish list of larger goals for himself. They were ambitions that anyone would want out of a career, though few would be that systematic about it.

Andrew's deliberate approach led him to a job in sales and project management as a professional engineer for a global renewable energies company. The new role encompasses his math and engineering skills, as well as his desire to be in a leadership role, working with a sales team. It allows for plenty of the human interaction and the variety he was missing in previous jobs. In addition to supporting his sales team, Andrew regularly gives presentations, attends conferences and business meetings and gets to be hands-on during the construction phase of various products. Andrew is not a detail-minded individual, so his present job leverages his skills in conceptualizing products and strategies. Once he has done the high-level thinking, he is able to delegate to each team with the necessary discipline for follow-through. In other words, Andrew's current job doesn't require him to be stuck at a desk, and allows him to take a more autonomous, entrepreneurial approach to his work. This role has kept him engaged ever since his breakthrough four years ago, at twenty-eight.

In addition to his day job, Andrew stays fulfilled and challenged by consulting for other firms, which he helps to come up with other product ideas. His experience trying to identify his passion also inspired him to launch a website, ADHD ReVamP, in 2013. The site offers some useful and specific suggestions for finding that dream gig, including doing a thorough self-assessment to determine what you enjoy and what you are good at, and even asking friends and associates for their take on your natural gifts. He also suggests reading and extensively researching possible fields and places to work at, again keeping track and taking notes.

I would also add, jump right in. Experiment with whatever job seems right, so you can get hands-on experience. If it doesn't work, don't try to force it, but take notes. Build something on paper so that you have an ongoing record of your likes and dislikes.

Of course, much of this advice is generic. But a key takeaway is to write it all down. This is especially true for ADHDers, because we have so many thoughts going on all at once, and are so easily distracted, that even the best ideas can be forgotten unless we make them concrete through the act of writing them down.

"The biggest issue with unsatisfied people is the lack of self-awareness," says Andrew. "We go through our lives in quiet resolution and just settle."

This is true for everybody, but especially ADHDers who spend their whole lives trying to contort themselves into the box labeled "other peoples' expectations." Instead, we need to have higher expectations for ourselves. We need to understand that we bring far more to an organization, or even our own businesses or consultancies, as self-starting leaders, strategists, inventors, networkers, risk-takers and multitaskers. We are much more inclined to be happy in our working lives when we know we are leveraging our strengths to contribute in our own unique ways.

This doesn't necessarily require changing careers. There are many ways we can make our careers fit our needs. Coming from a family where my father was a doctor, it was always understood I would become one too. But I hated premed, and switched to philosophy in college. Of course, after graduating, I couldn't find a job, so I figured I might as well go to med school, having already taken all the hard courses.

After graduating I got interested in pharmaceutical research, landed in internal medicine clinical research, hated it and lasted for about a year. While applying for jobs at pharmaceutical companies, I randomly met a psychiatry professor, and what he had to say was so fascinating it inspired me to go into the field. I loved psychiatry, but after seeing patients sixty hours a week, I lost interest. So I started a clinic, and then another, and another.

Mixing it up by seeing patients, recruiting other doctors, running a clinic, supervising nurse practitioners and others, serving as a hospital medical director and founding multiple new programs was my way of adapting the field of medicine to my strengths and passions. It was a circular process, but I discovered that I am as much a businessman as a doctor. This way, I can have the best of both worlds. I didn't have to fit the profession I was in, because I was able to make the profession fit me.

Trying It On for Size

Sometimes the process of searching for the right fit can continue through several years and multiple positions within a variety of fields. Conventional wisdom says this is less than ideal, because most employers want to see a more linear, streamlined résumé. But that's not a good enough reason to force yourself to stay in one thing and repress your desire to explore other interests. In fact, I would argue that in today's economy, the more diverse your experience, the better able you will be to adapt to the needs of this rapidly evolving marketplace. And all of those many things you dabble in, be they for weeks, months or years, will build a unique skill set that will help you hit it out of the park when you do eventually find that thing you love.

Lisa Castaneda, the educator from Chapter Five, tried several careers on for size, including training to become a police officer and, indulging in a lifelong interest in cars, as an auto insurance adjustor, going around to body shops and dealerships inspecting cars and negotiating on damages. Lisa even trained police dogs, for fun. She loved aspects of these jobs and pastimes and learned from them, but she wasn't passionate enough to stay in them for a lifelong career. Coming from a family of teachers, she got her teaching certificate, and loved teaching. But establishing her nonprofit, which is in many ways like launching a business, allowed her to leverage her passion as an educator with the people skills and risk-taking she learned in her other careers. Her many experiences have made her fearless, and have become fuel for the innovations she comes up with for education in the classroom and after-school programs.

"The impulsive part of ADHD helps me as a woman running an organization. I don't second-guess, I just need to go, and that has helped me a lot as an opportunity—that shiny new object I am excited about—presents itself."

Sometimes it's also simply a matter of enjoying yourself. Gordon Sanders, whom you first met in Chapter Five, lost count of the jobs he's had over the decades. His latest role is IT consultant for Cathay Pacific Airways in Hong Kong, and he moves all over Southeast Asia as a contractor helping various companies manage their IT projects. But he's done everything from fitness instructor, party deejay, sales, toy manufacturing, writer, print shop sales and specialty retail manager, to dating consultant and life coach. Gordon enjoyed most of these jobs while he lasted in them, which was often not for more than a year or two. Moving on quickly was his own prescription for happiness. But, as random as these jobs may seem, they also led him somewhere. Teaching people fitness and coaching them on dating gave him outstanding people skills, which helps him bring in more work. Being able to write makes him a great communicator, which is an asset in any field because "it helps me get the best out of people." Working in different industries also made him an adept IT project manager, because he can jump into any type of business and quickly understand their needs.

"Through my ADHD I realized that everything is related," says Gordon.

Role Models

Gordon found something he liked in every job and pastime he tried, taking it with him and adding it to a long list of interests that complement each other and blend together seamlessly in the career he has today. Nothing was wasted. Each experience also brought him closer to a balance of career and the lifestyle he loves.

Finding your passion is so crucial to our happiness as ADHDers that UK-based entrepreneur Daniel Sandler, whom you met in the previous chapter, decided to build a business around it: SeeMyPath, an online career advice platform that is now in the "beta" phase. The site is being designed to help young people make more informed career decisions and fill a void in the UK school system, "where career advice is terrible," says Daniel. He describes SeeMyPath as an online network that connects young people (and their parents) to career pathways through schools and employers, and highlights career role models, such as entrepreneurs in the digital media space. At the time of this writing, several businesses in the United Kingdom had already signed up to be a part of the service.

His business idea is not just for ADHDers, but it stems directly from his own experience as someone with ADHD who had no idea what he wanted to do with his life. Daniel hit a wall after completing a university degree in math and finance. It was part of a short-term plan to go into banking, but he wasn't inspired by the subject. Graduating in 2009 at the depth of the recession, he had no idea what he wanted to do in life, and the lack of focus caused him to panic. With the support of his understanding parents, he took a year off to find himself, working in a ski resort as a cook. The mental break gave him the space to reflect on what he desired most: to create and run a business.

He'd always struggled in school, but there were topics that ignited his passion. From the age of ten, when he should have been doing homework up in his room, Daniel was devising business ideas. "I must have scribbled down hundreds of ideas, although not all of them were that great."

By the end of his ski season, Daniel still hadn't come up with *the* idea, but he knew he had to at least continue his education and lay a foundation for whatever was to come next. So in 2010 he switched gears and embarked on a law degree.

Again, this subject didn't inspire him, and Daniel was miserable.

"I was never great at academia and could not focus or concentrate on anything in school for more than two minutes at a time; I felt imprisoned," he told me.

After graduating in 2012, he fell into the safety net of his father's law firm. But it's not for him.

"The normal route would be for me to progress to partner rapidly and go off into the sunset," he says. "To all my friends, this seems like winning the lottery, but not to me. The thought of sitting behind my desk every day and falling into a 'routine' gives me the same feeling as it did sitting in a classroom for all those years."

So he reverted to his usual creative outlet, dreaming up business ideas, and that's when he stumbled upon the idea for a career advice platform. He started exploring what was already out there, and what he found was standard career advice from adults telling children what they need to do, with a heavy emphasis on studying hard and getting the right degree. "It was everything teenagers hate," says Daniel.

Inspired by his own preferences and experiences as a teen, Daniel took the opposite approach, showing, rather than telling, his audience how they can be successful.

"I had greater sensitivity to what they wanted and needed to hear, and molded the actual business around it," says Daniel, who had always questioned academics as the be-all and end-all to success.

"People in positions of authority used to tell me that if I don't do well in school, I won't do well in life. Well, what about Steve Jobs, Sir Richard Branson or Bill Gates?"

While Daniel is not suggesting to his website subscribers that they quit school, "because everything you do in life can be utilized," he is trying to find more role models who can speak to school-age children who feel like they don't fit. He wants kids looking for their path to know that there are less conventional routes to success, and hopes they'll be inspired by self-made entrepreneurs, much like those we've profiled in these pages.

Anything and Everything Goes

Again, rule nothing out. There are so many possible careers, missions and occupations for which the ADHD mind is perfectly suited. Your possibility may even be something you'd never considered for an occupation.

Eileen, whom you met in Chapter Eight, took a few years to discover what makes her happiest. The fifty-six-year-old mother of three flitted from job to job for years, but nothing seemed quite right. It wasn't that she didn't work hard—some of these positions didn't require enough work, and she had no way to burn off that excess energy. She even took a training course to become a protection officer at a national oil reserve, but the job, which involved standing around for hours with nothing to do, was "deathly boring." She resorted to leading on-site exercise classes, jogging around the site and even pulling alarms to generate excitement and pass the time.

Fast-forward to today, and Eileen has found her niche as a high-end detail-oriented housecleaner. She absolutely loves to clean. She will spend hours in someone's home, cleaning every surface top to bottom, getting into the crevices with a toothbrush. She makes her own hours and works at her own pace, hyperfocusing to the point where everything she touches sparkles. Eileen is so good at what she does, and so passionate about it, that you could eat off the floors or walls or even the ceiling of any house where she has cleaned.

"I will it to perfection. I want everything I see to be shiny and clean, so I'll spend hours at it, until I lose track of time. It's either clean or it's not, and I won't quit until it meets my standards!"

It doesn't matter what you do. Eileen is successful because she has found something that makes her feel happy and fulfilled. Doing what she does gives her a sense of accomplishment she has not been able to find in any other job. Scrubbing, polishing, dusting, gives her a sense of well-being and calm most of us could only wish for.

Multiple Callings

Of course, finding your fit doesn't necessarily have to result in just one thing. Many ADHDers figure out their passion, or passions, through their natural propensity for multitasking, and could never be content specializing in just one field. You can be great at something, but don't assume it's your only calling. I am passionate about several things, and pursuing them all, or as many as I can, has been tremendously satisfying and productive. Sticking with something doesn't mean you have to get stuck.

Lee Mallett, the entrepreneur you first met in Chapter Eight, puts passion and drive into everything he does. Lee started on his path early in part because he didn't have a choice. When Lee was just twelve, his father, a local politician in Louisiana, got into trouble and had to serve five years in prison. As the eldest of five children, Lee became the man of the house and started planting small gardens to sell the produce and earn some extra cash for the family coffers. He would get up at four each day to pick mustard greens and turnips, wash the bundles and then deliver them to a warehouse before heading to school.

Making money awoke in Lee a burning passion to make more. He worked as a janitor, and bought himself a car as soon as he was old enough to drive. After graduating from high school, he got into the salvage business, driving around the South looking for deals. He then became a licensed general contractor, started cattle ranching, got into the construction business and established a construction company, a roof truss business, a rice mill and feed company, an air-vacuum business, a grain transfer business, a bar and restaurant, a halfway house and "one or two more I can't think of."

Unstoppable

Lee got into construction after watching a contractor assemble a pole barn—a kind of DIY barn kit—on his cattle ranch. He was fascinated with the materials that were used, and how quickly the structure went up, and decided to apply these methods to build apartments. At first, "people were laughing at me for making apartments out of pole barn materials," but he proved his concept, playing around with the designs. "I told them to keep laughing."

Lee sold thirty to forty buildings that first year, from triplexes to larger apartment and commercial buildings. Then he started manufacturing his own trusses, and today constructs about a thousand buildings a year across Louisiana and Texas. His construction company has spawned a number of other businesses, because Lee hates to order parts and materials from suppliers when he knows he can make them better and cheaper.

Recently, he took a U-turn and went into the corrections business. He established a kind of privately run halfway house that works with parolees for six months to two years, training them in job and life skills. With no state or federal money to fund his programs, Lee's facility offers about fifty training courses, as well as drug and alcohol treatment and anger management. Again, when he started the project, "a lot of people were against me," but it fired him up even more. Today, the men who get his training have a 22 percent recidivism rate, compared with 58 percent in the state. He even employs twenty-five of his "graduates" in his own businesses.

"These are human beings who've been beaten down and told they are nothing but trash," says Lee. "But I take these young people and pound them with the positive. I tell them, 'Don't be a sluggard,' and get on them like their daddies should have years ago. I mold them into men who want to work."

Work is all Lee ever wants to do. A few years ago he decided to take a year off and "I hated it." He realized that doing things he is passionate about day in and day out is like vacation for Lee.

"There is nothing I would rather do than get up at four in the morning, go to work and face the challenge."

In 2014, Lee was asked to give the commencement speech at the University Medical Center of New Orleans. Having only done one semester in college, Lee told me how honored and humbled he was to be able to give out all those diplomas to doctors and nurses.

"Y'all conceived it and believed it, and now you've achieved it," he told them, sharing his own words to live by.

To prepare for the big day, Lee wrote a résumé, and he found the process exhilarating. "I've gotten a taste of a lot of different things," he told me. "It's like eating different foods—you get to know what you enjoy in life."

But he credits his ADHD for the long list of accomplishments, and does not believe he would have pushed so hard, with such determination, energy and persistence, without the trait. Locking into something he found interesting, whether it was raising cattle, building apartments or rehabilitating troubled young men, Lee was able to hyperfocus and take it to the next level, creating a string of successful businesses.

"You have to have a passion," Lee says. "If you can combine that drive with the energy of an ADHD brain, there's just no stopping you."

He's right. Finding that passion is the key to unlocking all those ADHD strengths we've talked about in this book. It's the ignition, the spark, for the huge stores of energy you already possess, enabling you to leverage those gifts, exceed expectations and take you to places you never thought possible. It's the secret to your ADHD superpowers.

Remember, all those guidance counselors, teachers and bosses who underestimated you—were wrong. *You* were wrong. That full potential all those report cards said you weren't reaching is well within your grasp. It's not that you can't focus, pay attention or follow through. You are *not* destined to a life of being scattered, or late, or forgetful. Well, maybe a little. But once you've lit that fire, your ADHD strengths will burn past the weaknesses and you'll be unstoppable. And then, who knows? Maybe you can even change the world.

THE TOOL KIT

- Rule nothing out. There are careers to suit everyone with ADHD, and many you may never have even thought of.

- Figure out what excites you, and then write it down. Why? Because with an ADHD brain we may have a thought and quickly forget about it. Once you know what you love, your bingo brain will help you to figure out a way to monetize it.

- Don't blame yourself if you can't endure a nine-to-five desk job like everyone else. You were destined for something less conventional.

- Canvass friends, family, even teachers. Get another perspective on what you are good at from others. It may be a skill that never occurred to you, or something you took for granted.

- Know your strengths and weaknesses. How? By thinking about it—a lot. Self-awareness is crucial to finding a dream career that makes you feel accomplished.

- Take quizzes, draw up lists, do a systematic self-analysis and get it all down on paper.

- Look for role models and, if you can, speak to them. In particular, look for fellow ADHDer role models. You've already met plenty in this book!

- Seek out a career coach. There are plenty who specialize in ADHD. The Attention Deficit Disorder Association (http:// www.add.org/) can be a great resource in finding one of these professionals.

- Consider more than one job to fulfill your need to multitask.

- Raise your expectations. Shoot for more of what you enjoy doing. You deserve career fulfillment; it's the key to happiness that's within your reach.

- Try, try, try again. It's never too late to find your fit, and the journey itself is half the fun.

- Listen to your ADHD voice! Let your strengths guide you, and trust that they are taking you in the direction you were meant to go. If something doesn't ignite that passion, quit it! Life is too short to spend contorting yourself into that box called "normal."

In Their Own Words . . .

By now you know that ADHDers have a unique perspective on the world. Many also have a unique understanding of ADHD. Their insights on how to live a successful life *because* of the trait, not in spite of it, contain more wisdom and relevance than the opinions of many of the so-called experts. They've lived it, reaching their full potential and beyond largely through their own resourcefulness, resilience, self-awareness and self-acceptance. So I'll leave it to your fellow ADHDers—the CEOs, educators, homemakers and artists interviewed for this book—to have the last word:

> When you are young, find mentors who sense your greatness and let them lead you! That was me to a tee. Oh, and likely the mentors themselves are ADHD. Mine were!
>
> —KENNETH "BUCKY" BUCKMAN

> Every brain comes with its own challenges, but it is when you acknowledge those challenges and learn to optimize your strengths that you really begin to understand what you are capable of. In my experience, people who have brains that work like ours are capable of extremely interesting and valuable contributions to the world. But try to be understanding; not every-

one can think like we think. Sometimes you just have to be
patient.   —LISA CASTANEDA

Notice the things you do which give you energy and stimulate
you in a positive way. Choose to spend time on these every day.
                                            —SHANNA PEARSON

Accept your ADHD as a gift. Embrace it. Harness the creative
energy that ADHD gives you to dream differently.
                                            —BRIAN SCUDAMORE

To change your life, you must start with changing your daily
habits and creating healthy routines. Moreover, know that you
have an amazing mind and creative capacities. Success can be
unlocked through learning to harness your strengths and leveraging your ADHD abilities.   —AARON SMITH

Don't shy away from your ADHD, embrace it! For many it can
be a blessing in disguise, leading you to new places, new careers
and new people. Ultimately ADHD has the potential to enrich
your soul and create a fascinating life that others only dream of
having.   —TREY ARCHER

Learn what is important to you. Then choose to become intentional with your ADHD gifts, time and energy. You will be much
happier in living your life (and a by-product is you will be seen
as more productive by outsiders).   —DESHAWN WERT

Accept that there are many ways to be productive. Lighten up
on yourself!   —RUTH JOY BURNELL

I always say I "am ADHD" rather than "I have ADHD." It reminds others (and myself) that ADHD isn't a disease or disorder, it's just the way your brain processes, like being right- or
left-brained.   —ANITA ERICKSON

ADHD is the natural drug that motivates you and gives you the energy necessary to convert an idea into a business.

—Daniel Sandler

Finally, a few weeks after our interview, Spanish photographer Guadalupe wrote to me and made a brilliant observation about why her ADHD is such a gift:

Our conversation left me thinking about my ADHD for some days after. I do have mixed feelings about the disorder, since it never lets me rest . . . But there is one thing that I'm very thankful for, that is, a low tolerance for frustration.

I've always heard that the ability to tolerate frustration is something essential when becoming a mature adult—the possibility for happiness. But no matter how hard I've tried, I've never been able to stay for long in a situation that doesn't fully satisfy me. Whenever a job became dull, or a love relationship didn't appeal to me anymore, or something inside of me other than my will decided that I had to quit, no matter how unreasonable it seemed, I couldn't stand it any longer.

This sounds very immature. But looking back, I realize now it was right. Now that I've found the man that I feel excited being with every single day, even when I get mad at him. Or now that I've found a job I'm always excited about. I've learned that there's no need to put up with things that don't fulfill me just because maybe quitting them is a risk, and I thank ADHD for making me do it—I found out later that ADHD was the thing other than my will that decided it was over.

That doesn't mean no sacrifice, but sacrifice is no problem when things do fulfill me, like taking care of my son at night. I often hear people complaining about situations that they could easily quit or try to change. But I believe they could be a lot more satisfied with their everyday lives if they weren't afraid to quit what they don't actually enjoy, or what doesn't fulfill them. Then it would be easier for them to be passionate about their lives. And I thank ADHD for that habit.

I particularly love the way Guadalupe describes the trait as "the thing other than my will," as if it is some kind of guardian angel. In many ways, it is.

Like Guadalupe, the other individuals interviewed for this book are thankful for their ADHD. They understand that it can be a gift. They didn't always know it. In school, where many problems start, most struggled to fit in. Their ADHD was considered a learning disability, not a learning difference. But as they moved on from the rigid structure of grade school and high school into college, and then into the workforce, they figured it out. They experimented, suffered setbacks and learned from their mistakes, growing into their ADHD to become the success stories they are today. They found their fit and discovered the right contexts in which to leverage their strengths. They didn't have the benefit of a book to show them how, and yet they did it. So can you.

ACKNOWLEDGMENTS

There are so many people to thank for their support, knowledge and insights on this project, and I can think of no better place to start than with Dr. Allen Frances, who so generously donated his time to write the foreword for this book. Your outspoken views on the current state of ADHD diagnosis and treatment are as invaluable as they have been inspiring. Dr. Ned Hallowell, I am grateful for your words of encouragement. It's an honor to share this space with such esteemed colleagues.

I would also like to thank Christine Hoch, April Gower Getz and Susan Buningh with CHADD (Children and Adults with Attention Deficit/Hyperactivity Disorder), the nation's leading ADHD organization. Thanks to CHADD, I was able to connect with my fellow CHADD "Champions" Max Fennell, Marta Bota, Wendy Davis and Luca Furgeois.

My heartfelt thanks to the dozens of ADHDers who shared their inspiring stories in this book, as well as many of their spouses and partners. Most of you chose to be identified, and for those of you who did not, you know who you are. Your generosity and candor will help millions of readers. Many of you—including the Neeleman family, Howie Mandel and Christopher Lauer—have gone above and beyond with your support.

The insights and wisdom of experts and educators interviewed for this book have also been invaluable. Professor Johan Wiklund, Dr. Oren Mason, Francisco Ayala, Lucas Goodwin, P. J. McDonald and Michael Riendeau—thank you for your support and fresh perspectives.

I would also like to express my appreciation yet again for the winning team who worked with me on this project, including my literary agents, Todd Shuster and Jennifer Gates of Zachary, Shuster, Harmsworth.

The same goes for my collaborator, researcher, interviewer, co-writer, organizer and my non-ADHD alter ego, Samantha Marshall. Sam, your patience, organization and focus have been the perfect complement to my nonlinear, ADHD way of thinking. Thank you for unpacking the contents of my bingo brain and making this work. This book is as much yours as mine.

I am also most grateful to my editor, Caroline Sutton, at Avery (and her right hand, Brianna Flaherty), who understood immediately what I was trying to say and gave me the platform to say it.

A special thanks to Larry Graham, CEO of Memorial Hospital, for giving his support and allowing the time to write this book.

There is a long list of people at and affiliated with the Institute for Neuropsychiatry to recognize for their unwavering support, including Drs. Said Cantu, Charles Murphy, Kashinath Yadalam, Sreelatha Pulakhandam, Ramin Shahla, David Buttross III, Aneeta Afzal and Charles Woodard, as well as our team of therapists—Jerry Whiteman, Lloyd Kelley, Molly Larson, Jeanne Wolf, Art Schafer, Larry Cupit, Sheila Gilley and Mike Johnson. Thank you also to the best team of psychiatric nurse practitioners in the country: Sarah Cooling, Lisa Chavis and Catherine N. Udofia, and the rest of my team: Patricia Broussard, Mandra Hayzlett, Raegan Miller, Charlene Racca, Tammy Thomas, Keisha Fuselier, Tiffoni Mccomb, Sharon Jacko and Ashley Dupre. And a special thanks to Patsy Johnson, vice president of the institute and my right hand.

Finally, and most importantly, I must thank my father, Dr. Dale

Archer Sr., and mother, Val, who have been married for fifty-nine years and counting. My sister, Lee; my daughter, Adri, and her new husband, Andrew Ross (welcome to the family!); and my son, Trey, (whom you've read about in the book). You guys have put up with me and provided untold support during the arduous process of writing this book. Thank you!

To everyone named here, and many more who are not, you have played a huge part of this book's success. All the credit is yours; any mistakes are mine.

NOTES

Introduction: Why ADHD Can Be Your Greatest Strength

xviii **a national disaster:** Alan Schwarz, "The Selling of Attention Deficit Disorder," *New York Times*, December 14, 2013, http://www.nytimes .com/2013/12/15/health/the-selling-of-attention-deficit-disorder.html ?pagewanted=all&_r=0.

xviii **diagnoses have been climbing exponentially:** Alan Schwarz, "A.D.H.D. Seen in 11% of U.S. Children as Diagnoses Rise," *New York Times*, March 31, 2013, http://www.nytimes.com/2013/04/01/health/more diagnoses-of-hyperactivity-causing-concern.html?pagewanted=all.

xviii **unprecedented and unjustifiable levels:** Alan Schwarz, "The Selling of Attention Deficit Disorder."

xviii **an outspoken critic:** Dr. Allen Frances, "10,000 Young Toddlers Are on Stimulant Drugs for ADHD," *Huffington Post*, May 17, 2014, http:// www.huffingtonpost.com/allen-frances/adhd-toddler-diagnosis _b_5343766.html.

xviii **comparison with the United Kingdom:** "ADHD Statistics," last modified September 23, 2011, http://www.addrc.org/adhd-statistics/.

xviii **or France:** Marilyn Wedge, "Why French Kids Don't Have ADHD," *Psychology Today*, March 8, 2012, http://www.psychologytoday.com /blog/suffer-the-children/201203/why-french-kids-dont-have-adhd.

Chapter One: Born This Way

11 **club's next amateur night:** Howie Mandel and Josh Young, *Here's the Deal: Don't Touch Me* (New York: Bantam, 2008), 55.

16 **immersed in a story:** "At 40, Lisa Ling Gets Surprising Diagnosis of ADD," *Huffington Post*, June 12, 2014, last updated on June 13, 2014, http://www.huffingtonpost.com/2014/06/12/lisa-ling-add-adhd_n _5489924.html.

17 **there's a beauty in it:** Mary Kearl, "Interview with a Famous ADHD Chef," *ADDitude* [no date], http://www.additudemag.com/adhd/article /7431.html.

18 **A quiz developed and verified:** Dr. Dale Archer, *Better Than Normal: How What Makes You Different Can Make You Exceptional* (New York: Crown Archetype, 2012), 211.

Chapter Two: A Diagnosis of Boredom

21 **15 percent of school-age boys:** "State-based Prevalence Data of Parent Reported ADHD Medication Treatment," last updated October 6, 2014, http://www.cdc.gov/ncbddd/adhd/medicated.html.

21 **53 percent rise:** "Data & Statistics," last updated December 10, 2014, http://www.cdc.gov/ncbddd/adhd/data.html.

22 **800,000 received stimulant medication:** John Monczunski, "ADHD Diagnosis Overused for Children Youngest in Class, Notre Dame Research Concludes," *Notre Dame News*, August 18, 2010, http://news.nd .edu/news/16395-adhd-diagnosis-overused-for-children-youngest-in -class-notre-dame-research-concludes/.

22 **different signs and symptoms:** Maureen Connolly, "The Truth About Girls & ADHD," *ADDitude* [no date], http://www.additudemag.com/ adhd-web/article/4896.html.

24 **facilitated these epidemics:** Gary Greenberg, "Inside the Battle to Define Mental Illness," *Wired*, December 27, 2010, http://www.wired .com/2010/12/ff_dsmv/all.

26 **avalanche of overdiagnosis:** Alan Schwarz, "A.D.H.D. Seen in 11% of U.S. Children."

26 **trailing asthma:** Alan Schwarz, "The Selling of Attention Deficit Disorder."

27 **10,000 two- to three-year olds:** Alan Schwarz, "Thousands of Toddlers Are Medicated for A.D.H.D., Report Finds, Raising Worries," *New York Times*, May 16, 2014, http://www.nytimes.com/2014/05/17/us/among -experts-scrutiny-of-attention-disorder-diagnoses-in-2-and-3-year -olds.html.

27 **IMS Health:** "Watchdog Says Report of 10,000 Toddlers on ADHD Drugs Tip of the Iceberg—274,000 0–1 Year Olds and 370,000 Toddlers Prescribed Psychiatric Drugs," May 21, 2014, http://www.prweb .com/releases/2014/05/prweb11872059.html.

27 **other behavioral training:** Alan Schwarz, "Thousands of Toddlers."

28 **objective biomarker:** Jolynn Tumolo, "Low Brain Iron a Biomarker of ADHD?" *Psych Congress Network*, [no date], http://www.psych congress.com/article/low-brain-iron-biomarker-adhd-18044.

29 **foolproof diagnostic:** Jolynn Tumolo, "Involuntary Eye Movements May Diagnose ADHD," *Psych Congress Network* [no date], http://www .psychcongress.com/article/involuntary-eye-movements-may -diagnose-adhd-18673.

29 **present in more than one setting:** "Symptoms and Diagnosis," last updated September 29, 2014, http://www.cdc.gov/ncbddd/adhd/ diagnosis.html.

29 **need only exhibit five "symptoms":** "Symptoms and Diagnosis," last updated September 29, 2014.

31 **butts into conversations:** ibid.

31 **fifty-four thousand family doctors:** Alan Schwarz, "Doctors Train to Spot Signs of A.D.H.D. in Children," *New York Times*, February 18, 2014, http://www.nytimes.com/2014/02/19/health/doctors-train-to -evaluate-anxiety-cases-in-children.html.

31 **hands-on training:** ibid.

32 **leading predictors:** Elizabeth Landau, "ADHD: Who Makes the Diagnosis?" CNN, August 11, 2010, http://www.cnn.com/2010/HEALTH /08/11/adhd.medication.schools/index.html.

32 **Upgrade doctor training:** Alan Schwarz, "Doctors Train to Spot Signs."

33 **Ingvar Kamprad:** Laurie Dupar, "The ADHD Entrepreneurial Brain-Style," January 20, 2012, http://www.coachingforadhd.com/adhd -blog/adults/the-adhd-entrepreneurial-brain-style/.

34 **two genes involved in the trait:** Dr. Max Muenke, "The ADHD Genetic Research Study at the National Institutes of Health and the National Human Genome Research Institute," last reviewed March 17, 2014, http://www.genome.gov/10004297.

34 **parent who shares the diagnosis:** "When ADHD Runs in Families," January 20, 2003, last updated January 14, 2014, http://www.healthy place.com/adhd/articles/genetics-of-adhd-adhd-in-families/.

35 **identical twins share the condition:** Christine Margarete Freitag and Wolfgang Retz, "Family and Twin Studies in Attention-Deficit Hyperactivity Disorder," in *Attention-Deficit Hyperactivity Disorder (ADHD) in Adults, Key Issues in Mental Health*, W. Retz and R. G. Klein, eds. (Basel, Switzerland: Karger, 2010), vol, 176, pp. 38–57, http://www.karger.com/ProdukteDB/Katalogteile/isbn3_8055/_92/_37/KIMH176_02.pdf.

36 **Hallowell's groundbreaking book:** Edward M. Hallowell and John J. Ratey, *Driven to Distraction: Recognizing and Coping with Attention Deficit Disorder from Childhood Through Adulthood* (New York: Touchstone, 1995).

Breakout I: Medications for ADHD

40 **Medications for ADHD:** "ADHD Medication Chart," WebMD, last reviewed May 10, 2014, http://www.webmd.com/add-adhd/guide/adhd-medication-chart.

Chapter Three: Pop-a-Pill Culture

49 **twenty-four-year-old Richard Fee:** Alan Schwarz, "Drowned in a Stream of Prescriptions," *New York Times*, February 2, 2013, http://www.nytimes.com/2013/02/03/us/concerns-about-adhd-practices-and-amphetamine-addiction.html?pagewantedall&_r=0.

49 **a significant travesty:** ibid.

49 **drug and alcohol overdose:** Ted Gup, "Diagnosis: Human," *New York Times*, April 2, 2013, http://www.nytimes.com/2013/04/03/opinion/diagnosis-human.html.

50 **brilliant microbursts:** ibid.

51 **binge alcohol drinkers:** Crystal Karges, "Adderall Abuse Causes, Statistics, Addiction Signs, Symptoms & Side Effects," last updated September 26, 2014, http://www.addictionhope.com/adderall.

51 **emergency room visits:** Alan Schwarz, "Report Says Medication Use Is

Rising for Adults with Attention Disorder," *New York Times*, March 12, 2014, http://www.nytimes.com/2014/03/12/us/report-says-medication -use-is-rising-for-adults-with-attention-disorder.html?_r=0.

51 **prescriptions for adults:** Dr. David Muzina, "Report: Turning Attention to ADHD," March 12, 2014, http://lab.express-scripts.com /insights/industry-updates/report-turning-attention-to-adhd.

52 **sluggish cognitive tempo:** Alan Schwarz, "Idea of New Attention Disorder Spurs Research, and Debate," *New York Times*, April 11, 2014. http://www.nytimes.com/2014/04/12/health/idea-of-new -attention-disorder-spurs-research-and-debate.html?_r=0.

52 **getting this recognized as a legitimate disorder:** ibid.

52 **eroding the resilience:** Ted Gup, "Diagnosis: Human."

54 **misleading advertising:** Alan Schwarz, "The Selling of Attention Deficit Disorder."

54 **fifty thousand comic books:** ibid.

54 **multifront push:** Frank J. Granett, "ADHD Diagnoses Have Too Strong a Link to Drug Therapy," *Special Ed Post*, April 29, 2014, http://special edpost.org/2014/04/29/adhd-diagnoses-have-too-strong-a-link-to -drug-therapy/.

54 **operating on the dark side:** Katie Thomas, "Glaxo Says It Will Stop Paying Doctors to Promote Drugs," *New York Times*, December 16, 2013, http://www.nytimes.com/2013/12/17/business/glaxo-says-it-will -stop-paying-doctors-to-promote-drugs.html?pagewanted=1&nl =tdaysheadlines&emc=edit_th_20131217&_r=2&.

54 **landmark study:** Dr. Ashley Wazana, "Physicians and the Pharmaceutical Industry: Is a Gift Ever Just a Gift?" *JAMA* 283, no. 3, January 19, 2000, http://jama.jamanetwork.com/article.aspx?articleid=192314.

55 **reward its reps:** Virginia Harrison, "GSK to Scrap Targets for Sales Reps," *CNN Money*, December 17, 2013, http://money.cnn.com/2013 /12/17/news/companies/gsk-sales-targets/index.html.

55 **better ways of coping:** Scott O. Lilienfeld and Hal Arkowitz, "Are Doctors Diagnosing Too Many Kids with ADHD?" *Scientific American*, April 11, 2013, http://www.scientificamerican.com/article/are-doctors -diagnosing-too-many-kids-adhd/?page=2.

55 **physical and mental toll:** Edmund S. Higgins, "Do ADHD Drugs Take a Toll on the Brain?" *Scientific American*, July/August 2009, http://www

.scientificamerican.com/article.cfm?id=do-adhd-drugs-take-a
-toll&page=2.

56 **mood swings and dry mouth:** Jane Collingwood, "Side Effects of ADHD
Medications," *Psych Central*, 2010, last reviewed on January 30, 2013,
http://psychcentral.com/lib/2010/side-effects-of-adhd-medications/.

56 **eroding cognitive powers:** Edmund S. Higgins, "Do ADHD Drugs
Take a Toll?"

56 **2.7 kilograms less:** ibid.

56 **effectiveness in children:** "Follow-up of Major Study Reports on
ADHD Medication Effectiveness and Impact on Growth," *ADDitude*,
August 14, 2007, http://www.additudemag.com/addnews/42/2702
html.

57 **prone to anxiety disorders**: Edmund S. Higgins, "Do ADHD Drugs
Take a Toll?"

57 **difficulty experiencing joy:** ibid.

58 **lower levels of dopamine:** ibid.

58 **cautious eye on blood levels:** ibid.

Breakout II: You Are *Not* (Necessarily) What You Eat

62 **sugar plays no role in ADHD:** Stephanie Crumley Hill, "Effects of
Sugar on Attention Deficit Hyperactivity Disorder," Livestrong.com,
last updated August 16, 2013, http://www.livestrong.com/article
/28551-effects-sugar-attention-deficit-hyperactivity/.

63 **children were given aspartame:** "What Is Attention Deficit Hyperactivity Disorder?" National Institute of Mental Health, NIH Publication No.
12-3572, Revised 2012, http://www.nimh.nih.gov/health/publications
/attention-deficit-hyperactivity-disorder/index.shtml?utm_source=
REFERENCES_R7.

63 **hyperactive after ingesting:** "Hyperactivity and Sugar," *MedlinePlus*,
last updated May 10, 2013, http://www.nlm.nih.gov/medlineplus
/ency/article/002426.htm.

64 **impulsivity and hyperactivity:** Salynn Boyles, "Study Links Low Iron
to ADHD," WebMD Health News, December 17, 2004, http://www
.webmd.com/add-adhd/childhood-adhd/news/20041217/study
-links-low-iron-to-adhd.

65 **very small segment:** ibid.

65 **buzz about micronutrients:** "Micronutrients: What They Are and Why They're Essential," Fitday.com [no date], http://www.fitday.com /fitness-articles/nutrition/vitamins-minerals/micronutrients-what -they-are-and-why-theyre-essential.html#b.

66 **significantly better mood:** Julia J. Rucklidge, Chris M. Frampton, Brigette Gorman and Anna Boggis, "Vitamin-Mineral Treatment of At-tention-Deficit Hyperactivity Disorder in Adults: Double-Blind Ran-domised Placebo-Controlled Trial," *British Journal of Psychiatry*, January 30, 2014, http://bjp.rcpsych.org/content/early/2014/01/27/bjpbp.113 .132126.abstract.

66 **not an easy regimen:** "Can Vitamins Be Used to Treat ADHD in Adults?" *NHS Choices*, January 31, 2014, http://www.nhs.uk/news/2014/01 January/Pages/Can-vitamins-be-used-to-treat-ADHD-in-adults.aspx.

66 **study of six thousand women:** "Brain Food: Good Fats for Better Mem-ory," *LiveScience*, May 18, 2012, http://www.livescience.com/20429 -good-fats-good-brain.html.

Chapter Four: The Explorer Gene

70 **dopamine transporter gene:** Andrea L. Glenn, "The Other Allele: Ex-ploring the Long Allele of the Serotonin Transporter Gene as a Potential Risk Factor for Psychopathy: A Review of the Parallels in Findings," *Neuroscience Biobehavioral Reviews* 35, no. 3 (January 2011): 612–620, ac-cessed on July 30, 2011, http://www.ncbi.nlm.nih.gov/pmc/articles /PMC3006062/.

70 **died out millennia ago:** Dr. Dale Archer, *Better Than Normal*, 45.

71 **hunter in a farmer's world:** Thom Hartmann, *Attention Deficit Disorder: A Different Perception,* (Nevada City, CA: Underwood Books, 1997), 119.

71 **associated traits:** Peter S. Jensen, David Mrazek, Penelope K. Knapp, Laurence Steinberg, Dynthia Pfeffer, John Schowalter and Theodore Shapiro, "Evolution and Revolution in Child Psychiatry: ADHD as a Disorder of Adaptation," *Journal of American Child & Adolescent Psychi-atry* 36, no. 12 (December 1997): 1,672–79.

72 **movement and novelty:** David Dobbs, "Restless Genes," *National Geo-graphic*, January 2013, http://ngm.nationalgeographic.com/2013/01 /125-restless-genes/dobbs-text.

72 **unconventional ways:** Teresa Gallagher, "The Natural Born Scientist: Is There an ADD Connection?," *Born to Explore* [no date], http://www.borntoexplore.org/addsci.htm.

73 **diagnostic criteria:** ibid.

73 **something was taking place:** ibid.

77 **brain circuitry:** Daniel Goleman, "Exercising the Mind to Treat Attention Deficits," *New York Times*, May 12, 2014, http://well.blogs.nytimes.com/2014/05/12/exercising-the-mind-to-treat-attention-deficits/.

78 **improvements in mental focus:** Poppy L. A. Schoenberg, Sevket Hepark, Cornnelis C. Kan, Henk P. Barendregt, Jan K. Buitelaar and Anne E. M. Speckens, "Effects of Mindfulness-Based Cognitive Therapy on Neurophysiological Correlates of Performance Monitoring in Adult Attention-Deficit/Hyperactivity Disorder," *Clinical Neurophysiology* 125, no. 7 (July 2014): 1,407–16, published online: December 7, 2013, doi: http://dx.doi.org/10.1016/j.clinph.2013.11.031, http://www.sciencedirect.com/science/article/pii/S1388245713012285.

78 **brain images:** Anthony P. Zanesco, Brandon G. King, Katherine A. MacLean and Clifford D. Saron, "Executive Control and Felt Concentrative Engagement Following Intensive Meditation Training," *Frontiers in Human Neuroscience*, September 18, 2013, doi: 10.3389/fnhum.2013.00566, http://journal.frontiersin.org/Journal/10.3389/fnhum.2013.00566/abstract.

78 **control through meditation:** Daniel Goleman, "Exercising the Mind."

79 **use of the game:** Alison Abbott, "Gaming Improves Multitasking Skills," *Nature* 501, no. 7, 465 (September 4, 2013), doi:10.1038/501018a, http://www.nature.com/news/gaming-improves-multitasking-skills-1.13674.

81 **privilege of being alive:** Maria Popova, "Eleanor Roosevelt on Happiness, Conformity, and Integrity," *Brain Pickings* [no date], http://www.brainpickings.org/2012/11/16/eleanor-roosevelt-on-happiness-conformity-and-integrity/.

81 **Steve Jobs:** Bob Hathcock, "Steve Jobs ADHD?" Addventure Coaching [no date], http://addventurecoaching.com/stevejobsadhd/.

Chapter Five: Learning with ADHD

85 **simple immaturity:** Dr. Allen Frances, "Treat the Classroom, Not the

Kids," *Psychiatric Times*, April 2, 2014, http://www.psychiatrictimes
.com/adhd/treat-classroom-not-kids.

86 **alarming number of referrals:** Dana Barnes, "Teachers Confused About 'ADHD,'" Global Healing Center [no date], http://www
.globalhealingcenter.com/adhd/teachers-confused-about-adhd.

90 **different methods of teaching:** Ronald D. Davis, *The Gift of Dyslexia: Why Some of the Smartest People Can't Read . . . and How They Can Learn*, (New York: Perigree; revised and expanded edition, 2010).

93 **Tichelle has read:** Dr. Dale Archer, "ADHD: The Entrepreneur's Super-power," Forbes.com, May 14, 2014, http://www.forbes.com/sites /dalearcher/2014/05/14/adhd-the-entrepreneurs-superpower/.

98 **urban settings:** "Fast Facts: Teacher Trends," National Center for Education Statistics [no date], http://nces.ed.gov/fastfacts/display .asp?id=28.

104 *Exercise and the Brain:* John J. Ratey and Eric Hagerman, *Spark: The Revolutionary New Science of Exercise and the Brain* (New York: Little, Brown; reprint edition, 2013).

104 **twenty minutes of aerobic:** "Exercise: An Alternative ADHD Treat-ment Without Side Effects," *ADDitude*, December/January 2008 ex-cerpt, http://www.additudemag.com/adhd/article/3142.html.

105 **primed to learn:** ibid.

105 **learned helplessness:** ibid.

106 **press the reset button:** Harold W. Kohl II and Heather D. Cook, eds., "Educating the Student Body: Taking Physical Activity and Physical Education to School," Institute of Medicine of the National Academies, May 23, 2013, http://www.iom.edu/Reports/2013/Educating-the -Student-Body-Taking-Physical-Activity-and-Physical-Education-to -School.aspx.

Chapter Six: Resilience

111 **go out of business:** David Neeleman, "Seeing Failure as Opportunity," Stanford University's Entrepreneurship Corner, April 30, 2003, http:// ecorner.stanford.edu/authorMaterialInfo.html?mid=286.

113 **resilience in college students:** Linda Wilmshurst, Marella Peele and Luke Wilmshurst, "Resilience and Well-being in College Students

with and without a Diagnosis of ADHD," *Journal of Attention Disorders* 15, no. 1 (July 2011): 11–17, http://eric.ed.gov/?id=EJ907848; Cathy W. Hall, Keely L. Spruill and Raymond E. Webster, "Motivational and Attitudinal Factors in College Students with and without Learning Disabilities," *Learning Disability Quarterly* 25 (Spring 2002), http://faculty.uml.edu/darcus/47.375/ld/hall_spruill_webster_02 .pdf, 79–86.

116   *Raising Resilient Children*: Robert Brooks and Sam Goldstein, *Raising Resilient Children: Fostering Strength, Hope, and Optimism in Your Child* (New York: McGraw-Hill, 2002).

116   **islands of competence:** Laura Flynn McCarthy, "Teaching Resilience to ADHD Children: Advice for Parents," *ADDitude*, October/November 2013, http://www.additudemag.com/adhd/article/2525.html.

116   **turnaround people:** Dr. Paul B. Yellin, "Overcoming Obstacles: 3 Keys to Fostering Resilience in Children with Learning Disabilities and ADHD," *New Jersey Family*, March 25, 2014, http://www.njfamily.com/NJ -Family/April-2014/Overcoming-Obstacles/.

120   **human development:** Malcolm Gladwell, *David and Goliath: Underdogs, Misfits, and the Art of Battling Giants* (New York: Little, Brown, 2013).

121   **grievous disadvantages:** Alison Griswold, "Malcolm Gladwell Explains How 'Strategic Disadvantages' Can Make You a Great Leader," *Business Insider*, February 19, 2014, http://www.businessinsider.com /this-malcolm-gladwell-theory-upends-traditional-notions-about -learning-2014-2.

125   **deeply compassionate:** Carol Gignoux, "The Resilience of the ADHD Spirit," *Live ADHD Free*, March 6, 2014, http://liveadhdfree.com /resilience-adhd-spirit/.

Chapter Seven: Bingo Brain

128   **enough bandwidth:** Dr. Jory Goodman, "The ADHD Brain: Quintessential Supercomputer?" *Psychology Today*, June 20, 2010, http://www.psychologytoday.com/blog/attention-please/201006/the-adhd -brain-quintessential-supercomputer.

132   **let them marinate:** Brian Scudamore, "Given to Distraction," Profitguide .com, April 30, 2009, http://www.profitguide.com/manage-grow /leadership/given-to-distraction-29548.

132 **thirty-three percent fewer distractions:** ibid.

132 **weigh the benefits:** ibid.

136 **digital generation:** "Andreas Baum and Christopher Lauer—Pirates," *Content Lab Berlin*, September 23, 2011, http://www.contentlab-berlin .com/andreas-baum-and-christopher-lauer-pirates/.

140 **beautiful summer evening:** Zoë Kessler, "ADHD and Creative Thinking: A Blessing and a Curse," *Psych Central*, last reviewed June 12, 2013, http://blogs.psychcentral.com/adhd-zoe/2013/06/adhd-and -creative-thinking-a-blessing-and-a-curse/.

141 **dreams and goals:** ibid.

Chapter Nine: Cool in a Crisis

162 **every moment mattered:** Dr. Kenny Handelman, "ADHD Strategy: Use Deadlines Effectively," January 30, 2014, http://www.drkenny.com /adhd-deadlines-strategy.

Breakout III: Your Antidote to Boredom

170 **not very interesting:** Dr. Richard A. Friedman, "A Natural Fix for A.D.H.D.," *New York Times*, October 31, 2014, http://www.nytimes.com /2014/11/02/opinion/sunday/a-natural-fix-for-adhd.html?_r=0.

170 **walking around with reward circuits:** ibid.

172 **hardwired:** ibid."

Chapter Ten: The Entrepreneur's Superpower

177 **tendency to be self-employed:** Nicos Nicolaou, Scott Shane, Georgina Adi, Massimo Mangino and Juliette Harris, "A Polymorphism Associated with Entrepreneurship: Evidence from Dopamine Receptor Candidate Genes," *Small Business Economics* 36, no. 2 (December 16, 2010): 151–55, http://link.springer.com/article/10.1007/s11187-010-9308-1.

178 **chaos for breakfast:** Laurie Dupar, "The ADHD Entrepreneurial Brain-Style."

178 **Stockholm School of Economics:** Johan Wiklund, Holger Patzelt and Dimo Dimov, "Entrepreneurship and Psychological Disorders," Syracuse University, USA, and Stockholm School of Economics, Sweden; Technical University Munich, Germany University of Bath, United Kingdom. [Unpublished.]

178 **dearth of academic research:** Salvatore Mannuzza, Rachel G. Klein, Abrah Bessler, Patricia Malloy and Maria LaPadula, "Adult Outcome of Hyperactive Boys: Educational Achievement, Occupational Rank, and Psychiatric Status," *JAMA Psychiatry* 50, no. 7 (July 1993): 565–76, doi:10.1001/archpsyc, http://archpsyc.jamanetwork.com/article.aspx?articleid=496268.

178 **higher entrepreneurial intentions:** Ingrid Verheul, Joern Block, Katrin Burmeister-Lamp, Roy Thurik, Henning Tiemeier and Roxana Turturea, "AD/HD Symptoms and Entrepreneurial Intentions," Institute for the Study of Labor [no date], http://www.iza.org/conference_files/Entre Res2012/turturea_r7957.pdf.

181 **openness to experience:** Elfina Rohmah, *Entrepreneurship and the Big Five Personality Traits: A Behavioral Genetics Perspective*, Scribd, April 17, 2011, http://www.scribd.com/doc/53179237/Entrepreneurship-and-the -Big-Five-Personality-Traits.

189 **out-of-the-box thinking:** Brian Scudamore, "Given to Distraction."

Chapter Eleven: In the Zone

193 **Major League Baseball:** David Leon Moore and Jim Corbett, "The Strange Relationship Between Pro Sport Leagues, Athletes, and Adderall," *Business Insider*, November 28, 2012, http://www.businessinsider.com/adderall-in-pro-sports-2012-11.

193 **pro-athlete population:** Michael Linden, "Athletes with ADHD & Autistic Spectrum Disorder (ASD)," Futurehealth.org, April 27, 2010, http://www.futurehealth.org/populum/page.php?f=Athletes-with -ADHD—Auti-by-Michael-Linden-100424-956.html.

194 **intense bursts of attention:** Eileen Bailey, "The Many Faces of ADHD: Michael Phelps, Olympic Gold Medalist," *Health Guide*, August 11, 2008, http://www.healthcentral.com/adhd/c/1443/36969/olympic -gold-medallist.

195 **a natural at that:** Judy Dutton, "ADHD Athletes: Inspiring Sports Stars with Attention Deficit," *ADDitude*, June/July 2006, http://www.additude mag.com/adhd/article/989-2.html.

198 **going to remember:** "1990: Derrick Thomas Has 7 Sacks vs. Seahawks," *Today in Pro Football History*, November 11, 2009, http://fs64sports. blogspot.com/2009/11/1990-derrick-thomas-has-7-sacks-vs .html.

205 **children who exercised:** Matthew B. Pontifex, Brian J. Saliba, Lauren B. Raine, Daniel L. Picchietti and Charles H. Hillman, "Exercise Improves Behavioral, Neurocognitive, and Scholastic Performance in Children with Attention-Deficit/Hyperactivity Disorder," *Journal of Pediatrics* 162, no. 3 (March 2013): 543–51, http://www.jpeds.com/article/S0022 -3476(12)00994-8/abstract.

206 **children's physical activity:** "Exercise May Lead to Better School Performance for Kids with ADHD," *Michigan State University Today,* October 16, 2012, http://msutoday.msu.edu/news/2012/exercise-may-lead-to-better -school-performance-for-kids-with-adhd-1/.

206 **learning and memory:** "Adult ADHD and Exercise," WebMD, last reviewed May 31, 2012, http://www.webmd.com/add-adhd/guide/ adult-adhd-and-exercise.

206 **tae kwon do:** "Exercise: An Alternative ADHD Treatment Without Side Effects."

207 **It's never boring:** Gina Roberts-Grey, "Celebrities with ADHD: Karina Smirnoff of 'DWTS,'" *Lifescript,* January 2, 2015, http://www.lifescript .com/health/centers/adhd/articles/how_adhd_helps_dwts_pro _karina_smirnoff.aspx.

Chapter Twelve: Relationships

212 **divorce rate:** Melissa Orlov, "ADHD Isn't Just for Kids—Adults Feel Big Impact in Marriage," first published October 20, 2010 in May I Have Your Attention, accessed in *Psychology Today* (October 2012), http://www .psychologytoday.com/blog/may-i-have-your-attention/201010/adhd -isn-t-just-kids-adults-feel-big-impact-in-marriage.

212 **nearly twice as high:** nearly Melissa Orlov, *The ADHD Effect on Marriage: Understand and Rebuild Your Relationship in Six Steps* (Plantation, FL: ADD Warehouse, 2010), 5.

216 **vicious cycle:** ibid.

220 **respectfully negotiate:** Margarita Tartakovsky, "ADHD's Impact on Relationships—10 Tips to Help," *Psych Central,* last reviewed January 30, 2013, http://psychcentral.com/lib/adhds-impact-on-relationships -10-tips-to-help/0008563.

Chapter Thirteen: Find Your Fit

232 **dropout rate:** "Students with ADHD More Likely to Drop Out of High

School," *Clinically Psyched*, August 2, 2010, http://clinicallypsyched
.com/adhd-high-school-drop-outs/.

232 **long-term prison:** Ylva Ginsberg, Tatja Hirvikoski and Nils Lindefors,
"Attention Deficit Hyperactivity Disorder (ADHD) Among Longer-
Term Prison Inmates Is a Prevalent, Persistent and Disabling Disorder,"
BMC Psychiatry 10, no. 112 (2010), published online December 22, 2010,
doi: 10.1186/1471-244X-10-112, http://www.ncbi.nlm.nih.gov/pmc/
articles/PMC3016316/.

232 **alcohol abusers:** Gina Roberts-Grey, "Adult ADD/ADHD and Substance Abuse," *Everyday Health*, last updated June 16, 2011, http://
www.everydayhealth.com/adhd/adult-adhd/adhd-and-substance
-abuse.aspx.

INDEX